Delegating Powers

In this path-breaking book, David Epstein and Sharyn O'Halloran present the first unified theory of national policy making. Examining major U.S. policy initiatives from 1947 to 1992, the authors describe the conditions under which the legislature narrowly constrains executive discretion and when it delegates authority to the bureaucracy. In doing so, the authors synthesize diverse and competitive literatures, from transaction cost and principal-agent theory in economics, to information models developed in both economics and political science, to substantive and theoretical work on legislative organization and on bureaucratic discretion. Epstein and O'Halloran produce their own deductive specification of the conditions for making or delegating policy; gather a rich, original data set on delegation and discretion to test the propositions derived from their model; and devise appropriate statistical tests to assess the validity of their propositions. With its implications for the study of constitutional design, political delegation, legislative organization, administrative law, and the role of the executive in policy making, this book redefines the study of legislative–executive relations under separate powers.

DAVID EPSTEIN is Associate Professor of Political Science at Columbia University. He has also taught at Harvard and Stanford Universities. He is the author of more than twenty articles in such well-known journals as the *American Political Science Review, American Journal of Political Science,* and *Journal of Law, Economics, and Organization.* He has also won grants and fellowships from the Harvard University Research Training Group in Political Economy, the John M. Olin Foundation, the Hoover Institution, the World Bank, and the National Science Foundation.

SHARYN O'HALLORAN is Associate Professor of Political Science and International Affairs at Columbia University and has also taught at Harvard and Stanford Universities. She is the author of *Politics, Process and American Trade Policy* (University of Michigan Press) as well as twenty articles in leading journals, including the *American Political Science Review; American Journal of Political Science; Journal of Law, Economics, and Organization;* and *International Organization.* Professor O'Halloran has also won grants and fellowships from the Harvard University Research Training Group in Political Economy, the Hoover Institution, the World Bank, the Chazen Center for International Business Education, the Dirksen Foundation, the John M. Olin Foundation, and the National Science Foundation.

DELEGATING POWERS

A TRANSACTION COST POLITICS APPROACH TO POLICY MAKING UNDER SEPARATE POWERS

DAVID EPSTEIN
Columbia University

SHARYN O'HALLORAN
Columbia University

PUBLISHED BY THE PRESS SYNDICATE OF THE UNIVERSITY OF CAMBRIDGE
The Pitt Building, Trumpington Street, Cambridge, United Kingdom

CAMBRIDGE UNIVERSITY PRESS
The Edinburgh Building, Cambridge CB2 2RU, UK http://www.cup.cam.ac.uk
40 West 20th Street, New York, NY 10011-4211, USA http://www.cup.org
10 Stamford Road, Oakleigh, Melbourne 3166, Australia
Ruiz de Alarcón 13, 28014 Madrid, Spain

First published 1999

Printed in the United States of America

Typeface Sabon 10/12 pt.   *System* Penta [BV]

A catalog record for this book is available from the British Library.

Library of Congress Cataloging in Publication data

Epstein, David, 1964–
    Delegating powers : a transaction cost politics approach to policy
making under separate powers / David Epstein, Sharyn O'Halloran.
    p.   cm.
    Includes bibliographical references.
    ISBN 0-521-66020-3. – ISBN 0-521-66960-X (pbk.)
    1. Delegation of powers. 2. Delegation of powers – United States –
Case studies. 3. Transaction costs. I. O'Halloran, Sharyn, 1964–
. II. Title.
JK585.E67 1999
320.473'04 – dc21
                                                                    99-12787
                                                                    CIP

ISBN 0 521 66020 3 hardback
ISBN 0 521 66960 X paperback

To Bob and Barbara Morrison

Contents

ix

5
DATA AND POSTWAR TRENDS

6
DELEGATION AND CONGRESSIONAL–EXECUTIVE RELATIONS

7
DELEGATION AND LEGISLATIVE ORGANIZATION

8
DELEGATION AND ISSUE AREAS

9
CONCLUSION

Contents

AN AFTERWORD ON COMPARATIVE INSTITUTIONS

APPENDICES

Figures and Tables

Figures

Tables

Preface

The aim of this book is to develop and test theories of legislative–executive relations in a separation of powers system. We apply transaction cost analysis to the study of relations among political actors, arguing that delegation is, at its heart, a choice between congressional policy making and policy made through executive branch agencies. To understand the contours of delegation, and hence the administrative state, one must therefore first understand the strengths and weaknesses of policy making through both of these two modes and the trade-offs that legislators face when choosing between them. In this sense, our work is partly synthetic, bringing together two literatures already well established within political science, and it is partly generative, illuminating and expanding on these literatures by juxtaposing them, seeing them as alternatives, and elucidating the reciprocal influences that the branches have on each other.

We were aided by many of our colleagues in the process of preparing this work, especially, but not exclusively, Chris Achen, John Aldrich, Jeff Banks, Bob Bates, Kathy Bawn, Jonathan Bendor, John Brehm, John Carey, Gary Cox, Rui DeFigueredo, Avinash Dixit, John Ferejohn, Andrew Gelman, Oliver Hart, Will Heller, John Huber, Simon Jackman, Bob Jervis, Phil Keefer, Gary King, Ken Kollman, Matt McCubbins, Douglass North, Sunita Parikh, Torsten Persson, Roberta Romano, Ken Shepsle, Bob Shapiro, Kaare Strøm, Craig Volden, Barry Weingast, and Greg Wawro, and participants at the Harvard Political Economy Book Seminar, the Stanford Public Choice and Political Economy Seminars, and the Columbia University Political Economy Workshop. Jim Alt, David Brady, and Morris Fiorina were especially encouraging, and we thank them for their support. Excellent and much appreciated research assistance was provided by Boyan Belev, Judy Chase, Allyson Ford, Eric Groothius, Kim Johnson, Barak Jolish, Jonah Kaplan, Noah Kaplan (no relation), Alissa Kosowsky, Nedim Nomer, Kathleen O'Neill, Ray

Smith, Sean Theriault, and Alan Yang. Finally, we would like to thank our families, especially Ted Epstein, who first introduced us to the wonders of relational database management. Special thanks go to Bob and Barbara Morrison, whose hospitality saved our sanity more than once.

Financial support for this project was provided by the National Science Foundation under grant SBR-95-11628, the Hoover Institution, the Dirksen Congressional Research Center, the Stanford Institute for the Quantitative Study of Society, and the John M. Olin Foundation. Most of the data collection was completed at Harvard while the authors were postdoctoral fellows in the Harvard/MIT Research Training Group in Positive Political Economy under NSF grant DIR-91-13328. Columbia University generously provided research support through the Lazarsfeld Center for Social Sciences. The assistance of these institutions is greatly appreciated.

1

Paths of Policy Making

No axiom is more clearly established in law, or in reason, than that wherever the end is required, the means are authorized; wherever a general power to do a thing is given, every particular power necessary for doing it is included.

James Madison, *Federalist 44*

THE POLITICS OF MILITARY BASE CLOSINGS

In 1988 the U.S. Congress established a blue-ribbon Base Realignment and Closure (BRAC) Commission. Its powers were broad: to recommend a list of military establishments to be closed, which would become law unless Congress voted to override the commission's decision. Its impact was immense, with foreseen economic consequences, calculated in terms of lost jobs and economic growth, that could devastate the local communities surrounding targeted military bases. Why would Congress delegate authority over a policy area so obviously vital to constituents? And why did delegation take the shape of an independent commission?

Let us examine the problem from legislators' point of view. They have three choices: (1) ignore the issue entirely and close no bases; (2) pass a law listing which bases will be closed; or (3) delegate this decision to the executive. Congress had taken the first option after a round of base closings following the Vietnam War, nearly five hundred in all, had left members unhappy both over the loss of jobs in their districts and with the perception that the cuts were politically motivated, coming largely at the expense of Democrats. In retaliation, Congress in 1976 imposed the requirement that any base closings be preceded by a full environmental impact statement (EIS), which promptly put an end to further military closings for the next dozen years.

A typical case was the Loring Air Force Base in Maine. Once a vital outpost for B-52 bombers that could reach Russia from the mainland,

1

Loring's strategic importance declined with the increasing range of modern aircraft and the advent of nuclear submarines. Accordingly, the Defense Department planned to reduce Loring from a Strategic Air Command base to a military airfield with a minimal crew. However, the process of obtaining the necessary environmental clearances gave opponents time to marshal their forces, bringing "enormous political pressure to bear on the Congress and the Department," according to Frank Carlucci, secretary of defense under Reagan. A "Save Loring Committee" was formed, after which the Senate passed a bill prohibiting the downgrading of the base. Before the House had a chance to act, the Defense Department abandoned its plan to scale down the base altogether.

In the late 1980s, however, the political climate began to change. The combination of lessening cold war tensions and a budget crunch made base closings, with an estimated savings of between $2 and $5 billion a year, politically attractive. Then Rep. Dick Armey (R-Tex.) offered a floor amendment to the 1988 Defense Authorization bill to make base closing easier, which surprised observers by coming within seven votes of passage. It was now clear that the idea of closing at least some bases had considerable support among rank-and-file members.

If base closings were to happen, though, some institutional mechanism had to be devised to select which bases would be targeted. Choosing a list of bases by enacting a law through the normal legislative process seemed both technically and politically unattractive. To preserve the benefits of unified decision making and action, the details of defense policy have usually been left to the executive branch, which has subsequently acquired a considerable degree of expertise in these matters. Given the complexity of the task and the possible consequences of ill-considered policy – namely, a reduction in the nation's capacity for self-defense – legislators had an understandable desire to delegate the task to experts.

It is also true that legislators feel much more comfortable passing bills that distribute benefits widely rather than bills that take benefits away from a few districts. Thus, highway bills are legislative perennials, but bills proposing selective cuts are seldom introduced. Even when some cuts are necessary, members fear that the legislative process will give extra weight to those in key positions, such as party and committee leaders, rather than distribute burdens fairly. As a result, legislation singling out one or a few districts is rarely passed.

Consider, for example, the fate of the Staten Island Home Port. In 1990, with the navy shrinking, the House Armed Services Committee proposed closing down the Staten Island naval base. The port had long been considered superfluous, and Defense Secretary Dick Cheney had recently ordered a freeze on any further construction there, pending a

2

report from the navy defining its priorities. The committee also knew that many liberal Democrats from surrounding New York districts opposed the base. However, then-freshman representative Susan Molinari (R-NY) staged a counterattack, claiming that she had been unfairly singled out and lining up support among Republicans and other representatives with bases in jeopardy, warning, "Your military installation could be next." In the end, Molinari was able to pass a substitute amendment that gutted the proposal and saved the base from closure.

In the face of these difficulties, delegation became an attractive alternative, much as Congress has delegated authority to the executive to overcome its logrolling tendencies in the area of trade policy. This option had its drawbacks as well, however, as delegation to executive officials with political appointments might lead to politically targeted reductions, which majority Democrats, recalling the events of the early 1970s, wanted to avoid at all costs.[1] Hence, both traditional legislative action and wholesale delegation to the Department of Defense (DoD) were seen as unappealing. This left Congress with the possibility of delegating to an independent commission whose suggestions would receive minimal political interference from either the legislative or executive branches. Policy made this way would be unpredictable, but at least the process would be fair *ex ante*, allowing legislators to escape their own logrolling dilemma without surrendering control to executive agencies with contrary partisan aims.

The final delegation regime balanced these concerns. First, a twelve-member commission was to be chosen by the secretary of defense in consultation with Congress. In fact, Congress was so eager to make the BRAC Commission independent that the enacting legislation included the unusual stipulation that no more than half of the commission's staff could have been previously employed by the Defense Department. The commission was to recommend a set of military bases to be closed or downsized, provided that the expected savings from the closure would exceed the associated costs in six years or less.[2] These recommendations were not subject to the requirement of an environmental impact statement, and although actual base closings would have to be accompanied

---

[1]These fears were not necessarily ill founded. Two years later, Dick Cheney, President Bush's secretary of defense, proposed a list of potential base closings in which over 99% of the lost jobs would come from Democratic House districts. He accompanied this list with the suggestion that Democrats clamoring for defense cuts should start by sacrificing obsolete bases in their hometowns.

[2]This provision was added to the bill at the behest of Rep. Herbert Bateman (R-VA), whose Fort Monroe base was at risk. However, the base was laden with so many years of refuse – it still contained unexploded Confederate artillery shells – that the cleanup costs would have outstripped savings for at least twenty-five years. The plan worked; Fort Monroe was spared in the final list.

by an EIS, legal challenges to these statements had to be filed within sixty days.

The commission's list would have to be accepted or rejected by the secretary of defense in its entirety, without the possibility of amendment, within fifteen days. If the secretary accepted it, the list would then go to Congress, which had forty-five working days to pass a joint resolution of disapproval. This resolution had to be enacted by both houses, with the possibility of a presidential veto, and again they could not amend the list of bases. Thus, both the executive and legislative branches were faced with a closed rule; that is, an up-or-down decision. If no disapproval resolution was passed, then the list of closings would automatically go into effect.

Events proved the efficacy of this procedure: The commission recommended that eighty-six bases be closed and a further fifty-four be realigned, and a disapproval motion was overwhelmingly defeated in the House. In fact, Congress used a nearly identical procedure for subsequent base closings in 1991, 1993, and 1995, resulting in overall estimated savings of $5.6 billion a year.

In the end, then, most of the crucial policy decisions regarding base closings were made by an independent commission, with relatively little room for political interference. It is possible, indeed likely, that in this case the decision-making structure coincided quite closely with one whose sole objective would be the making of good public policy. However, the commission structure was not chosen primarily for its policy benefits; otherwise, Congress could have established such a commission anytime in the previous twelve years. Neither would it have included the provision that all closings pay for themselves within six years, thus exempting those bases that were in the worst shape.

Rather, the commission structure was adopted because it best served legislators' need to close some bases without handing over too much power to the Defense Department. Congress examined its expected costs and benefits under alternative policy-making structures and selected the one that provided the most possible expected net political benefits, allocating decision-making authority across the branches and constraining it in such a way as to reap the benefits of delegation while minimizing the associated political costs. It is this type of choice over alternative policy-making procedures, and their impact on policy outcomes, that this book will explore.

DELEGATING POWERS: THE PUZZLE

The United States Constitution divides the responsibilities of policy making among the various branches of government: Congress writes the

4

laws, the executive branch implements them, and the courts interpret them. While the Constitution provides a general framework for government, though, many of the details concerning the interaction among the branches and the daily functioning of the state were left unresolved. In many ways, the history of American political development from 1789 to the present can be viewed as an attempt to arrive at a manageable arrangement that allows government to be effective yet responsive.

We see this inherent tension between effectiveness and responsiveness most clearly in the dramatic changes in the structure of government and the powers and functions of the bureaucracy that have arisen since the New Deal. What divides the modern administrative state from its predecessors is the delegation of broad decision-making authority to a professional civil service. But this delegation of authority from Congress to the executive has never been monolithic; it has varied over time, by issue area, and with national political and economic trends.

Consider Figure 1.1, for example, which examines a set of 257 important laws enacted in the postwar era.[3] The vertical axis represents the number of provisions in a given law that delegate policy-making authority to the executive, as a proportion of the total number of provisions in that law. The horizontal axis identifies the committee in the House of Representatives that considered and reported the bill that eventually became law.

What is most striking about the figure is the considerable amount of variation across the different issue areas. Predictably, Congress delegates least authority in bills reported out of Ways and Means, Budget, Rules, and the House Administration Committees. But perhaps counter to intuition, bills reported from the Agricultural and Public Works Committees, usually considered "pork-barrel" policy areas that legislators jealously guard, do in fact delegate significant authority to the executive. Finally, the Armed Services Committee delegates the most.

Or take a few specific examples. In many cases, we observe Congress delegating broad mandates to executive agencies. The 1934 Reciprocal Trade Agreements Act, for instance, gave the president authority to reduce tariffs unilaterally by up to 50 percent, and the 1970 Clean Air Act required that industries use the "best available control technology" to reduce emissions but left the definition of the crucial term "best" to the EPA's discretion. These decisions on the structure of policy making have cleared the way for a sharp reduction in trade barriers in the former case and tough environmental standards in the latter.

---

[3]These comprise the enactments included in Mayhew's (1991) analysis of important postwar legislation, updated through the 102d Congress. Chapter 5 describes these data in detail.

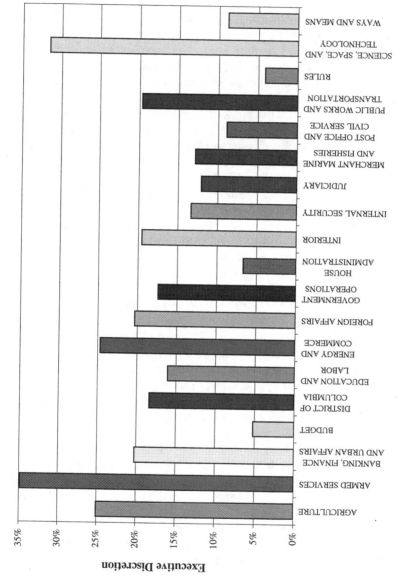

Figure 1.1. Average Discretion by Reporting Committee

6

In other cases, Congress enacts painfully detailed legislation, leaving administrative agencies with little or no leeway. For example, in 1973 Social Security benefits were increased by exactly 11 percent; in 1974 Congress increased the minimum wage to $2.30 in three staged hikes; and in the Tax Reform Act of 1986 Congress specified that the existing fourteen tax brackets would be collapsed to two and mandated a sharp reduction in overall rates. In each of these instances, the executive branch was limited to carrying out Congress's explicitly stated wishes without having much independent impact on the content of these policies.

It is clear from these examples that where policy is made – in Congress or through delegation to the executive – has a significant impact on policy outcomes. The central puzzle to be explained, then, is why does Congress delegate broad authority to the executive in some policy areas but not in others? Does this delegation reflect the particularities of an issue area, such as who are its benefactors, who are adversely affected, and what are its complexities? Does it reflect deeper structural factors, such as legislative organization, committee composition, or congressional–executive conflict (divided government)? Is executive branch decision making different from the internal workings of Congress, and how does this affect the decision to delegate? Can Congress perfectly control delegated authority through administrative procedures, oversight, and administrative law? Does it want to? In the end, what are the implications of delegating discretionary authority for our separation of powers system and the incremental mode of policy making that it was meant to encourage? Can the virtues of separate powers intended by the Founders be maintained alongside significant delegation to the executive?

A TRANSACTION COST POLITICS APPROACH

Our approach to this question begins with the observation that policy can be made in Congress, through delegation of authority to executive agencies, or by some mixture of these two. Furthermore, the amount of discretionary authority delegated is a decision made by Congress, which can write either detailed legislation that leaves the executive with little latitude in implementation or vague laws that leave executive actors with broad discretionary powers. And when deciding where policy will be made, Congress trades off the internal policy production costs of the committee system against the external costs of delegation. Thus, Congress's decision to delegate is similar to a firm's make-or-buy decision; hence our usage of the term "transaction cost politics."

What are the costs associated with each alternative? Legislators can enact direct, detailed laws through normal congressional procedures, but the necessary information to make well-formed policy may be costly to obtain; bicameralism and supermajority requirements inhibit speedy, flexible action; and legislative logrolls tend to inflate the costs of even the simplest policy initiatives. Alternatively, Congress can delegate authority to the executive branch to escape this dilemma, but bureaucrats may be motivated as much by the desire to pursue their own policy goals, inflate their budgets, and increase their scope of control as by their desire to follow congressional intent. Neither option is without its faults, but in different circumstances one or the other may be relatively more attractive from legislators' point of view.

In some cases, delegation may offer legislators an appealing – or irresistible – alternative to making policy themselves. Consider the issue of airline safety, which is characterized on the one hand by the need for technical expertise and on the other by an almost complete absence of potential political benefits. That is, policymakers will get little credit if things go well and no airline disasters occur, but they will have to withstand intense scrutiny when things go wrong: Airline regulation is an issue with only a political downside, and failures tend to be spectacular and well publicized. Furthermore, legislative and executive preferences on this issue will tend to be almost perfectly aligned: have fewer accidents rather than more as long as the costs to airlines are not prohibitive. The set of individuals receiving benefits, the flying public, is diffuse and ill organized, while those paying the costs of regulation, the airline companies, are well organized and politically active. And, keeping in mind the easy observation of deficiencies in the system, delegated power is relatively simple to monitor. For all these reasons, even if legislators had unlimited time and resources of their own (which they do not), delegation to the executive would be the preferred mode of policy making.

By contrast, in other policy areas legislators will be loath to cede authority to the executive. Consider tax policy, where Congress uses considerable resources to write detailed legislation that leaves the executive branch with little or no leeway in interpretation.[4] The political advantages of controlling tax policy come not from the duty of setting overall rates, which taxpayers tend to resent, but from the possibility of granting corporations and other well-organized lobby groups special tax breaks, so-called corporate welfare. If designed correctly, these benefits can target a specific industry or group and are paid for by the general public, either through taxes paid into general revenues or the decrease in

---

[4]The *Congressional Quarterly* summary of the Tax Reform Act of 1969, for instance, listed 136 major provisions, of which only 3 delegated substantive authority to the executive.

revenue stemming from the tax break. Such political benefits are not lightly forgone, and they would be difficult to replicate through a delegation scheme with open-ended mandates. Thus, Congress continues to make tax policy itself, despite the demands of time and expertise that this entails.

Our theory predicts, then, that policy will be made in the politically most efficient manner, be it through direct legislative action, through delegation to executive branch agencies, or through some combination of these two. Note the term "politically" efficient; we make no claim that policy making under separate powers will be *technically* or *economically* efficient, allocating resources to their greatest advantage. Indeed, as some features of the base-closing case demonstrated, policy making may be quite inefficient according to a strict economic benchmark. Rather, we claim that policy will be made in such a way as to maximize legislators' political goals, which we take to be reelection first and foremost. Legislators will prefer to make policy themselves as long as the political benefits they derive from doing so outweigh the political costs; otherwise, they will delegate to the executive.

DELEGATION AND BROAD THEMES IN AMERICAN POLITICS

Our approach to delegation has significant implications for a number of issues in American politics, one of which is the debate over whether Congress can control unelected regulatory agencies when delegating authority. Some critics, most notably Lowi (1969), argue that congressional delegation of authority has become equivalent to an abdication of Congress's constitutionally assigned policy-making role, in which legislators have over time surrendered their legislative powers to unelected bureaucrats. The result has been a system where special interests reign supreme, cozying up to the very bureaucrats set up to regulate them, as legislative actors turn a blind eye to the situation. Policy, then, reflects the demands of these interests at the expense of consumers and the public at large.

The counterargument, as posed for example by McCubbins and Schwartz (1984), McCubbins, Noll, and Weingast (1987; 1989) and Kiewiet and McCubbins (1991), is that legislators can control bureaucrats through oversight and administrative procedures such as congressional hearings, reporting requirements, and enfranchising third parties into the decision-making process. If Congress can curtail bureaucratic excesses through these means, then delegation need not be as deleterious as previously assumed.

Our perspective emphasizes that delegated authority cannot be judged in a vacuum: One must compare bureaucratic policy making with the next best alternative, which is policy making through committees. Indeed, special interests may receive protection through favorable agency regulations, but is this more widespread or morally more opprobrious than having them protected through a tax loophole or a targeted provision in a bill?

Or consider the other side of the coin: The proposal that Congress can control delegated authority through fire-alarm oversight and administrative procedures. In our model, Congress delegates those areas in which the legislative process is least efficient, and, accordingly, we should not expect oversight to be either perfect or desirable. Legislators lacking the time, expertise, and/or political will to make hard policy choices themselves in an issue area will not magically find these resources when it comes time to oversee the executive. Nor should we necessarily want them to try, if this would decrease agencies' incentives to invest in policy expertise. In essence, we claim that a selection bias is at work here: A theory of oversight divorced from a theory of delegation will overlook the fact that those issue areas in which the executive makes policy differ fundamentally from those in which Congress makes policy itself.

Legislative Organization and Delegation

We also address what has come to be known as the "information versus distribution" debate in the legislative organization literature; that is, whether committees primarily serve members' distributive, pork barrel needs or their desire to avoid the consequences of ill-formed policy. We assert that this question must be a false dichotomy: Some policy areas are characterized more by informational concerns, others by distributive, and still others by both. The right question to ask, from our perspective, is how the informational or distributive content of an issue area affects the types of procedures used to implement policy. Specifically, we shall argue that informationally intense policy areas will be good candidates for delegation, while distributive issues will tend to be made in Congress.

Along these lines, our analysis carries implications for the study of committee outliers and excessive legislative logrolling. In the congressional-organization literature, the cost of these committee-based pathologies is simply less efficient legislation. In our view, the poorer the performance of the committee system, the more likely it is Congress will delegate to the executive. So even though committees have monopoly power internally, they face external competition from the executive branch, and this may be sufficient to rein in committee excesses. Similarly, the possibility of delegating authority to executive actors affects

10

legislators' incentives to invest in issue-specific expertise: In some cases it gives committees greater incentives to make such investments; at other times, less incentives.

We also claim that legislative organization is directly affected by its broader environment of separate powers: Congressional committees will be organized differently given the possibility of delegation to the executive. Their preferences will not be extreme, as predicted by a purely distributive approach, nor will they meet the informational theory's expectations of precisely matching the median floor voter's preferences. Rather, committees will tend to be moderately biased in a direction opposite to the preferences of the executive branch; they will be *contrary outliers*. This highlights the differences between a policy-making perspective that begins and ends within Congress, and one that incorporates executive branch decision making into the analysis.

Divided Government and Delegation

Our findings also cast a new light on the divided-government debate, specifically, the question about whether divided government has significant policy consequences. As the term "gridlock" creeps into the popular vernacular, it has become commonplace to assume that divided government is synonymous with policy making even more convoluted and incremental than the Founders imagined, so much so that it challenges the ability of the national government to respond to pressing issues of the day. On the other hand, some authors – most notably, Mayhew (1991) – argue that the same number of important pieces of legislation get passed under unified and divided government, so perhaps the claims of gridlock are overdrawn.

We reply that it is not only the quantity of legislation that matters, but the quality as well, and that the laws passed under divided government differ significantly from those passed during times of unified government. We reanalyze all 257 pieces of legislation that Mayhew counts as significant postwar enactments and ask whether any appreciable difference in executive branch discretion is discernible under unified and divided government. Our findings indicate that, in fact, Congress delegates less and constrains more under divided government. Thus, split partisan control of our national policy-making institutions, even if it does not lead to legislative gridlock, may result in procedural gridlock – that is, producing executive branch agencies with less authority to make well-reasoned policy and increasingly hamstrung by oversight from congressional committees, interest groups, and the courts.

11

Separated Powers and the Dynamics of Policy Change

Finally, our approach has implications for broader questions concerning our separation of powers system. The traditional wisdom holds that, given our constitutional design of bicameralism, separation of powers, checks and balances, and federalism – the U.S. system of government is conservative in the classic sense of the word. Policy change is hard, requiring large and persistent majorities. Parties, and the platforms they espouse, have arisen to bridge the gaps between the various elected branches, but they are in general too weak and fragmented to bring government anywhere near the system of responsible party government called for by a series of mid-century scholars.[5]

Our theory turns this account on its head by noting that the same mechanisms that impede policy making through the normal legislative process also insulate bureaucrats from external control. When it is hard to make new policy, it is hard to overturn what bureaucrats have done. In this account, parties are not the only key to policy movement, as a single branch of government is empowered to make regulations with the binding force of law. Thus, the overall impact of a separation of powers system may be not to reduce the amount of policy made but merely to change its location.

OUTLINE OF THE BOOK

The following chapters elaborate our argument in greater detail. The next chapter reviews a number of relevant literatures, including the large literatures on congressional organization and legislative oversight of the bureaucracy, and the rather svelte body of work on the question of what policy areas Congress chooses to delegate to the executive. Chapter 3 reviews some of the recent insights into the economic theory of the firm and hierarchical organizations, which we then use as a basis for our theory of transaction cost politics. Chapter 4 describes the theoretical building blocks of our study and details a game theoretic model of Congress's decision to delegate. We predict in which cases Congress will choose to delegate rather than make policy itself, derive several propositions relating political conditions to delegation and agency discretion, and detail the empirical hypotheses that follow from our model. Chapter 5 describes the data used in our study and presents basic trends in executive branch discretion in the postwar era. Chapters 6, 7, and 8 test the implications of our model for congressional–executive relations, leg-

---

[5]See, for instance, Schattschneider (1942), Key (1947), and APSA Committee on Political Parties (1950).

islative organization, and patterns of policy making across issue areas, respectively. The final chapter summarizes our findings, combines them into a single analysis, and draws out their implications for delegation and policy making in our modern separation of powers system.

2

Choosing How to Decide

It is only against a background of hard reality that choices count.
Ben Shahn, *The Shape of Content*

Our approach to congressional delegation states that legislators cede
substantive discretionary authority to the bureaucracy in policy areas
where the legislative process is least efficient relative to bureaucratic
decision making. In this chapter, we provide background for our argument by reviewing recent work on both congressional policy making
and legislative oversight of the bureaucracy. We then discuss previous
treatments of the question of when Congress delegates and conclude
by arguing that to understand delegation one must measure it against
the hard reality of making policy through congressional committees.

LEGISLATIVE ORGANIZATION

The starting point of modern congressional analysis is David Mayhew's
book *The Electoral Connection* (1974), which lays out a vision of congressional organization as a rationally constructed, conscious choice
made by reelection-seeking individuals. Mayhew emphasized the importance of the committee system as a basis for members to pursue their
electoral goals and consequently downplayed the role of parties. His
study has remained influential mainly due to its methodological focus: It
took a ground-up view of legislative organization and built upon this
edifice a theory of public policy. Mayhew's incentive-based approach
and deductive style of argumentation are typical of economic analysis,
even if no explicit formal models, economic or otherwise, were employed.

Social Choice Roots

The second strand of modern theories of Congress has its roots in social-choice theory, a rather abstract branch of study somewhere in the intersection of mathematical economics and decision theory. The intellectual history of this field has been retold many times: It starts with Arrow's (1951) famous Impossibility Theorem, which states that any rule for aggregating individual preferences into a social ordering must violate one of five seemingly innocuous conditions. In essence, Arrow had rediscovered and sharpened the intuition of Condorcet's (1785) voting paradox: Individuals may be rational in the sense of being able to choose between any two alternatives, but aggregating their preferences via majority rule may lead to collective irrationality, or the cycling of social preferences. Politically speaking, this means that "the will of the people" is not a well-defined concept as long as the issues involved are complex and individuals' preferences over them do not fall neatly along a one-dimensional continuum. This point, which was not well appreciated by political scientists at the time, has become a cornerstone of the modern view of political institutions.[1]

Against this backdrop, Black's (1958) median voter theorem provided a ray of hope. If policy alternatives can be arrayed along a line, and if all voters have single-peaked preferences (meaning that they have a favorite policy on that line and their utility declines as outcomes move away from that policy), then the outcome of successive majority rule votes will be the median voter's most preferred policy. This finding held out the possibility of stable collective choices if the only task were to pick a single policy, rather than order all possible alternatives (as Arrow's Theorem demanded). Unfortunately, Plott (1967) showed that in more than one dimension the median voter result breaks down. To be precise, it holds only under razor-edge circumstances (the "Plott conditions"); otherwise, once again, no stable policy exists. Further, the chaos theorems of McKelvey (1976) and Schofield (1978) showed that when the Plott conditions fail, successive majority rule voting can lead to any outcome whatsoever, or it can be manipulated to produce the favorite policy of a centralized agenda setter.

---

[1] In fact, it might well be argued that herein lies the fundamental difference between economics and politics. The basic theorems of economics are the First and Second Welfare Theorems, which establish baselines of efficiency and a means of achieving efficient outcomes through competitive markets. The basic theorem of politics – Arrow's Theorem – is one of disequilibrium, a lack of universal standards, and a statement that no one political system is necessarily better than any other.

The New Institutionalism and the Distributive Synthesis

It is in the light of these chaos theorems that we must evaluate Shepsle's (1979) article on congressional structure. Shepsle claimed that a committee system that divided complex policy into many one-dimensional issue areas could solve the chaos problem, as long as committees were given the right to initiate all legislation within their substantive domain. Thus, even if preferences alone could not produce definite policy outcomes, the addition of a committee system could create a "structure-induced equilibrium." As with Mayhew, Shepsle argued that a legislative system with strong committees solved a fundamental problem, creating orderly, stable policy outcomes even when preferences alone would tend toward disorder and chaos.

The years that followed saw the rise of what has come to be known as the "new institutionalism." Its battle cry was that "institutions matter," meaning that in the details of legislative procedures, including floor voting and amendment rules, committee referral precedents, and conference committee proceedings, lay the secrets of congressional power. What Congress did was seen as inseparable from how it did it. Thus were launched a number of studies concerning the theoretical properties of amendment agendas, gatekeeping powers, and proposal rights, all showing the links between institutional arrangements and policy outcomes.[2]

Along the way, Shepsle's original thesis was somewhat modified and supplemented, so as to synthesize Mayhew's approach with social-choice theory. Rather than solving a chaos problem, the committee system was posited to solve a distributional puzzle: how to pass programs that benefit a few members intensely when all floor votes must be made by majority rule? The answer was that, via the committee system, legislators requested (and were granted) membership on the committees that most directly affected their constituents. Then committees could legislate on their subject areas in peace, free from outside interference. These committee jurisdictions were upheld through the use of various procedural devices: gatekeeping powers, closed rules, and domination of conference committees. Thus, legislative organization is designed to maximize district-specific benefits and help ensure members' reelection. Weingast and Marshall (1988) capped off a decade of research with a summary of this *distributive view* of congressional organization (a rather cynical view, by the way, which makes very little mention of which policies are good for

---

[2]Key articles in this tradition include Romer and Rosenthal (1978), Denzau and Mackay (1983), and Ordeshook and Schwartz (1987), to name but a few. Book-length expositions include excellent works by Oleszek (1984), Bach and Smith (1988), and Smith (1989).

the nation as a whole) in their article "The Industrial Organization of Congress."

The Informational Approach

The counterargument to the distributive view came not from "outside," which is to say from traditional congressional scholars who eschewed the methods of the new institutionalists, but from "inside." Building on game-theoretic models by Crawford and Sobel (1982) and Austen-Smith and Riker (1990), Gilligan and Krehbiel (1987; 1989) presented an alternative view of the committee system. They argued that the central problem that legislators face is producing reasonable policy in the face of an uncertain, complex environment. Committees (once again) solve this problem: They are populated by experts who put their expertise to work when fashioning legislation. Thus, any procedural advantages that committees receive, such as closed rules, can be read as inducements to gather information, and any deference they receive on the floor is due to their superior expertise. This *informational theory* of committees (much less cynical than the distributive view, but still not necessarily wrong) is laid out at length by Krehbiel (1991) and stands as a major competitor to the distributive theory.[3]

Even so, both theories share much in common. First, they put committees at the forefront when discussing Congress; committee power plays an important role in both analyses, even if the two sides cannot agree on its basis. This committee-based structure is no accident; legislators designed it that way, along with its attendant procedural accouterments, in order to maximize their reelection chances. And under both views, the committee system has built-in inefficiencies. For the distributive view, it is unrestrained logrolling, the most spectacular instance of which is probably the 1930 Smoot-Hawley Tariff Act, but less disastrous examples of wasteful pork barrel legislation occur every session. For the informational view, the problem is that committees and floor members may differ in their preferences, so policy making will display some residual uncertainty over outcomes, unable to fully incorporate committees' expertise.

Presently, the congressional organization literature has reached somewhat of a breathing spell, as scholars attempt to reconcile the fundamental insights of these two competing camps.[4] Research on Congress has

---

[3]See for example, a well-known published debate between Shepsle and Weingast on one side and Krehbiel on the other, titled "Why Are Congressional Committees Powerful?" (Shepsle and Weingast 1987a, 1987b; and Krehbiel 1987).

[4]See the essays in Shepsle and Weingast, eds. (1995).

also exhibited a renewed interest in the role of political parties, as institutions that work through the committee system to formulate and implement political agendas (Rohde 1991; Cox and McCubbins 1993; Aldrich 1995). This perspective thus draws on both distributive and informational elements, adding the possibility that committees are responsive to the policy goals of party caucuses as well as the chamber as a whole.

We take two lessons from the legislative-organization debate. First, we use the research tradition as a whole, and especially the points of agreement between the competing views, as one building block for our analysis of the policy-making process. Second, we find it a bit curious that these views of legislative organization should be seen as diametrically opposed, mutually exclusive theories of committees. Drawing upon a long tradition in political science, including Fenno (1973) and Wilson (1974), we believe that some issue areas are characterized more by informational concerns while others are distributive; on that account, different policies have different politics. Rather than seeing an opposition between these views of policy making, then, we take distributive and informational concerns as a useful typology of issue areas to be used in our analysis of where policy is made.

DELEGATION AND OVERSIGHT

Our other building block comes from the recent literature on delegation, in which a long normative debate has taken a positive turn. The normative debate centers around the basic dilemma of legislative–executive relations. According to our separation of powers system, Congress is supposed to make the laws while the executive carries them out, but this distinction becomes difficult to sustain in practice. On the one hand, since Congress can never supply every single detail pertaining to the execution of its laws, the executive will always have some freedom to specify the exact process by which legislative intent becomes reality. On the other hand, Congress cannot delegate unrestricted authority to the executive without violating the "nondelegation doctrine," which states that legislative power may not be delegated to any other person.[5] In

[5] For excellent discussions of the nondelegation doctrine, see Jaffe (1965), Davis (1978), and Bruff and Shane (1988, 64–88). Interestingly, the nondelegation doctrine used to have a lesser-known cousin, the non-subdelegation doctrine, which stated that power delegated to one executive branch actor could not be subdelegated to another actor not explicitly empowered by Congress to receive such authority. Like the nondelegation doctrine, this mandate also fell into disfavor and was eventually overruled explicitly when Congress passed the Presidential Subdelegation Act of 1947 (3 U.S.C. Section 301–33 [1976]), which allowed subdelegation unless specifically forbidden by the governing statute.

between these two extremes, who is to say where execution ends and legislation begins? Executive branch actors must make some decisions in carrying out Congress's laws, but in doing so they may potentially change outcomes away from legislators' original intent. Determining the boundaries of the legislative and executive spheres is certainly a line-drawing exercise, but it is unavoidable in any separation of powers system.

The Growth of Administrative Law and the Decline of Oversight

The first response to this dilemma was simply to state that Congress should not be allowed to delegate any responsibilities that would require significant executive branch discretion. This solution worked for a while; the Supreme Court in its 1825 *Wayman v. Southard* decision allowed that Congress could delegate authority if the person receiving the authority only had to "fill up the details."[6] And as long as the central government did not do very much, this benign view of delegation was workable. Indeed, as late as 1888 Lord Bryce could write, "It is a great merit of American government that it relies very little on officials and arms them with little power of arbitrary interference."

The ICC and the Death of the Nondelegation Doctrine

However, events overtook this arrangement. The year before Bryce's assessment, Congress had passed the Interstate Commerce Act, which created the Interstate Commerce Commission (ICC), charged with regulating railroad rates. The courts first opposed this delegation, insisting on reviewing every ICC decision and changing the ICC's ruling if they disagreed. But when Congress strengthened the ICC's hand in the 1906 amendments to the Interstate Commerce Act, the court gave way and acceded to ICC findings of fact in the cases it considered, reserving for itself the role of ensuring that the ICC appropriately interpreted the statute. It was now impossible to claim that Congress only left detail filling to the executive; the establishment of rail rates was a major issue in American politics at the time, and Congress gave the ICC wide latitude in exactly what rates would be permitted.[7]

After the ICC's constitutionality was upheld, the nondelegation doctrine was on its last legs. Americans increasingly turned to the national government to solve social problems, and the government responded

---

[6] *Wayman v. Southard*, 23 U.S. (10 Wheat.) 1 (1825).
[7] This history is retold well in Skrowronek (1982).

with a spate of new agency-based laws in the first decade of the twentieth century. Then came FDR and the New Deal, and a host of new agencies were created, often charged with regulating only "in the public interest." This explosive growth in the executive branch has led to a fivefold increase in the number of civil service employees since 1930.

It was during the New Deal that the nondelegation doctrine made its bloody last stand. In the 1935 *Schechter Poultry* and *Panama Refinery* cases, the Supreme Court struck down key provisions of the National Industrial Recovery Act (NIRA) as overbroad delegations of authority, not only to executive branch officials, but also to private-industry boards as well, who were to be allowed to set their own rules of conduct.[8] After these cases, as is well known, Roosevelt waged a war against the Court by trying to expand it from nine to fifteen members; Congress refused to go along, but the Court backed down anyway, upholding New Deal legislation (the "switch in time that saved nine") and announcing that from then on they would concentrate more on social issues than economic ones. The nondelegation doctrine is now moribund, although various law review articles try to breathe life into it every so often.[9]

Judicial Control of the Bureaucracy

Having conceded the legitimacy of delegating discretionary authority to the executive, the next question was how to stop bureaucrats from running amok and abusing this discretion for personal or partisan gain. Thus began the study of bureaucratic control through the courts.[10] Following the passage of the 1946 Administrative Procedure Act (APA), which set out basic guidelines for agency decision making, scholarly attention focused on how bureaucrats could be made to follow Congress's statutory intent and serve the public interest. The main answer was to make agencies look as much like (idealized) legislatures as possible. Agencies were to give advance notice of rules and regulations under consideration and afford all parties with even a tangential interest in the outcome a chance to speak their mind (that is, they were to engage in "notice and comment" rule making). Furthermore, agencies should re-

---

[8]*Panama Refining Co. v. Ryan*, 293 U.S. 388 (1935); *Schechter Poultry Corp. v. United States*, 295 U.S. 495 (1935). The NIRA was actually an extraordinarily ambitious act, and it would probably be struck down today too.

[9]See Aranson, Gellhorn, and Robinson (1982), Schoenbrod (1983), and Macey (1988). The nondelegation doctrine's primary supporter on the Supreme Court has been Chief Justice Rehnquist; see his dissents in *Industrial Union Dept. v. American Petroleum Institute*, 448 U.S. 607 (1980) and in *American Textile Mfrs. Inst., Inc. v. Donovan*, 452 U.S. 490 (1981), where he was joined by Burger.

[10]These developments are summarized and evaluated in Shapiro's (1988) excellent treatise on administrative law.

spond to all suggestions, and their eventual decision must be supported by a lengthy, specific record of their deliberations (which, ironically, was incorporated into the "concise and general statement" that the APA required all rules to include).

In short, the main thrust of administrative law was to make agencies look like pluralistic enterprises, open to the public and reviewable by higher courts. Correspondingly, the focus of the administrative law literature was the role of interest groups and courts as checks on bureaucratic power, ensuring that agencies would act, in the words of Stewart (1975, p. 1675), "as a mere transmission belt for implementing legislative directives in particular cases." The literature was explicitly normative in orientation; indeed, many of the procedural innovations imposed by courts on agencies (such as the "rational basis" test and "hard look" review) began as suggestions in the scholarly community.

The Supposed Absence of Congressional Oversight

For the most part, this literature saw Congress as less important in the ongoing control of agencies. Much of the support for this viewpoint came from the observation that Congress rarely exercised its most obvious levers of control.[11] Agency budgets were seldom cut, Congress did not spend much time revising their original mandates, and presidential nominees were hardly ever rejected (a commonly cited example was the fact that the average Senate confirmation hearing lasted seventeen minutes).

For some, this lack of congressional involvement was seen as a positive development. Scholars of the public administration school argued that bureaucrats were by and large dedicated public servants who could do their jobs well if they could be assured that political meddling would be kept to a minimum.[12] Indeed, Huntington (1971) claimed that Congress does best by restricting its role to constituency service, leaving detailed regulation to policy experts in the bureaucracy. This view harks back to the turn-of-the-century Progressive civil service revolution, where agencies were established to "take the politics out of policy." Accordingly, mechanisms that insulated agencies from political control were seen as beneficial to the smooth functioning of government.

Others, however, took the lack of active congressional participation to be a sign of failure in our democratic institutions. This point was forcefully made by Lowi (1969), who accused legislators of abandoning

---

[11]This lack of direct oversight was noted by Bibby (1968), Pearson (1975), Seidman (1975), and Hess (1976), among others.

[12]See, for instance, Wilson (1973), Heclo (1977), and Shefter (1978).

their duties by delegating power to unelected bureaucrats and omnipotent congressional committees. Lowi believed that the original delegations of power, as in the ICC, were well conceived and structured so as to make agencies hew to congressional intent. But, over time, delegation became less and less tied to specific mandates and more open-ended, allowing agencies an illegitimate amount of discretion. Legislators had abdicated responsibility for the execution of public policy, to be replaced by "interest-group liberalism," meaning that agencies reacted to the wishes of those organized groups that pressured them for favorable policy decisions. This, in turn, was wont to devolve into agency "capture" – public power exercised for the benefit of a few private interests, against the public good and unsupervised by democratically elected legislators.

Positive Theories of Legislative–Executive Relations

This, then, was the intellectual milieu as of the late 1970s, and it was ripe for a reassessment of Congress's impact on bureaucratic proceedings. The key starting point is Fiorina's (1977) book, *Congress: The Keystone of the Washington Establishment*, which sets forth an exceptionally cynical thesis: Congress delegates broad power to bureaucrats knowing in advance that they will make mistakes. When they do so, legislators can step in, undo any wrongs imposed on their constituents, and reap all the credit for making things right. As Fiorina (1977, 48) writes:

Congressmen earn electoral credits by establishing various federal programs. The legislation is drafted in very general terms, so some agency, existing or newly established, must translate a vague policy mandate into a functioning program. . . . Aggrieved and/or hopeful constituents petition their congressmen to intervene in the complex decision processes of the bureaucracy. The cycle closes when the congressman lends a sympathetic ear, piously denounces the evils of bureaucracy, intervenes in the latter's decisions, and rides a grateful electorate to ever more impressive electoral showings. Congressmen take credit coming and going.

So agencies are created not to serve the public good but to muddle along and make mistakes every so often, hopefully without any irreparable consequences. In this story, interest groups still matter, but they work through the legislative process rather than through the courts. Indeed, it is hard to imagine in this account how any court could scrutinize bureaucrats' actions and decide whether or not they had complied with legislators' intent.

Fiorina's view of congressional–bureaucratic relations rests heavily on

22

the notion of "shifting responsibility," also known as blame shifting. There are two senses in which Congress might delegate to the executive branch in order to shift blame. First, there may be policy areas where, even if great care is taken, things will go wrong every so often. For instance, consider the regulation of food and drug safety. Even under the best of circumstances, some products brought to market will have unforeseen adverse side effects; and when they do, people will naturally seek to pin the blame on the responsible party. Witness the recent furor over Dow-Corning breast implants; what politicians would ever want to be held responsible for approving their use? Emergency disaster relief is another case in point; there is no upside for getting things right, only a downside for making a mistake. In both areas, Congress has delegated to the bureaucracy on the assumption that, without executive branch expertise, outcomes would be even worse. Contrast this type of blame shifting with Fiorina's, in which groups do not blame legislators for the results of agency actions even if that agency has merely carried out Congress's instructions. This stronger sense of blame shifting is much more difficult to motivate in a world where groups are organized, informed, and conscious of the implications of different procedures.

Notice the similarities between Fiorina's theory of legislative–executive relations and Mayhew's book on congressional organization. In both cases, legislators deliberately establish systems that enhance their chances of reelection. Both approaches are positive rather than normative, and their ultimate purpose is to predict the shape of public policy. Just as Mayhew's treatise set the stage for an explosion of interest in legislative procedures, so Fiorina provoked further discussions on the impact of delegation.

The Limits of Congressional Oversight

Congressional Dominance Theories

Due largely to Fiorina's efforts, the early 1980s saw a sharp peaking of scholarly interest in congressional–bureaucratic relations. The battle lines were drawn clearly in Weingast and Moran (1983), who distinguished the "bureaucratic" approach (bureaucrats are not influenced by Congress) from the "congressional dominance" approach (Congress does exert significant influence).

Weingast and Moran made the important point that the behavioral patterns emphasized by advocates of the bureaucratic approach – the scarcity of conspicuous oversight activities – were indeed consistent with a world in which Congress has little influence over bureaucrats. However, they are also consistent with a world where Congress perfectly controls the bureaucracy. If the mere threat of congressional retaliation is enough to cow executive branch agents into submission, then these agents will never step out of line and legislators need never impose any overt sanctions. Thus, it is possible that the traditional tools of congressional control are so effective that they are never actually used – this is the problem of "observational equivalence." Weingast and Moran went on to examine Federal Trade Commission (FTC) decisions in the late 1970s and concluded that changes in enforcement patterns corresponded to changes in the preferences of the relevant congressional oversight committees, interpreting their findings as support for the congressional dominance viewpoint.

This theme of congressional oversight-at-a-distance was also the subject of McCubbins and Schwartz (1984), who examined the question of how a relatively uninformed Congress could possibly control bureaucrats who were much more knowledgeable about their particular policy area. True, they could go out and gather their own information or force the agent to disclose information at oversight hearings ("police patrol" oversight), but this would quickly become prohibitively costly, consuming legislators' scarce time and energy. On the other hand, legislators have access to a cheap source of information: namely, those interest groups affected by the agency's decisions. These groups are generally well informed about the relevant issue area and are more than willing to let their representatives know when an agency is acting contrary to their interests. Thus, legislators can control agencies simply by sitting back and waiting to see if any groups come to their doors with complaints ("fire alarm" oversight). As in Weingast and Moran, if the fire alarm system works perfectly, then bureaucrats will never step out of line and no fire alarms will actually be sounded.

Administrative Procedures and Agency Discretion

In a similar vein, McCubbins, Noll, and Weingast (1987; 1989) point to administrative procedures as a key mechanism of congressional control. Along with establishing an agency and imbuing it with an initial mandate, Congress also specifies the procedures that agencies must follow in reaching decisions. These procedures may influence bureaucrats to favor a certain constituency, avoid making rulings in a certain area, or otherwise bend them to legislators' will. Thus, congressional control is woven into the very fabric of the agency, exerting influence in a powerful yet subtle manner. Notice the kinship between this argument and those of the new institutionalist congressional scholars: One controls outcomes by controlling the procedures by which they are reached.

Kiewiet and McCubbins (1991) build upon this literature, noting that

24

congressional parties have delegated power both to committees and to executive agencies in the appropriations process. But unlike those who see this delegation as tantamount to committees' being all-powerful or as abdication to agencies, the authors show that the majority party has many procedural devices and levers through which it continues to exercise influence over key budgetary decisions. Thus, the Budget and Appropriations Committees reflect the composition of the majority party both geographically and ideologically, and the president's budget requests are frequently amended when fashioning the final congressional budget resolution, with more dramatic changes coming under divided government.

According to this literature, the basic problem that Congress faces when delegating authority is *bureaucratic drift*, or the ability of an agency to enact outcomes different from the policies preferred by those who originally delegated power. This phenomenon, illustrated in Figure 2.1 (taken from McCubbins, Noll, and Weingast 1989) arises from the fact that agencies can make regulations that can only be overturned with the combined assent of the House, Senate, and president. For instance, let the ideal points of these three actors be H, S, and P, respectively, and assume that Congress passes and the president signs legislation designed to implement policy X. Now assume that the agency has policy preference A. The agency maximizes its utility by setting policy equal to X', the point in the Pareto set closest to its ideal point. Even though this policy is not what Congress and the president originally intended, the necessary coalition to overturn agency decisions cannot be formed.

As detailed in Epstein and O'Halloran (1994), two general categories of administrative devices have been identified as means of controlling bureaucratic drift. The first category, *ex ante controls*, concerns issues of agency design. What are the procedures, including reporting and consultation requirements, that an agency must follow in making policy? Who are the agency's key constituents and how will they influence decision making? What standards or criteria must an agency consider when promulgating regulations? In which executive department will the new agency be located, and how far down the organizational ladder will political appointments reach? These are all questions that legislators must answer when drafting the authorizing legislation.

The second category consists of *ongoing controls*, those institutions or procedures that check agency actions on a regular basis. These include instruments of congressional oversight, such as the direct and indirect monitoring discussed above, and renewing or withholding appropriations (Calvert, Moran, and Weingast 1987). They also include judicial oversight implemented through existing administrative law (Mashaw 1990) and presidential appointment powers (Calvert, McCubbins, and Weingast 1989; Spulber and Besanko 1992). Both *ex ante* and ongoing

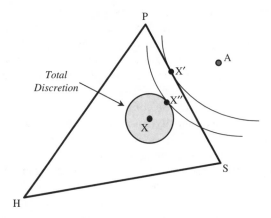

Figure 2.1. Bureaucratic Drift and Agency Discretion

controls, then, serve to limit the degree to which agencies can act contrary to congressional intent.[13]

On the other hand, we argue that a much more direct method of circumscribing agency influence is also available, one that avoids the problems of costly monitoring and complicated administrative procedures: explicitly limiting the *discretion* of an agency to move outcomes from the status quo. Assume, as shown in Figure 2.1, that the relevant statute allows the agency to move policy only a limited distance away from X, say by limiting agricultural price support levels to lie between 60 and 90 percent of parity. Outcomes are now equal to X", which is much closer to Congress's original intent than X'. Whereas McCubbins, Noll, and Weingast (1989) define discretion as those actions that no political coalition can overturn, equating discretion with the limits of bureaucratic drift, we argue that Congress may prefer to set limits on agency discretion *more stringent* than those implied by their *ex post* power to overturn agency decisions alone.

In fact, Congress limits executive branch discretion in this manner all the time, simply by passing specific, detail-filled legislation. If Congress had specified in the 1970 Occupational Safety and Health Act that airborne concentrations of benzene emissions were to be limited to 1 part per million, then the secretary of labor would have had little choice but to implement these standards. Any attempt to do otherwise would have been overturned, not by a coalition of the House, Senate, and president, but by the courts, which, in turn, could not disregard Con-

---

[13]Classic political science treatises on bureaucratic policy making and delegation include Landis (1938), Harris (1964), and Woll (1977). For an overview, see Ripley and Franklin (1984, 16–19).

gress's explicit mandates without losing credibility. Thus, the discretion continuum connects congressional and executive policy making; saying that there is no discretion is equivalent to saying Congress makes policy on its own.[14]

Why, then, does Congress not always control agencies by passing detailed legislation and limiting bureaucratic discretion to a minimum? The answer, of course, is that there are costs to limiting agency discretion in this way. Making explicit laws requires legislative time and energy that might be profitably spent on more electorally productive activities. One of the reasons that bureaucracies are created in the first place is to implement policies in areas where Congress has neither the time nor the expertise to micromanage policy decisions, and by restricting flexibility, Congress limits the agency's ability to adjust to changing circumstances. This trade-off is captured well by Terry Moe (1990, 228) in his discussion of regulatory structure:

> The most direct way [to control agencies] is for today's authorities to specify, in excruciating detail, precisely what the agency is to do and how it is to do it, leaving as little as possible to the discretionary judgment of bureaucrats – and thus as little as possible for future authorities to exercise control over, short of passing new legislation. . . . Obviously, this is not a formula for creating effective organizations. In the interests of public protection, agencies are knowingly burdened with cumbersome, complicated, technically inappropriate structures that undermine their capacity to perform their jobs well.

Administrative procedures, then, play an important role in limiting executive branch authority. But it is incorrect to conclude that Congress wants only to restrict agency discretion; legislators want to strike a balance between granting agencies too much leeway and constraining them so tightly that there is no room to incorporate bureaucratic expertise into policy outcomes.

Principal–Agent Models of Oversight

The congressional dominance theorists generated vociferous opposition from within the community of public administration scholars. Part of the debate was genuinely substantive; critics pointed out that many sources other than Congress influence bureaucrats, including the president, interest groups, and the courts (Moe 1985). On the other hand, part of the debate also stemmed from an unfortunate disagreement over semantics. The congressional dominance scholars made frequent reference to principal–agent analysis, a theoretical paradigm developed in

---

[14]See the essays in Hawkins (1992) for further discussions of agency discretion and its legal ramifications.

economics to describe situations in which one party (the agent) takes actions on the behalf of another party (the principal). Hundreds if not thousands of articles have been generated in the past two decades on the general theme of principal–agent relationships, with the punch line being that principals can usually mitigate conflicts of interest through the careful design of incentive contracts but can rarely control agents perfectly.

In the bureaucratic-control literature, however, principal–agent analysis became synonymous with the view that legislators do perfectly control executive branch agents to whom they have delegated authority. This, confusion was exacerbated by the fact that, as Bendor (1988) put it, "principal–agent models are more talked about than written down." Thus, there emerged a debate over the question of whether or not bureaucrats were really the "agent" of their political "principals." This discussion has generated rather more heat than light and has served to bog down more-substantive investigations of the procedural mechanisms by which Congress controls bureaucratic behavior.

Those investigating congressional–bureaucratic relations imitated not only the logic of the new institutionalists working on Congress but their style as well. The field quickly became quite mathematically intense, blending social-choice approaches (Hammond and Miller 1985; Hammond 1986; Calvert, McCubbins, and Weingast 1989) with theories based on budget-maximizing bureaucrats who have issue-specific expertise (Miller and Moe 1983; Bendor, Taylor, and Van Gaalen 1985, 1987; Banks 1989).[15] This literature argues that, although legislators may try to control agency actions through administrative procedures, these controls can only ameliorate, but never completely resolve, the basic problem. As Moe (1989, 271) states:

> Experts have their own interests – in career, in autonomy – that may conflict with those of [legislators]. And, due largely to experts' specialized knowledge and the often intangible nature of their outputs, [Congress] cannot know exactly what its expert agents are doing or why. These are problems of conflict of interest and asymmetric information, and they are unavoidable. Because of them, control will be imperfect.

The conclusion is that Congress must solve the problem of delegating just the right amount of authority to agencies in just the right way. Too little or too tightly constrained delegation will deny Congress the benefits of agency expertise and reduced workload that motivated the initial

---

[15]It must be acknowledged that this latter tradition has its roots in the pioneering work of Niskanen (1971), who argued that agencies inflate their budgets above the efficient level. Niskanen was far ahead of his time; he even formalized his theory at a time when few political treatises contained equations of any kind.

delegation of authority. On the other hand, delegating too much power to an agency runs the risk of allowing policies to be enacted that are contrary to the wishes of legislators and their constituents. It is this trade-off between expertise and control, informational gains and distributive losses, that lies at the heart of this view of administrative procedures. Note that the same themes from the congressional organization literature – information and distribution – resonate in the oversight literature as well.

In the end, like the literature on legislative organization, the congressional–bureaucratic relations literature has also reached a bit of an impasse. While work continues on formalizing some of the notions previously set forth (Banks and Weingast 1992; Lupia and McCubbins 1994; Epstein and O'Halloran 1994, 1995; Bawn 1995), the general consensus has been reached that legislators have more-effective means of control than was previously realized, but bureaucrats still retain significant amounts of discretion in setting policy.

WHY DELEGATE?

These findings, however, raise a further question: If congressional control of the bureaucracy is imperfect, then which policy areas are decided in Congress and which are delegated to the executive branch? This is clearly an important question, for behind its answer lie the boundaries of the modern administrative state; it goes right to the heart of our separation-of-powers system, defining where legislation ends and where implementation begins. Yet few authors have tackled it head on. Most concentrate on reasons why legislators cede authority to executive branch actors at all. The typical answer, as given for instance by Ripley and Franklin (1984, 17), is that Congress delegates to take advantage of reduced workload and executive branch expertise:

Government has assumed increasing responsibility in an ever-expanding number of issue areas in the twentieth century, and Congress of necessity has delegated a great deal of authority vested in it by the Constitution to various parts of the executive branch. The sheer volume and technical complexity of the work are more than Congress, with its limited membership and staff, can manage alone.

On the other hand, the "original sin" hypothesis, advanced by Stigler (1971), asserts that bureaucracies are created by politicians specifically to serve constituency needs, with the amount of protection being determined by the point where supply meets demand; that is, where the costs to the politician of adding more protection equal the benefit to the affected constituents. Similarly, "iron triangles" or subgovernments may form, in which congressional committees, interest groups, and bureau-

29

crats combine in an unholy trinity to deliver benefits to the interest group's members at public expense. This line of reasoning, then, dovetails with Lowi's (1969) attack on delegation as an abdication of legislative responsibility.

This view also converges with the concerns of legal scholars, such as Aranson, Gellhorn, and Robinson (1982), who decry delegation as a means of delivering private benefits to favored constituents, and who urge a resuscitation of the nondelegation doctrine. Similarly, Schoenbrod (1993) argues forcefully that Congress oversteps its constitutional bounds when delegating broad discretion to executive agencies, that it could find the time and resources necessary to write detailed laws if it really wanted to, and that in practice delegation leads to such nonsensical policies as burning oranges during the Great Depression. "Delegation allows Congress to stay silent about [regulatory costs and benefits], so it severs the link between the legislator's vote and the law, upon which depend both democratic accountability and the safeguards of liberty provided by Article I" (17).

These theories fall into the category of general reasons for delegation and, as such, are not tailored to answer the question of which policy areas in particular Congress chooses to delegate over others. Thus legislators may wish to reduce their workload and hand difficult issues over to the executive. However, Congress does retain policy-making authority in some issue areas, including such complex areas as tax policy. And certain interests may extract rents from the regulatory process, but one would certainly not want to argue that Congress does not also deliver benefits to targeted constituencies through the legislative process. What is needed, then, is a theory that distinguishes those policies that are delegated from those that Congress decides itself.

The extant literature offers three broad categories of explanations for why Congress delegates in some issue areas rather than others. First, Congress might choose to delegate for reasons of constituency relations; and within this category, in turn, we are presented with three variations. In order, beginning with the most benign: (1) legislators may wish to free up time to spend on constituency service, simultaneously taking advantage of agency expertise. By this reckoning, legislators will begin to delegate authority at the point where the marginal returns to favored constituents from enacting specific policy equal the marginal returns from casework; (2) as in Fiorina's (1977) original work on the subject, legislators may gain by exposing their constituents to the vagaries of administrative regulation, content to play the role of ombudsmen who intervene if this process goes awry; (3) the most sinister interpretation casts legislators in the role of leading an organized "protection racket," threatening uncooperative constituents with harmful regulation if they do not contribute to legislators' coffers.[16]

This class of explanations rests on a view of the legislative process as concentrating almost exclusively on the provision of private benefits. Legislators desiring to maximize casework-related dividends might indeed find delegation (or in some cases, the mere threat of regulation) a useful tool. But this view of legislative activity is certainly a bit simplistic; legislators also spend their time dealing with issues of general import, delivering benefits to large classes of constituents rather than small, targeted interest groups (witness Social Security and Medicare). Legislators can and do combine general and specific benefits in the same piece of legislation (take the budget, for example), but the statement that Congress is never wholly public spirited is not evidence for the statement that they are entirely private minded.[17]

The second category of explanations revolves around the notion of a "regulatory lottery." As detailed in Fiorina (1982), this supposes that interest groups who come to loggerheads in the legislative process, unable to resolve their differences, will agree that authority be delegated to agencies. That is, they prefer the uncertainty of the regulatory process at some point down the road to any certain outcome in the present. This theme is also echoed in McCubbins (1985), who assumes that a legislative coalition might be more easily constructed around a bill that delegates than one that enacts specific policies. Fiorina (1986) later offered a slight variant on this theme, examining the delegation choice as one of deciding between two uncertainties. If Congress delegates, then the agency may implement a range of possible outcomes, perhaps with some bias toward one policy direction or the other. But direct legislation is subject to interpretation by the courts, which may also cause some distortions. Thus, legislators' preferences over whether or not to delegate rest on their expected benefits from bureaucratic policy making as opposed to judicial policy making.

These uncertainty-based explanations, though provocative, are also subject to a number of possible critiques. Those that assume that interest groups will choose the regulatory lottery are predicated on these interests having risk-loving preferences. That is, if they prefer an uncertain outcome in the future to a present outcome with the same expected value, then they must gain independent utility from taking risks. This runs counter to the normal economic assumption that actors are risk

[16]See Niskanen's comments in Manne and Miller (1976) for an argument along these lines pertaining to the auto industry.

[17]This corrective view of legislative motivation, directed at a legal audience, is spelled out well by Farber and Frickey (1991, chap. 1).

averse or, at the worst, risk-neutral. The "competing uncertainties" theory, on the other hand, assumes that judicial enforcement of statutes will result in a large degree of variation in outcomes. If Congress writes detailed legislation, though, the courts will have little recourse but to follow the exact letter of the law, so Congress could wring most of the uncertainty out of legislation if it chose to do so. In addition, delegating to the executive does not remove the judicial component of uncertainty, for courts could overrule agency decisions at least as easily as they could change the intent of congressional statutes.

Third – synthesizing the work of Wilson (1974) and Weingast, Shepsle, and Johnsen (1981) – Fiorina (1982) posited that when groups of unequal size clash, delegation may offer legislators the best of all possible worlds. Large groups will be mollified by delegation to a neutral third party accompanied by general exhortations to regulate in the public interest. The more concentrated group can then bring its resources to bear on the agency and sway particular regulations in its favor. Based on this difference in information costs, Congress can shift the blame for unpopular policies to regulatory agencies. Therefore, legislators prefer to delegate to bureaucrats whenever the policy in question has concentrated benefits and dispersed costs and make policy themselves when the opposite is true.[18] Similarly, Arnold (1990, 101) argues that delegation allows legislators to enact unpopular policies through hidden means:

One method of masking legislators' individual contributions [to policies that impose costs on their constituents] is to delegate responsibility for making unpleasant decisions to the president, bureaucrats, regulatory commissioners, judges, or state and local officials. . . . Sometimes legislators know precisely what the executive will decide, but the process of delegation insulates them from political retribution.

The blame-shifting model undoubtedly captures some of the motivations behind legislators' decision to delegate – who would not want to relinquish the responsibility for making difficult policy choices with clear winners and losers? But, for both empirical and theoretical reasons, the situation is probably a bit more complicated. First, the theory implies that constituent benefits will be delivered via delegation, while broad, general policy will be passed in the legislature. This assumption runs counter to the usual notion that legislators are engaged almost entirely in providing constituency benefits through pork barreling and casework. Also, for this logic to work, voters must constantly be fooled by delegation, lacking any political entrepreneur to inform them of its deleterious

---

[18]See also Kafka (1996) for an argument relating agency structure to the distribution of costs and benefits.

nature. As argued by Farber and Frickey (1991, 81), we should expect that under such situations rational voters would either develop some appropriate "legal technology" to monitor executive officials or look askance at all delegation as simply means for delivering particularized benefits at their expense.

We do not wish to argue too strenuously against any of these previous theories, for each contains more than a grain of truth. But although each captures part of the story, none treats all players as fully strategic actors with their own goals, sets out a clear decision-making process, and arrives at an equilibrium choice of institutions.

We argue that the answer to the question of "Why delegate?" lies in the previous two literatures reviewed in this chapter. Theories of legislative organization and congressional oversight are both well developed in their own right but have heretofore matured in relative isolation from one another. We contend that these two lines of thought are best seen as describing alternative ways of producing policy, either through normal legislative processes or through delegation. The following chapters integrate the insights of these previous approaches into a single theory that predicts why certain policy areas are consistently decided by direct legislation and others are left to the executive.

3

Transaction Cost Politics

Without some knowledge of what would be achieved with alternative institutional arrangements, it is impossible to choose sensibly among them.

Ronald Coase, *The Firm, The Market, and The Law*[1]

Our view of legislative–executive relations, similar to the studies cited in Chapter 2, attempts to motivate delegation from the ground up as a rational institutional choice made by utility-maximizing legislators. In constructing our framework, we draw an analogy with recent insights from the economic theory of the firm. Particularly of interest is work on the subject of transaction cost economics and vertical integration – that is, a firm's make-or-buy decision. We argue that Congress has a similar make-or-buy decision when making public policy; it can specify the details of legislation itself or it can subcontract them to executive agencies. Furthermore, the central concepts of transaction cost economics can help us construct a theory of political delegation, so that we can make predictions about the location of policy making in a separation of powers system.

Our objective in this exercise is not simply to impose transaction cost analysis on a political context but to use its key notions as organizing principles. In particular, the concepts of boundaries, incomplete contracts, and the holdup problem shed new light on issues of legislative organization and congressional–executive relations. The committee system and delegation both have their strengths and weaknesses, and the transaction costs associated with policy production in either mode will vary from case to case. The basic prediction is that legislators will arrange the institutions of governance – the boundaries between legislative

[1]Coase (1988, 30).

34

and executive policy making – to minimize their overall average political transaction costs.

This chapter first recounts in some detail the logic of transaction cost analysis in economics, including its assumptions, key elements, and style of reasoning. We then apply this approach to politics, discuss which assumptions hold in a political context and which do not, and elucidate the implications of the transaction cost approach for our central question of why legislators will delegate some issue areas rather than others to the executive.

LESSONS FROM THE THEORY OF THE FIRM

Elements of Transaction Cost Analysis

The best way to understand transaction costs is to imagine a world where they do not exist. This is a Coasian world, in which economic actors can bargain with each other to reach an efficient allocation of resources.[2] In the classic example, if a plot of land is more valuable when used for farming than when it is used for ranching, then the farmer will buy or lease it from a neighboring rancher. Or, if the farmer already owns the land, the rancher will not wish to pay the amount necessary to obtain it. Note that the initial allocation of property rights will affect actors' *ex post* utilities – the rancher would rather start with the land and lease it out, of course – but it will have no impact on the actual production of goods and services. Note, too, that the final contract may be quite complex – the farmer's rent may vary with the amount of rainfall, for instance, or the lease may be canceled entirely if the price of corn drops below a certain level.

A transaction cost, then, is anything that makes reality deviate from this Coasian world; in Dixit's words, "anything that impedes the specification, monitoring, or enforcement of an economic transaction is a transaction cost" (1996, 38). As such, transaction costs are necessarily a broad, catchall category, a general rubric rather then a single, easily definable set. For instance, the arrangement between the farmer and the rancher may break down if the farmer knows more about the land's quality than does the rancher (asymmetric information), if the farmer must buy specialized equipment to work the field (asset specificity), or if the rent paid depends on improvements made to the land but the effort put into these improvements is hard to observe (principal–agent problems). Transaction cost economics thus provides a conceptual frame-

---

[2]We refer here to Coase's (1960) seminal article on economic efficiency and the allocation of property rights.

work for analyzing a large class of problems endemic to markets, organizations, and, as we shall argue, politics: To the extent that any of these systems departs from the Coasian benchmark, transaction costs are at work.

Despite the wide variety of interactions described as potentially plagued with transaction costs, all transaction cost analyses do share some common elements.[3] First, they focus on the *contract* as the unit of analysis. Two or more parties wish to make an exchange, and they devise a contact to embody the terms of this exchange. To claim that a transaction departs from the Coasian ideal, then, is to say that the contract the parties wish to enter into is in some way deficient. Second, contracts are assumed to be enforceable by some *neutral third party*, usually taken to be the courts, although in some cases the contracting parties may wish to rely on another outside arbitrator instead. Third, transaction cost analyses assume the existence of multiple possible *governance structures;* for instance, economic exchanges can be governed by one-time spot contracts, by long-term contracts, by custom, or by integration into a single firm. Governance structures are important insofar as they influence the magnitude and shape of the transaction costs associated with a given interaction – different structures imply different costs. Fourth, economic actors are assumed to be *boundedly rational*, due to the fact that they exist in a complex, uncertain, dynamic environment. As Milgrom and Roberts (1992, 128) state, "Real people ... cannot solve arbitrarily complex problems exactly, costlessly, and instantaneously, and they cannot communicate with one another freely and perfectly." In such a setting, no one agent or even set of agents can know the exact state of events now or in the future, so they cannot eliminate transaction costs by simply contracting around these events from the outset.

Whenever some departure from the efficient Coasian world is identified, transaction cost analysis proceeds along the following lines. First, one makes sure that the elements of the transaction cost setting hold: that is, enforceable contracts, multiple governance structures, and bounded rationality are all present. Second, a search is made for the transaction costs that could have caused this deviation. Third, alternative governance structures are evaluated according to their ability to mitigate these and possibly other related transaction costs.

The central concern of the transaction cost perspective, then, is comparative institutional analysis; a given set of transactions may be plagued with a variety of costs, and different governance structures might affect

---

[3]What follows is necessarily a summary of this rich literature. For lengthier treatments, see Holmstrom and Tirole (1989), Williamson (1989), Milgrom and Roberts (1992, chap. 9), and Dixit (1996).

the magnitude of each of these costs. The farmer and rancher might merge into a single farm-products corporation, for instance; they might enter into a complicated leasing arrangement; or they might agree to let a third party develop the land as she sees fit and each take a percentage of the profits. The task is to predict how optimal governance structures change as this menu of transaction costs changes, the assumption being that rational economic actors will structure their relationships so as to minimize the overall transaction costs.[4]

Transaction Costs and Incomplete Contracts

Recent years have seen an explosion of interest in transaction costs, as economists have begun to appreciate the importance of two closely related issues: incomplete contracts and power relations among economic agents. In a world where contracts are complete, every provision that is or will be relevant to a transaction can be written down and bargained over by the contracting parties. Once the initial contract is signed, all that remains is a mechanical unfolding of its provisions over time. This does not mean, of course, that at the time the contract is signed the parties know what events will happen in the future. But it does mean that every possible eventuality is *knowable*, and so contractual obligations can be made contingent on all future events. In this world, the *ex post* division of power among parties has no meaning, since every action they take has been specified in the contract. And the job of enforcing the contract is straightforward; courts need only examine the relevant clause of the contract and oblige one party or the other to act in the specified manner.

When significant transaction costs exist, on the other hand, and individuals are boundedly rational, contracts will in general be incomplete; that is, they will have missing provisions and ambiguous clauses. This incompleteness is caused by a number of factors: thinking costs, trying to imagine every possible future state of the world; negotiation costs, arising from the fact that haggling over difficult clauses may be more costly than it is worth; and writing or enforcement costs, since many factors affecting the value of the relationship may be difficult or impos-

[4]Consequently, the analyst must be judicious when evaluating any given organizational form, as seemingly inefficient practices might be necessary to avoid other, even larger transaction costs. Therefore, a system should be judged on its average efficiency over time rather than on any one instance or task. For example, Wilson (1989, 319–20) defends centralized military procurement practices resulting in the purchase of $435 hammers as a precaution against decentralization that would result in many more, but less observable, wasteful practices. (As it turns out, as Wilson explains, even the $435 hammer is a myth.)

sible to credibly verify to a court. Thus, there may very well arise situations in a contractual relationship that neither party counted on when entering into the original agreement and whose resolution is not explicitly described in the contract.[5]

When contracts are incomplete, the process of negotiation never really ends, as parties to a contract will be continuously adjusting their actions in response to changing circumstances. Under these conditions, *ex post* power relations matter exceedingly. The party who has the right to determine how assets will be used when a gap in a contact is reached will have considerable influence over the final allocation of costs and benefits across the contracting parties. The question of who controls assets when an uncontracted eventuality occurs is thus an important one in transaction cost analysis and goes by the name of residual rights of control. Also, the job of the arbitrator becomes much more difficult, for she may be called upon to determine how ambiguous or partial contract terms apply to a given real-world situation.

Incomplete contracts are important not only in understanding the ongoing dynamics of contractual relationships; they are also crucial in explaining the types of contracts that are entered into in the first place and the form that these contracts will take. Consider an employee in a firm who has an idea of how to make the production process more efficient. If the employer has all residual rights to the benefits of the employee's new process (he owns the patent), then the employee might be hesitant to reveal her idea, for she would reap none of the benefits. To counter such a possibility, many companies have explicit policies governing the treatment of employee innovations, including profit-sharing agreements, bonuses, and promotions. These in turn are devised so that the company can attract imaginative, high-quality employees. Thus *ex post* control rights may exert strong influence over *ex ante* contractual arrangements.

The Economics of Boundaries

Transaction cost analysis has found its most important application in the study of firm boundaries, also known as vertical integration or the firm's make-or-buy decision. To understand the basic questions involved in the economic theory of vertical integration and their relation to political organization, it is useful first to have a visual representation of

[5]For instance, suppose Sally agrees to supply Fred with 100 widgets for the price of $100. Then Sally's factory is hit by a tornado. What happens now? Must Sally buy the widgets from a competitor and hand them over to Fred? Must Fred rebuild Sally's factory?

the problem. As shown in Figure 3.1, a firm consists of a related set of nodes in the process of producing a final product. At the bottom of the figure are raw materials, which are combined with each other in successively more complex intermediate products until the final product is sold on the consumer market. Firms are defined by their position in this hierarchy; some deal mainly or wholly in raw materials, others produce intermediate goods, while others concentrate predominantly on consumer goods.

At some point, each firm stops making its own inputs and instead relies on the market to supply them; after all, even highly integrated firms buy their pens, pencils, and other office supplies from other companies. The question is therefore one of boundaries. What are the natural limits of firms? Where does one stop and another begin? Why do firms not branch out to other markets; conversely, why do they not concentrate on doing only one thing but doing it well? In the limit, these boil down to two more-fundamental questions: Why do firms exist at all, and conversely, why is the economy not organized as one large firm?

Neoclassical and Principal–Agent Approaches

The two predominant literatures within economics offer little guidance in answering these questions. Neoclassical economics, based on the familiar supply-and-demand curves, can predict well the overall output of an industry, monopoly and oligopoly behavior, and the way in which prices react to changing market conditions. But it has little to say about the division of output across firms or the size of firms in relation to each other. Nor is it helpful in studying questions about mergers or vertical integration – that is, the scope of activity within firms.

The principal–agent literature, on the other hand, is well suited to analyzing behavior within firms or within hierarchical organizations in general. For instance, the prototypical principal–agent problem analyzes the difficulty that one actor (the principal) will have getting another actor (the agent) to work on her behalf in the presence of incomplete information. But it is not clear how this analysis relates to the theory of the firm. The principal could be the agent's supervisor within a firm, or they might be in an arms-length market relation – nothing in the theory tells us which organizational structure would minimize agency losses. Or consider Jensen and Meckling's (1976) principal–agent theory of the firm as a "nexus of contracts," in which the authors conceive of transactions within a firm as taking place on a basis of constant negotiation. Even so, their theory tells us little about the origin of this nexus or why two nexuses do not merge to form a single nexus.

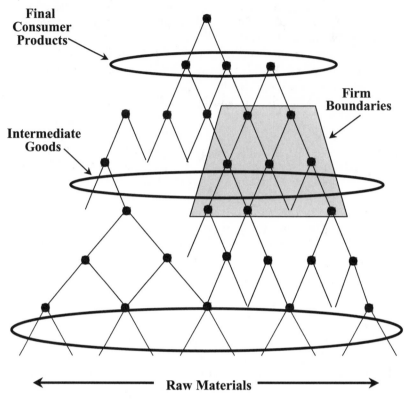

Final Consumer Products

Firm Boundaries

Intermediate Goods

← **Raw Materials** →

Figure 3.1. Schematic Representation of the Boundaries of a Firm

Coasian Analysis of Boundaries

Coase (1937), in his classic article on the subject of firm boundaries, tackled this problem by noting first that a good deal of economic activity takes place within firms; that is, through the suppression of the price mechanism. Coase then proposed that the genesis of firms lies in the fact that market transactions may involve significant costs of negotiation, while transactions in firms operate on a command-and-control basis; bringing transactions within the ambit of the firm, then, can economize on these negotiation costs. But when firms become too large, they become bureaucratic and unwieldy as well, making it difficult for any one individual to allocate a firm's resources efficiently. Therefore, the size of the firm is determined by the point at which these two costs balance. Although he did not label it so at the time, Coase's arguments are forerunners of the modern transaction cost approach: Economic actors

40

negotiating in the market might not achieve the best possible outcomes because the costs of finding a reasonable contract are too high; therefore, an alternative governance structure – unified ownership – might minimize overall transaction costs.

Coase's insights lay fallow for a number of years, until they were picked up in the 1970s due to a renewed interest in the subject of vertical integration. At that point a number of scholars, particularly Williamson (1975, 1979, 1985), Goldberg (1976), and Klein, Crawford, and Alchian (1978), began to delve more deeply into the exact nature of the inefficiencies and transaction costs that plague market interactions, for the costs of negotiation alone seemed insufficient to account for the amount of economic activity that occurs in firms rather than markets.

The Holdup Problem

In the end, attention focused on a particular combination of asset specificity and time consistency problems, known as the *hold-up problem*. A prototypical example of the hold-up problem, due to Joskow (1985), occurs between a coal mine and an electricity generating plant. Economically, it may be most efficient for the generator to be located as close to the coal mine as possible to conserve on transportation costs (so-called mine mouth generating plants). But the owner of the generator will be reluctant to spend the resources necessary to move her plant, for then she would be at the mercy of the coal producer, who would try to raise the price of coal and take advantage of their proximity; that is, she may be "held up" by the mine owner. The firms might want to sign a contract specifying the price to be charged for coal, but if each firm can take actions that affect the value of the investment but are nonobservable or nonverifiable – if contracts are incomplete, in other words – then this solution may be insufficient. The end result might be that the plant operator will refuse to make an economically sound investment (moving her plant closer to the source) for fear of being held up.

Naturally, firms will anticipate the hold-up problem and attempt to devise ways around it. One inventive solution was practiced for many years in the computer chip industry.[6] Manufacturers of new computer chips used to hand over their design to a second company immediately, often helping to establish that company, in order to generate competition for their new product. This was done to convince computer manufacturers to adopt their new chip without fear of being held up once the investment in the new chip technology was made. This practice came to

[6]This example is drawn from Shepard (1987) and Farrell and Gallini (1988).

an end with Intel's 80386 chip; they reasoned that they would have to keep prices low in order to compete with the previous generation of their own chips.

The more usual solution to the hold-up problem is for the upstream and downstream firms simply to merge, as in fact often happens with coal mines and generating plants. The advantage of a hierarchically structured firm is that one person controls all physical assets of both companies, and she can then engage in relationship-specific investments that would not otherwise be made for fear of the hold-up problem. So the owner of a joint mine-plant venture could move her plant closer to the mine, secure in the knowledge that if the mine *manager* (no longer owner) tries to hold her up, the manager can simply be fired. Hence, in a world of incomplete contracting, unified ownership structures may encourage relationship-specific investments that would not be entered into between separate firms. The importance of controlling the physical assets involved in production is the keystone of the *property rights* approach to vertical integration.[7]

The problem with vertical integration, on the other hand, is that employees within firms have little incentive to make relationship-specific investments, since they reap few of the rewards for doing so. Thus, two firms that have little relation to each other should not merge, because doing so would only result in the loss of what Williamson (1985) terms "high powered market incentives" captured by competitive prices. These problems could be solved by intense monitoring, but such supervision is itself costly, and any attempt to replace direct monitoring with a system of internal prices (called transfer prices) is again subject to manipulation.[8] Thus, large firms tend to become "bureaucratic" and inefficient, and coordination among subunits becomes difficult to achieve.

The bottom line is that firm structure – whether firms merge or stay independent – will trade off these two forms of inefficiencies. To the degree that integration helps achieve coordination that would be lost in arms-length market relations, mergers will occur and firms will grow in size. But bloated firms that try to carry on economically unrelated activities will be prime targets for selloffs and decentralization. The boundaries of the firm are therefore in constant flux, and, at each moment, they should reflect the current trade-offs imposed by market conditions and the technologies of producing various goods and services in different market sectors.

---

[7]In fact, this is the principal advantage of the property rights paradigm, as traditional transaction cost approaches have difficulty explaining exactly why mergers can solve the hold-up problem. See Hart (1995) for a lucid exposition.

[8]See Milgrom and Roberts (1992, 550–1). For an interesting and more detailed account of the costs of intrafirm transactions, see Miller (1992).

A THEORY OF TRANSACTION COST POLITICS

We are now in a position to relate this new economic literature on the structure of the firm to our main question of where policy is made. Our theory, in brief, is that delegation to the bureaucracy is subject to the political equivalent of the hold-up problem, so Congress will delegate to the executive when the external transaction costs of doing so are less than the internal transaction costs of making policy through the normal legislative process via committees. Thus, policy will be made in the manner that is politically most expedient from legislators' point of view – that is, in a manner that minimizes the costs of producing policy. In this section, we first show that the basic elements of a transaction cost approach hold in the political setting as well. We then apply the transaction cost theory of firm boundaries to address the question of the boundaries of the modern administrative state. Finally, we examine the implications of this argument for the study of legislative organization, delegation, and national policy making.

Political Equivalents of Transaction Cost Analysis

The transaction cost literature reviewed above describes market relations as potentially plagued with costs of their own, and these costs in turn will influence whether the transactions take place within or between firms. The concepts set forth in this analysis, however, are not necessarily applicable only to economic questions; indeed, they would seem to have relevance for any system characterized by a series of agreements between rational, utility-maximizing individuals.

Our claim is that this scenario certainly includes political exchange as one application, and so it would not be out of place to speak of a theory of transaction cost politics. In fact, this term is not new; Wilson (1989, 358–9) briefly mentions the idea of applying transaction cost analysis to the question of which services the government performs itself and which it contracts out to private firms. The phrase "transaction cost politics" itself was first used by North (1990) in connection with individual decision making; North asserted that the presence of various transaction costs will prevent actors from behaving in complete accordance with the norm of "instrumental rationality."

More recently, Dixit (1996) presents an absorbing overview of the ways in which transaction cost economics may serve both as an organizing principle for various political literatures and as a fruitful area of future research, paying particular attention to the problem of common agency in political principal–agent relations. As illustrated in Figure 3.2, though, Dixit's analysis focuses mainly on questions of government intervention in the economic marketplace, where transactions between economic actors can be disrupted by inefficient government policies; that is, his is a theory of politically imposed transaction costs. For instance, Dixit argues that compensation to declining industries often takes an economically inefficient form – tariffs, quotas, price supports, or subsidies – because more-efficient relocation policies are politically infeasible due to politicians' inability to commit to future benefits and voters' inability to commit to future electoral support for current officeholders.

In contrast, we use transaction cost analysis to examine the relation of various political actors to each other. We claim that some transactions among political actors may potentially generate benefits for all concerned. Yet, just as in economic situations, these may not take place due to the existence of transaction costs, such as time consistency problems, principal–agent losses, and incomplete and asymmetric information. Ours, then, is a theory of transaction cost politics, and in particular we shall argue below that delegation from Congress to the executive is subject to a form of the political hold-up problem. When we refer to political transaction costs, then, we mean transaction costs that arise in interactions among political actors, not costs imposed by political actors on the economic marketplace.

Economics versus Politics: Differences

Before launching into our own application of transaction cost politics, we must note some essential differences between the economic and political spheres that will affect our analysis. First and foremost, politics has no equivalent of the free market or price system in economics. Private-sector firms cannot compete freely for the right to receive delegated authority; this role may constitutionally be played only by the executive branch of the government. Therefore, the correct baseline for our analysis is not economic market efficiency but rather political efficiency in terms of reelection probabilities – insofar as legislators design the institutions of delegation and these legislators care primarily about being reelected, power will be delegated to the executive in such a way as to maximize legislator's reelection chances.

Second, Congress is ultimately limited by the size of the parent chamber. Firms can always expand, contract, or merge, but the House and Senate, at least in the short run, are fixed in size.[9] Given its limited resources, then, Congress realizes that it can only effectively manage a certain amount of public business; the rest it must either refuse to con-

---

[9]True, more staff can always be hired, but this creates ever more intense problems of supervising and monitoring the staff's activities.

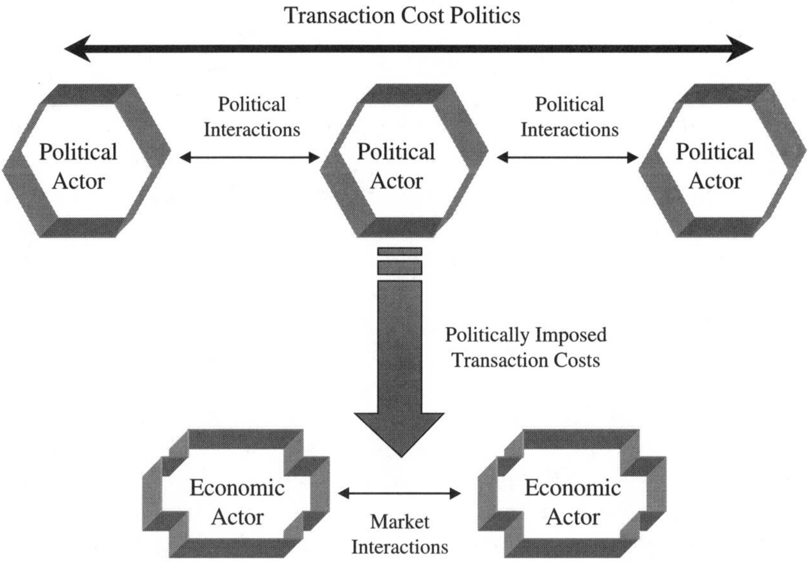

Transaction Cost Politics

Figure 3.2. Differences between Political Transaction Costs and Transaction Cost Politics

sider or delegate to the executive branch. Third, contracts between Congress and the executive are not the result of a normal bargaining process. The president may veto the implementing legislation, but this veto may be overridden by a two-thirds vote, and the president has no power to make counteroffers. Thus, Congress has a much greater degree of control over agencies than one firm would ever have over another, including power over budgets, operating procedures, and even the very existence of the agency.

Economics versus Politics: Similarities

Despite these differences, we claim that the major themes of transaction cost analysis apply in a political context as well. Consider first the political equivalents of the four elements of transaction cost analysis given above: (1) a focus on the contract as the unit of analysis; (2) third-party enforcement of these contracts; (3) multiple possible governance structures; and (4) bounded rationality.

For our purposes, the unit of analysis will be a specific piece of legislation. Just as a contract specifies the obligations of the relevant parties, so a law specifies the obligations of public officials in their relations with the populace at large. It details the actions that may or

45

may not be taken by both legislators and bureaucrats, and it regulates the relations between them for the duration of the law. In politics, like economics, third-party enforcement of these contracts is provided by the court system; if public officials fail to execute their obligations under law, then they can be sued in court for nonperformance.

Note that our approach implies that legislation is equivalent to an incomplete political contract. To convince oneself that this is so, assume the opposite and then imagine the details that would have to be included in order to make contracts between Congress and the executive complete: Every possible adjudication would have a predetermined result based on the facts of the case, every regulation would be specified in advance depending on the outcome of agency research, the timing of mailing every benefit check would be written down, and so on.[10]

The existence of multiple governance structures in politics is crucial to our analysis. Just as in economics there exist two basic modes of organization – intrafirm production or purchase in the market – we argue that when making public policy the basic choice is between production within Congress or delegation to the executive; the details of policy either will be spelled out in legislation or will be left for the executive branch to determine.

Williamson (1975) emphasizes that the true range of possible economic governance structures is wide and varied, and political organization provides a wealth of possibilities here as well. Delegation can be broad (regulation "in the public interest"), or it can be accompanied by a variety of procedural constraints. Power can be delegated to an independent agency or commission, to the executive office of the president, or to a government corporation. Congress can refer bills to one or more committees, with or without time limits, and under such restrictive amendment procedures as the floor wishes to adopt. Executive agencies can be limited by a variety of administrative procedures, including sunset provisions, reporting and rule-making requirements, exemptions, and compensations for affected parties. Just as transaction cost economics assumes that governance structures will be chosen so as to minimize the transaction costs associated with economic exchange, so political governance structures should minimize the political transaction costs associ-

---

[10] It is interesting to note that almost identical language was used by Madison in *Federalist 44* to justify the fact that the "necessary and proper" clause of the Constitution did not itemize every power that might fall into this category: "Had the Convention attempted a positive enumeration of the powers necessary and proper for carrying their other powers into effect, the attempt would have involved a complete digest of laws on every subject to which the Constitution relates; accommodated too not only to the existing state of things, but to all the possible changes which futurity may produce."

ated with the implementation of a given policy where, again, these costs should be assessed from legislators' reelection perspective.

Finally, it should be clear that the assumption of bounded rationality is at least as applicable to political decision making as to economic; given the enormous complexity of the national economy, military and defense issues, social welfare policy, and so on, political actors will not be able to anticipate all possibilities that may arise as policy implementation unfolds over time. In fact, it is often the very complexity of the policy area at hand that prompts Congress to delegate power in the first place.

THE POLITICAL HOLD-UP PROBLEM

This brings us to our basic questions: Why are some issue areas delegated to the executive and not others? When should we expect to see the details of public policy spelled out in legislation, and when will they be left to the executive to determine? The transaction cost approach is to identify the costs associated with each possible mode of production and then find the governance structure that minimizes total transaction costs. Our task is therefore to specify the political transaction costs of internal policy production in Congress and external production through delegation to the executive. This is where the legislative organization and oversight literatures reviewed in the previous chapter will come to the fore.

Reasons Not to Delegate

To begin with, the choice of whether or not to delegate rests with Congress. Legislators can either write detailed laws, in which case the executive branch will have little or no substantive input into policy, or delegate the details to agencies, thus giving the executive a substantial role in the policy-making process. Since legislators' primary goal is reelection, it follows that policy will be made in such a way as to maximize legislators' reelection chances; delegation will follow the natural fault lines of legislators' political advantage.

Next, note that delegation to agencies displays many of the same transaction costs that beset exchanges between firms. When Congress delegates authority to regulatory agencies, it makes a relationship-specific investment in both senses of the word, since it invests the executive with the power to fill in the details of legislation. Delegation is also plagued by a time-consistency problem. Congress might like to delegate broad discretionary authority if agencies would agree to use their power only for the benefit of the median floor voter. And agencies might like to receive such authority, increasing their flexibility to implement regulations. But the presence of incomplete contracts implies that Congress cannot specify the details of all future agency actions, and agencies themselves cannot promise not to abuse wide discretionary authority; presidents and heads of agencies change over time, and there is no legal means for one executive to bind the actions of his successors.

Therefore, potential executive abuse of discretionary authority is the political equivalent of the hold-up problem. Given agencies' inability to commit to a future course of action, potentially valuable transactions between legislators and bureaucrats may never take place. Congress might write specific legislation based on the information that it has at the time, or it may delegate and attach restrictive administrative procedures that in certain cases hobble the agency and induce inefficient policy making. Where oversight and monitoring problems do not exist, legislators would happily delegate authority to the executive branch, taking advantage of agency expertise and conserving on scarce resources of time, staff, and energy. But given that delegation implies surrendering at least some residual rights of control over policy, legislators will be loath to relinquish authority in politically sensitive policy areas where they cannot be assured that the executive will carry out their intent.

These costs of delegation, furthermore, are exactly the costs that have been identified in great detail in the oversight literature reviewed in Chapter 2. Legislators can control bureaucrats to some degree, but insofar as the preferences of legislative and executive branch actors differ and delegated authority is difficult to monitor, Congress will be reluctant to cede discretionary authority or, if it does delegate, will impose procedural constraints on the executive's actions. Thus, we can reinterpret the agency losses of delegation as political transaction costs from legislators' point of view.

Reasons to Delegate

This answers the question of why Congress does not delegate everything to the executive, so why does Congress delegate at all? Why does Congress not specify all details of legislation itself? Two obvious answers to this question come from the traditional literature on policy making: Congress delegates to reduce its workload and to take advantage of agency expertise. But the legislative organization literature reviewed in Chapter 2 offers another, more subtle reason, namely, that Congress delegates to avoid the inefficiencies of the committee system. Committees introduce delay, logrolling, and informational inefficiency into the policy-making process, so in many cases it is politically more advantageous for the median floor voter to leave the details of policy making to the executive.

In short, then, the legislative organization and oversight literatures identify the internal and external political transaction costs of making policy, respectively. Neither alternative is perfect, but in specific cases one or the other will be relatively more attractive from the median legislator's perspective. Thus, delegation follows a logic of political efficiency. When legislators feel that delegation will increase their electoral opportunities relative to policy making in Congress, then the executive will be given discretionary authority. When legislators perceive greater advantage in making policy themselves, despite the investment of their own scarce time and resources that this involves, they will write specific legislation that leaves the executive with little latitude.

To illustrate this point, Figure 3.3 summarizes the process of policy making, parallel to Figure 3.1. One difference between the figures is that the flow of action works the opposite way: In the economic diagram, basic goods and services are slowly combined to make a final product. In politics, the basic policy decisions are made first, then elaborated step by step until they reach the fine details of policy implementation. The essential points of both diagrams are the same, though: Congress must make the fundamental policy decisions in any law (or run afoul of the nondelegation doctrine), but it will usually not find it useful or even possible to specify the most intricate details of policy implementation (when to mail benefits checks, which contractor to use for a specific project, and so on). So the scope of detail in a given piece of legislation will be limited, making explicit some policy choices and leaving others to executive actors.

To recap, our logic in a nutshell is as follows. Policy can be made either through direct legislation or by delegation to the executive branch – this is the make-or-buy decision. Congress has the power to decide which of these options will be used either by writing specific, detailed legislation or by leaving the details to be filled in by the executive. Therefore, the decision on how to form policy will be made to maximize legislators' utility, which we assume means maximizing their chances of reelection. There are political transaction costs associated with either option: the costs of making policy internally come from the inefficiencies of the committee system, while the problems of delegation stem mainly from Congress's principal–agent problems of oversight and control, which we describe as a political hold-up problem. Therefore, the boundaries of the administrative state will be determined by the trade-off between these two sets of transaction costs. To the extent that one option or the other becomes more attractive to legislators' reelection chances, it will be the preferred mode of policy production.

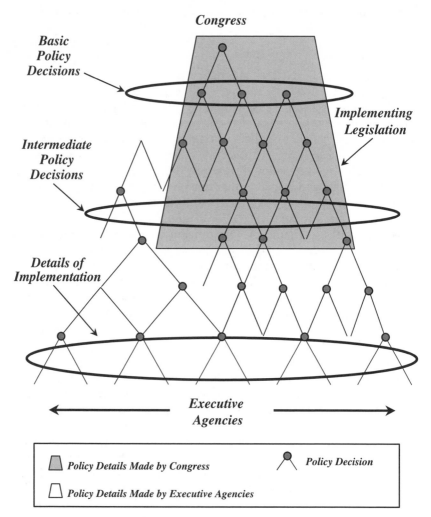

Figure 3.3. Boundaries of the Administrative State

Implications for Policy Making

At first blush, our transaction cost politics argument, once stated, may seem obvious. But our approach has a number of significant implications for the study of governmental institutions and the making of public policy. First, we join together two literatures – legislative organization and oversight – that have previously been treated separately, and we pose them as alternative modes of producing policy. The internal workings of Congress and the details of delegation to and oversight of the

50

executive should not be viewed as distinct, but rather as interconnected pieces in the grand puzzle of designing policy. Where one alternative is less attractive, the other will perforce be more attractive. In a world with no delegation to the executive, legislative organization would look very different than it does now; and if Congress were not structured as it is – including bicameralism, different election cycles for the House and Senate, and a strong committee system – delegation would change significantly as well.

Our approach casts a new light on executive branch discretion, characterizing it as a point along a continuum. When legislators make all important policy decisions themselves, which is equivalent to congressional policy making, agencies have no discretion. When laws leave the details of public policy to the executive to fill in, then agencies have greater discretion. And it is Congress that chooses a point along this continuum by writing detailed or broad legislation.

We have also emphasized that Congress can arrange the institutions of policy making in myriad ways: Delegation can be accompanied by a variety of administrative procedures, and policy making within Congress can be carefully structured through the use of restrictive amendment rules. The options available to Congress, however, do not include either a perfect market or efficient government intervention in the market. In other words, we should judge the outcomes of delegation to the executive, not against the theoretically most efficient policy or a lack of government involvement in the economy, but rather against the next best political alternative, which is policy making through the committee system. Viewed against this backdrop, many of the problems associated with delegation, such as clientelism, iron triangles, and a bias toward special interests, should be seen as general problems of policy making in the presence of well-organized pressure groups. These difficulties would not magically disappear were Congress to make policy itself; indeed, in many cases they would be exacerbated.

Finally, posing the problem of making policy as one of competing transaction costs implies that, as external conditions change, so, too, should the boundaries of the administrative state. Variations in political factors – such as conflict between the legislative and executive branches, the politics of different issue areas, the supply and demand of expertise, legislators' electoral environment, and interest group competition surrounding an issue, will engender variations in the extent and nature of legislative delegation to the executive. It is these types of correlations that the ensuing theoretical and empirical chapters will examine.

4

The Decision to Delegate

$$\frac{a + b^n}{n} = x \; donc \; Dieu \; existe, \; respondez?$$

Euler to Diderot before the Russian Court

The famous eighteenth-century mathematician Euler befuddled the French philosopher Diderot with his proof of the existence of God, not by its elegance and force of logic but by its mere formalism. The existence of God has nothing to do with the relation between a and the exponential power of b or, if it does, Euler never proved it so.

The appeal of mathematics lies in its ability to simplify complex phenomena. But math, like all languages, is simply a series of logical expressions from which we derive meaning. The strength of the argument rests wholly on the soundness of those logical statements. Of course, the well-trained modern scholar would never fall prey to Diderot's dilemma, but it does caution the reader to be wary; formalism adds nothing unless the model relates to the complex process being studied. Specifically, a good model will accomplish at least one of two tasks: It will illuminate the subject matter being investigated and/or produce testable, falsifiable predictions. All the better if these predictions are nonobvious or even counterintuitive, but this need not be a requirement. After all, for every "obvious" hypothesis produced by a model, there may exist many other seemingly obvious predictions that are contradicted by it.

With this in mind, the present chapter captures the central logic of our transaction cost approach to policy making through a game theoretic model in which Congress decides whether to delegate to an executive branch agency or make policy internally. Our model not only captures the key elements of policy making under separate powers and produces testable predictions, it also sheds new light on the interrelation between legislative and executive policy making and their reciprocal influence on each other's structure. We first present our theory and then derive predictions concerning where policy will be made. The model is presented informally in the text; the technical details are reserved for presentation in Appendix A. The last section summarizes the empirical predictions that follow from the model, which will be tested in subsequent chapters.

THE ELEMENTS OF POLICY MAKING

The previous chapters argued that with the rise of the administrative state there are now two alternative methods for making policy: through the normal internal practices of the committee system or through the external delegation of authority to executive branch agencies. Each option is plagued with its own types of political costs. Committees may try to benefit their own constituents at the expense of others by strategically withholding information from the floor or by inserting pork barrel benefits into legislation. Agency policy making carries its own dangers too, as even carefully designed administrative procedures may be insufficient to prevent bureaucrats from pursuing policy agendas different from those of the enacting legislative coalition.

Given the transaction cost politics approach we outlined in Chapter 3, a formal model of Congress's decision to delegate must contain the following elements: (1) a focus on legislation as the basic unit of analysis; (2) an enforcement mechanism for interbranch contracts; (3) residual rights of control combined with multiple possible governance structures; (4) bounded rationality, leading to incomplete contracts; (5) the political hold-up problem; (6) internal transaction costs of production; and (7) a decision mechanism predicting which governance structure will be chosen by legislators whose first concern is reelection. These components are all captured in the following model of the policy-making process.

The relevant players in our game consist of the median Floor voter in Congress, a congressional Committee, the President, and an executive branch Agency, identified as F, C, P, and A, respectively. Consistent with our theory of transaction cost politics, our unit of analysis is a bill; therefore, these players will combine to make policy in a one-dimensional policy space $X = \Re^1$. This assumption of unidimensionality is seemingly simple but nonetheless crucial, as the most important division in formal models of political processes is between one-dimensional and multidimensional policy spaces. If policy can be accurately portrayed as falling along a single left–right spectrum, and if political actors have single-peaked preferences, then there exists a median voter who will be pivotal in the choice of legislative organization, administrative procedures, policies, and so on.[1]

Each actor has a most-preferred policy, or ideal point, in this unidimensional space; if the policy in question is agriculture, then this could represent the actor's preferred level of aid to farmers. If actor i has ideal point X_i and the final policy outcome is X, then the actor gains utility equal to $-(X-X_i)^2$, known as a quadratic loss function. Without loss of generality, we assume that the floor's ideal point $x_F = 0$ and the president's ideal point $x_P > 0$.

This quadratic loss function has two important implications. First, actors will prefer outcomes that are closer to their ideal point than those further away; this is the distributive component of their utility. But actors will also be risk-averse, meaning that they will dislike uncertainty over policy outcomes; this is the informational component. Even though actors want outcomes close to their preferred policy, then, they may nonetheless be willing at the margin to accept a system that biases policy away from their preferences if they can simultaneously reduce the uncertainty associated with these outcomes.

Although players' preferences are defined over final outcomes, these are not necessarily the same as the policies that emerge from the political process. Formally, we assume that $X = p+\omega$, where p stands for the policy passed and ω represents other factors that might impact real-world outcomes – for instance, the weather affecting next year's crops. Players start the game with probabilistic beliefs over what value ω might take; we assume that these beliefs are initially uniform in some interval $[-R, R]$. During the play of the game, committees and/or agencies may have the opportunity to gather more information about the exact value of ω. In this way, they obtain expertise about the policy issue at hand, and they can use this information when making proposals or promulgating regulations. Given our assumption of risk aversion, this information

---

[1]Note that even our one-dimensional model can address well certain distributional concerns. For instance, if preferences over farm policy can be usefully described as pro- and anti-agriculture as measured by the percentage of constituents employed in agricultural-related businesses, then a one-dimensional model will accurately describe the nature of the resulting politics. When these interests splinter, so as to pit corn versus soybeans versus sugarcane, then models that collapse preferences down to a single left–right dimension may lose some richness – for instance, in describing the types of coalitions and cleavages that will appear among various agricultural interests. Nevertheless, our approach does allow us to consider both informational and distributive concerns and predict the impact of different institutional arrangements (governance structures) on each of these components and on policy outcomes. The differences between multidimensional and unidimensional models are thoughtfully analyzed in Krehbiel (1991, 260–1), Shepsle and Weingast, eds. (1995, 24–6), and Maltzman and Smith (1995, 253–7).

can potentially benefit all players in the game by allowing more fully informed policy choices.

The game is played as follows. First, committees gain some information about the policy issue being discussed, and then they send a bill or report to the floor player. Based on this report, the floor player must decide whether to enact specific legislation that gives the executive no substantive input into policy or to allow the executive some latitude. If she chooses to delegate, F can set both a baseline policy $\hat{p}$ and give the executive some (possibly limited) discretion to move policy away from $\hat{p}$. For example, Congress may allow the secretary of agriculture to set price support levels for certain crops anywhere between 60 percent and 90 percent of parity. Then the president sets the agency's ideal point, and the agency gathers information (e.g., weather conditions and yields) and sets final policy within the limits of the discretion afforded by Congress. Figure 4.1 provides a game tree, breaking this process into three stages – the institutional design stage, the policy-making process, and final outcomes – and showing the order of moves in the game along with the information available to the players at each point in the decision-making process.

Institutional Choice

We now proceed to examine the game in greater detail. In the first stage, committee members hold hearings, gather information, deliberate, write reports, and draft a bill (b), which is then sent to the floor. The committee's bill may contain suggestions as to what policy should be enacted, whether or not to delegate, what administrative constraints should be placed on any delegation, which interest groups should be enfranchised into the decision-making process, and so on.

Thus far, our setup is similar to previous models of committees and legislative organization under imperfect information.[2] Where we depart from this tradition is by assuming that committees' expertise in the relevant issue area is incomplete and that they have less information than an agency would have when promulgating regulations.[3] We assume that while the agency observes the exact value of ω, the committee observes only whether ω lies in the range $[-R, 0]$ or the range $[0, R]$; that is, the committee sees only the sign of ω. This agency advantage might arise through greater numbers of staff and more time to analyze

[2] See, e.g., Gilligan and Krehbiel (1987; 1989), Austen-Smith (1993), Epstein (1997; 1998).

[3] To be precise, we assume that the agency's information first-order stochastically dominates that of the committee, which is to say that the agency's information is more fine-grained than that available to committees.

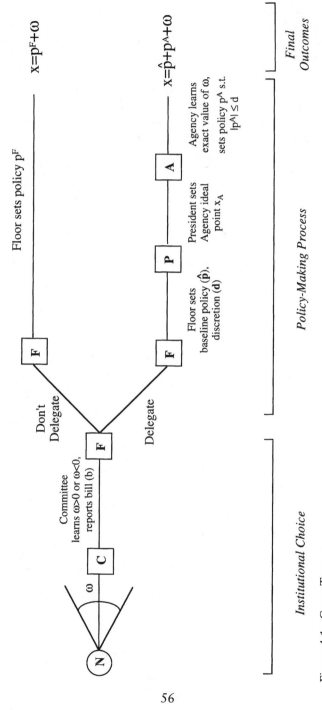

$x = p^F + \omega$

Floor sets policy p^F

$x = \hat{p} + p^A + \omega$

Agency learns
exact value of ω,
sets policy p^A s.t.
$|p^A| \leq d$

A

President sets
Agency ideal
point x_A

P

Floor sets
baseline policy ($\hat{p}$),
discretion (**d**)

F

F

Don't
Delegate

Delegate

F

Committee
learns $\omega > 0$ or $\omega < 0$,
reports bill (b)

C

ω

N

Institutional Choice

Policy-Making Process

*Final
Outcomes*

Figure 4.1. Game Tree

56

the technical issues at hand, or it might simply be due to the fact that some time will elapse between the passing of the law and making regulations, giving the agency access to new information revealed in that period. Continuing with our agricultural example, the committee may have only the *Farmer's Almanac* to rely on, whereas the agencies setting price support levels may have more-sophisticated models of supply and demand, plus they can make policy decisions closer in time to the growing season. Thus, our model is one of sequential signaling and screening: Committees and then agencies in turn gather information and apply their expertise to the formulation of legislation and regulatory policy.

After receiving the committee's bill, the median floor voter, F, makes the key decision as to whether policy will be made through Congress alone or if substantive discretionary authority will be delegated to executive branch agencies as well. We represent this as the floor's choosing the value of an indicator variable $\mathcal{D}$. If F chooses to make policy internally without delegating substantive authority ($\mathcal{D} = 0$), then the legislation passed by Congress will be specific, leaving the executive with no discretionary authority.

If the floor chooses to delegate to the executive branch ($\mathcal{D} = 1$), then it must also determine the procedures under which the agency will operate. In particular, F sets a status quo policy ($\hat{p}$) and specifies the level of discretionary authority (d) that the agency has to move outcomes away from $\hat{p}$.[4] As discussed in Chapter 3, agency discretion results from the complex set of administrative procedures attached to the delegation of authority. If the agency is mandated simply to regulate "in the public interest," then it will have unfettered discretion. The more specific the statutory language and the more constricting the administrative procedures, the lower the value of d.[5]

Paths of Policy Making

After the institutional design stage comes the policy-making process, the details of which depend on the institutional choices made in the first

---

[4]Equivalently, the floor could set minimum and maximum policies p^- and p^+ and require that agency actions fall somewhere within the $[p^-, p^+]$ interval. For instance, Congress may require airborne benzene emissions standards to fall between two and ten parts per million. Given values of p^+ and p^-, the translation to our notation is straightforward:

$$\hat{p} = \frac{p^+ + p^-}{2} \text{ and } d = \frac{p^+ - p^-}{2}.$$

[5]Of course, agencies may derive discretion from other sources as well, through such means as policy entrepreneurship. Here we focus on statutory discretion – that is, the policy latitude intentionally left to executive agents in the implementing legislation.

stage of the game. If Congress decides to retain control and enact specific policy, then the bill reported out of the committee is considered by Congress as a whole, and the median floor voter is free to amend the committee's recommendation and pass p^F, the final policy. The executive branch must implement p^F, of course, but in doing so executive agents will not be able to change important details of policy away from those set by Congress without being overturned by the courts.

On the other hand, if legislators elect to delegate authority to the executive, then the president enters the scene by choosing an administrator for the agency, which we assume means that the president determines the agency's policy goals. This can be done in a number of ways. Congress might establish a new agency or program, for instance, and allow the president to appoint its head. For preexisting agencies, the president might replace the previous director and name a new agency chief or inform the existing chief which policy should be pursued, using the presidential power to dismiss or reduce an agency's budget as leverage. The important aspect of this order of moves is that the president cannot precommit to any one set of preferences for the agency before Congress acts.

Two points concerning the role of the president in the policy-making process are important to note here. First, our simplifying assumption that the president can unilaterally set X_A, the agency's ideal point, clearly understates the importance of other institutional actors who also affect agency preferences, such as interest groups, congressional committees, and other agencies.[6] There is also a large literature discussing the independence career bureaucrats have from the directives of agency heads, and how, at times, the goals of the appointed cabinet members may be in direct conflict with the goals of the career bureaucrats running the agency.[7] All that is necessary for the implications of our model to be correct is that presidents have some sway over agency policy making, and that conflict between legislative and executive goals increases during times of divided government as opposed to unified government. Also, the model does lead to the interesting implication that presidents may have incentives to "stack" agency appointments to counterbalance existing pressures that push agency policy making in the other direction; perhaps appointing bureau chiefs with preferences even more extreme than the president's own, so that overall the agency pursues his policy goals as nearly as possible.

[6]See Moe 1985. Below, we discuss a variant of our model in which agencies can have more independence from presidential influence.

[7]For example, Casper ("Cap the Knife") Weinberger was appointed by Nixon to head the Department of Health, Education, and Welfare with the explicit objective of cutting the agency's budget. See Wilson (1989, 209–11) for a discussion.

Second, for the sake of simplicity our model ignores the role of the presidential veto in determining policy. This possibility could be integrated into our analysis in the following manner. Given our order of play, the president always prefers more discretion to less, so his ideal delegation regime is $\hat{p} = x_P$ and $d = R + x_P$. As shown below, Congress in general prefers $\hat{p} = x_F$ and lower levels of discretion. A bargaining process over final policy would lead to some compromise between Congress and the president, resulting in a level of executive discretion greater than Congress prefers but less than the unfettered discretion that the president desires. This would lead to higher levels of discretion in equilibrium, but the comparative statics derived from the model and therefore all empirical predictions would remain unchanged.

Given the authority delegated by Congress, the agency gains information about the issue area by conducting fact findings, undertaking investigations, or holding hearings. As stated above, we assume that the agency learns the exact value of the hidden variable, ω. The agency then promulgates a regulation within the limits of its discretion afforded by Congress. In particular, the absolute value of the agency's policy, $|p^A|$, can be no greater than d, the amount of agency discretion.

Final Outcomes

After the mode of policy making is selected and after all bills, delegations, amendments, and final regulations are issued, a single policy outcome will result. In the congressional policy-making game, outcomes are simply the sum of the policy set by the floor and the realization of the true state of the world, so $X = p^F + \omega$. Final outcomes in the delegation game combine the baseline policy set by Congress, the policy set by the agency, and the realized state of the world; consequently, $X = \hat{p} + p^A + \omega$, where, as explained above, $|p^A|$ is constrained to be less than or equal to d.[8]

EQUILIBRIUM ACTIONS AND OUTCOMES

We now analyze the game described above to identify its set of Nash equilibria. As usual, we solve the game starting from the end and work-

[8]In our model, then, all policy outcomes are realized at the end of a single period of play. Some interesting questions also arise from multiperiod considerations; for instance, if Congress anticipates a shift in partisan control of the presidency, it might adjust the level of executive discretion accordingly. Or if proponents of the legislation being considered fear that their coalition will dissolve in the near future, they may constrain discretion to lock in their gains; this is Moe's (1989) explanation of the EPA's structure. See Epstein and O'Halloran (1994) for a model of agency structure in an intertemporal setting.

ing backward, so the equilibrium analysis proceeds in three steps: We first determine equilibrium behavior if the floor delegates authority to executive agencies; then we determine the equilibrium outcomes if the floor chooses the detailed legislation option; and finally, we combine these results to predict the conditions under which one alternative or the other will minimize political transaction costs.

Delegation Game

Agency Policy Making

Consider the agency's problem if it has to make policy. Congress has specified a baseline policy $\hat{p}$, and the agency has discovered the value of ω. Final policy will be $\hat{p} + \omega + p^A$, and the agency would like to bring this outcome as close to X_A, its ideal point, as possible. If the agency were free to set policy as it pleased, then it would simply set $\hat{p} + \omega + p^A = X_A$, so that $p^A = X_A - \hat{p} - \omega$; call this p^{A*}.

However, the agency is also working under the constraint that $|p^A| \leq d$, its total discretion, so the agency might not be able to enact its first-best policy option. The agency's actions are then clear; if $|p^{A*}| \leq d$, the agency will set $p^A = p^{A*}$ and receive its ideal point X_A. If $|p^{A*}| > d$ and $\hat{p} + \omega < X_A$, then the agency will set $p^A = d$; conversely, if $|p^{A*}| > d$ and $\hat{p} + \omega > X_A$, then the agency will set $p^A = -d$. In both these latter cases, the agency uses the full amount of discretion at its disposal to move final outcomes as close to its ideal point as it can, given the legislative limits placed on its discretion.

Presidential Appointments

Working backward, the next question is what ideal point the president will select for the agency. The answer is straightforward: In equilibrium the president will always choose an agency head with policy preferences identical to her own, so that $X_A = X_P$; loyalty to the president's goals will be the primary factor in choosing executive branch officials. Given the discussion above, this is not too surprising. The agency will use the discretion Congress affords it to move policy as close to its ideal point (X_A) as possible. Knowing this, presidents are best off when the agency's preferences mirror their own $(X_A = X_P)$, so that the agency is bringing policy near the president's ideal point as well.

Baseline Policy and Constraints on Agency Discretion

With this in mind, the median floor voter in Congress must decide on the baseline policy and how much discretion to give the agency, based on its beliefs about ω and its knowledge of the president's preferences X_P. In equilibrium, no matter what the ideal point of the president may be, Congress sets $\hat{p}$ so that, in expectation, the median floor voter gets her most-preferred policy (which is 0 by assumption) if the agency were to adopt $\hat{p}$. The exact policy, though, depends on F's beliefs about ω. As shown in Figure 4.2, if F believes that $\omega \in [-R, R]$ (as she does at the beginning of the game with no further information), then the range is already centered around x_F, and the floor sets $\hat{p} = 0$. If F believes that $\omega \in [-R, 0]$, then she will set $\hat{p} = \frac{R}{2}$ so as to center this range on her ideal point, changing the set of possible outcomes to $[-\frac{R}{2}, \frac{R}{2}]$. Similarly, if F's beliefs are uniform on the interval $[0, R]$, then she will correct this positive bias by setting $\hat{p} = -\frac{R}{2}$, so final outcomes again fall into the $[-\frac{R}{2}, \frac{R}{2}]$ range.

And what about agency discretion? This depends on the relation between X_F, X_A, and the range of possible values of ω. For instance, assume that the floor believes that ω is in the range $[-R, R]$. Then as shown in the appendix, if $X_A \le -R$ or $X_A \ge R$, the floor sets $d = 0$, meaning that the agency will have no discretion to move outcomes away from the baseline policy. Similarly, if the floor believes that ω is in the range $[-\frac{R}{2}, \frac{R}{2}]$, then it will give no discretionary authority to agencies whose ideal points fall outside of this range.[9] Note two important points: (1) when the preferences of Congress and the president diverge too greatly, agencies receive no discretion; and (2) the floor player's beliefs about ω will have an impact on her decision to delegate. For instance, when $\frac{R}{2} < X_A < R$, then F will delegate when she believes ω is in the range $[-R, R]$ but not if she believes that ω is in $[-\frac{R}{2}, \frac{R}{2}]$.

If Congress does delegate, then the agency is given more discretion the more closely aligned are the interests of Congress and the president. If ω is believed to be in $[-R, R]$, for instance, the agency will receive discretion $d = R - X_A$. When Congress and the executive share the same goals, agencies will be given unfettered discretion to make policy, and when they disagree, agencies will be put under tighter reins through the imposition of restrictive administrative procedures. Agencies will have greater latitude to set policy, then, the lower the level of legislative–executive conflict.

The final outcomes from the agency delegation game, incorporating

[9]Technically, the floor does not know X_A when setting discretion; it only knows the value of X_P and *anticipates* what the value of X_A will be. The discussion in the text is thus a bit of an abuse of notation in the service of a clearer exposition.

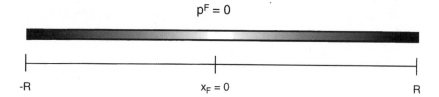

$p^F = 0$

-R $x_F = 0$ R

Case 1: Committee Reveals No Information about ω
Floor Sets $p^F=0$

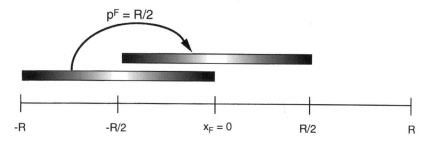

$p^F = R/2$

-R   -R/2 $x_F = 0$ R/2   R

Case 2: Committee Credibly Signals ω ≤ 0
Floor Sets $p^F = R/2$

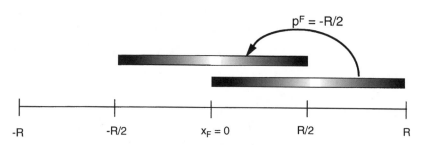

$p^F = -R/2$

-R   -R/2 $x_F = 0$ R/2   R

Case 3: Committee Credibly Signals ω ≥ 0
Floor Sets $p^F = -R/2$

Figure 4.2. Information, Outcomes, and the Status Quo

the president's equilibrium choice of X_A and the floor's choice of $\hat{p}$ and d, are as follows. For extreme negative values of ω – those between $-R$ and $-R + 2X_A$ – the agency uses the full extent of its discretionary authority to move outcomes to the right, so that final policy ranges from $-X_A$ to X_A. For all other values of ω – those greater than $(-R + 2X_A)$ – the agency has enough discretion to obtain its ideal point, so policy outcomes remain constant at x_A. The fact that outcomes remain unchanged while ω varies from $(-R + 2X_A)$ to R is an indication that agency expertise is being used to reduce the uncertainty associated with policy making in a complex environment. But for this enhanced information the median floor voter must pay the price of outcomes that are on average biased toward the executive's preferred policies: agency policy making presents a trade-off between informational gains and distributive losses.

Congressional Policy Choice

Legislative Policy Making

In comparison, the analysis of the congressional policy-making game is much simpler than the delegation game. After the floor player sets policy, the outcome will be $p^F + \omega$, so F will set policy to maximize her expected utility given her beliefs about the state of the world, knowing that no further moves will be made. Given the information conveyed by the committee's bill, then, the median floor voter will set p^F so that she obtains her ideal point in expectation.

This is, in fact, the same problem that the floor solved when setting the status quo for the agency, so her policy choices in setting p^F are exactly the same as those illustrated in Figure 4.2. If the committee credibly signals that ω is low ($\omega \in [-R, 0]$), then F will set $p^F = \frac{R}{2}$; if the committee signals that that ω is high ($\omega \in [0, R]$), then F will adjust policy so that $p^F = -\frac{R}{2}$. If the committee has given no useful information, then F must make policy based on her original knowledge about ω and simply set $p^F = 0$.

This similarity between congressional policy making and delegation is not accidental; in fact, it is a necessary result of our approach. Were the floor to delegate to agencies but set discretion equal to 0, then the baseline policy would be the outcome, just as p^F is the outcome in the congressional policy-making game. In other words, delegating with no discretion is the same as not delegating at all – Congress chooses the policy to be implemented and the executive has no choice but to follow the legislature's wishes. This is the basis of our model of interbranch relations; the degree of discretion given to the executive lies along a continuum, with one endpoint being complete abdication and the other being direct legislation by Congress. If delegation to the executive would be accompanied by zero discretion, then, we count this to be equivalent to no delegation.

Notice that in the congressional policy-making game, the floor always receives her ideal point in expectation. Thus congressional policy making does not show the same policy bias as the agency delegation game. On the other hand, the floor player is denied the benefits of agency expertise that can be captured if substantive discretionary authority is allotted to the executive. Compared to agency delegation, then, direct legislation trades off distributive gains for the median floor voter against informational losses.

Committee–Floor Signaling

We now arrive at the first stage of the game, where the committee sends a bill to the floor after having observed some information about the state of the world, ω. Although this bill might contain any provisions or suggestions that the committee wishes to include, as far as the floor is concerned the only variable of interest will be whether the committee bill conveys any information about ω. Therefore, we will stylize the bill as a simple report about what the committee observed, so that $b \in \{\omega^-, \omega^+, \varnothing\}$, where ω^- means the committee announces that ω is less than zero, ω^+ means the committee announces ω is greater than zero, and $\varnothing$ means the committee reveals nothing about its observation of ω.

The floor player, though, must be wary of how it treats the committee's bill: Just because the committee claims that it observed $\omega < 0$, for instance, does not mean that F should necessarily believe it. Consider, for instance, the example of an Agriculture Committee reporting on the expected weather conditions for the upcoming growing season. If members of the committee want greater subsidies for their constituents, then they are liable to report that bad weather is ahead, no matter what the actual forecast conditions.[10] The committee, then, will resemble a broken record, always reporting the same thing, and is therefore useless to the floor as a reliable source of information.

What, then, are the possibilities for committee signaling in our model? A moment's thought will reveal that in equilibrium there are, in fact, only two: Either the committee truthfully reports what it knows about

---

[10]In much the same way, it seems that for years the CIA purposely overestimated the strength of the Soviet economy, presumably so that the agency would continue to receive high levels of funding.

ω in every case, or it essentially says nothing.[11] For instance, the committee cannot choose to report b = ω⁻ when ω is negative and b = Ø when it is positive, for then the floor could infer that b = Ø really meant that ω > 0. The committee of course can try to mislead the floor regarding its information, but in equilibrium the floor will not heed such a committee.

If the committee can credibly signal whether it has observed a high or low value of ω, this is called a "separating" equilibrium (because the committee sends separate messages for different values of ω). When the signal is the same for all observations of ω or when the floor simply ignores the committee's bill, this is called a "pooling" equilibrium (because the committee pools all its information into a single signal).[12] A separating equilibrium, then, is synonymous with the committee's transmitting information to the floor; pooling indicates that the committee's bill conveys no useful information.

Example

As a baseline case, and to get a feel for the dynamics of costless signaling models, consider a world where no agency exists but the committee and floor play the same game considered here. So the committee finds out if ω is positive or negative, makes a speech (sends a bill) to the floor, and then the floor sets policy outcomes. We must ask ourselves for which values of X_C a separating equilibrium can be sustained, for if it cannot, then a pooling equilibrium will be the only alternative remaining. To figure this out, we must first assume that a separating equilibrium does exist, and then determine if any player has an incentive to defect from the equilibrium.

We know from our discussion of the agency delegation game that in a separating equilibrium the floor will respond to an announcement of ω⁻ with a policy of $p^F = \frac{R}{2}$, and an announcement of ω⁺ will elicit policy $p^F = -\frac{R}{2}$. For concreteness, assume first that R = 1 and $X_C = \frac{3}{5}$. Say that the committee observes ω ∈ [−1, 0]. Then in a separating equilibrium, if

---

[11]When the committee's bill is not informative, then the committee might report b = Ø for all values of ω; it might report b = ω⁺ no matter what the true value is; it might report that ω was positive when it was really negative and vice versa; and so on. When external conditions (the values of X_C, X_A, and R) do not support truth telling, then the floor player will simply ignore whatever the committee chooses to report, so the committee's actual strategy is not important.

[12]As readers who have experience with costless signaling games will recognize, a pooling equilibrium, also known as a "babbling" equilibrium, always exists. We shall focus our analysis on the most informative equilibrium, so we shall select a separating equilibrium when it can be sustained, since it produces Pareto superior results.

the committee tells the truth and reports $\omega = \omega^-$, the floor will set policy equal to $\frac{1}{2}$, so the possible outcomes will shift to the range $[-\frac{1}{2}, \frac{1}{2}]$. If the committee lies and reports $\omega = \omega^+$ when in reality $\omega = \omega^-$, the floor will set policy equal to $-\frac{1}{2}$, shifting possible outcomes to the range $[-\frac{3}{2}, -\frac{1}{2}]$. Given that the committee's ideal point is greater than 0, it certainly would not want to mislead the floor in this instance.

On the other hand, say the committee observes $\omega = \omega^+$. Then if the committee tells the truth, the floor will, as before, set policy in the range $[-\frac{1}{2}, \frac{1}{2}]$. But now a false statement (lie, misdirection, credibility gap, what have you) that $\omega = \omega^-$ will elicit a response of $p^F = \frac{1}{2}$, giving a range of possible outcomes of $[\frac{1}{2}, \frac{3}{2}]$. Given the choice of these two ranges, the committee now prefers to mislead the floor, for its ideal point of $\frac{3}{5}$ falls within the latter range but not the former.[13] The committee will thus report $\omega = \omega^-$, no matter what it actually observed – it acts like a broken record. So the floor, looking ahead, will refuse to believe the committee's report. That is, the hypothesized separating equilibrium breaks down, and so the players will be relegated to a pooling equilibrium.

Had the committee's ideal point been positive but less than $\frac{1}{2}$, however, then it would have had incentives to tell the truth both when ω was negative and when it was positive. In this circumstance, the separating equilibrium could be sustained, for neither player would have incentives to defect. In general, as long as the absolute value of X_C is less than $\frac{R}{2}$, a separating equilibrium will exist; otherwise, only the pooling equilibrium will be available. This is a general lesson that is replicated in other costless signaling models of this type: The closer the preferences of the committee and floor, the more information can be transmitted between them in equilibrium.

This discussion leads us to a number of questions about committees and signaling in our game. First, under which conditions will a separating equilibrium arise? Second, under which conditions will committees prefer separation to pooling? Third, if information acquisition were costly, when would committees spend the resources necessary to become experts? Finally, how does the presence of an agency change the answers to all of the above questions? Just as previous models explored the

---

[13]This is a shorthand way of saying that the committee's expected utility, given that outcomes are uniformly distributed in the set [½, 3⁄2], is greater than if they were uniformly distributed in the set [−½, ½].

impact of legislative procedures such as closed rules (Gilligan and Krehbiel 1987), multiple referrals (Austen-Smith 1993), and gatekeeping (Epstein 1997) on the informational role of committees, we ask how the possibility of delegating to the executive affects these incentives. We shall return to these questions below.

Choosing the Lesser of Two Evils

We are now in a position to address our key question of when Congress will choose to delegate substantive authority to the executive and when it will enact detailed policy on its own. Three variables will affect this decision: X_C, the ideal point of the committee; X_A, the ideal point of the agency; and R, the degree of political uncertainty in the environment (recall that the floor's ideal point X_F is defined to be zero). An equilibrium to our game will also tell us the committee's pattern of signaling – separating or pooling – as these variables change.

Equilibrium Diagram

The answers to these questions are contained in Figure 4.3. The horizontal axis denotes the committee's ideal point, while the vertical axis shows the agency's ideal point. In both cases, the further these preferences are from the floor's ideal point of zero, the greater the degree of policy conflict. The shaded areas represent the combinations of committee and agency ideal points for which $\mathcal{D} = 0$; that is, the floor does not delegate to the executive. The unshaded areas represent values for which substantive authority is delegated. For easier explanation, the diagram has been broken down into a number of regions, each with a distinct pattern of behavior.

In Region 1, denoted by the encircled number 1 and appearing in both the top left and top right sections of the diagram, both the committee and the agency have ideal points relatively far away from the floor. Given the difference in preferences between the committee and floor $(|X_C| > \frac{R}{2})$, the committee's signal to the floor is uninformative, so F will only know for sure that ω falls in the range $[-R, R]$. Even so, the agency is too far away from the floor to merit any delegated authority; $X_A > R$, meaning that the agency's ideal point falls out of the range of values that would receive substantive discretion. In this case, both the committee and the agency are preference outliers; that is, their ideal points are too extreme relative to the floor's to play a significant role in the policy-making process.

The analysis of Region 2 is the same from the agency's perspective; it

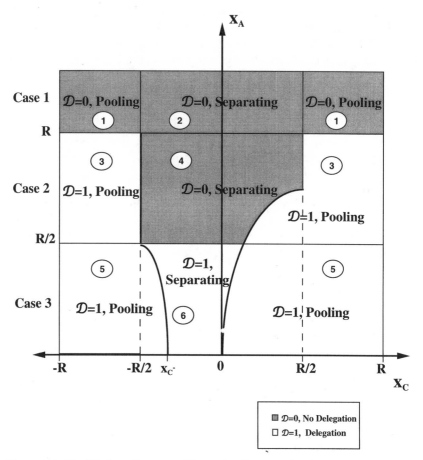

Figure 4.3. Equilibrium Outcomes Illustrating Ranges of Delegation

is too much of an outlier to receive discretionary authority. But now the committee can credibly convey information in its message, as it lies within the critical $[-\frac{R}{2}, \frac{R}{2}]$ range. Whereas the signaling equilibrium in Region 1 was pooling then, it is separating here. In both Regions 1 and 2, the executive's preferences are too extreme relative to the legislature, so that the game will be played as if the possibility of delegation did not exist. In other words, these cases are identical to the baseline game, discussed above, between the committee and floor with no agency at all.

Consider next Regions 5 and 6 at the bottom of the figure. Here, the absolute value of the agency's ideal point is less than $\frac{R}{2}$, so no matter what information the committee conveys to the floor, the agency will receive some delegated authority; $\mathcal{D} = 1$ for both regions. As in the previous two cases, we have pooling for extreme values of X_C and separation for moderate values, but compared to Regions 1 and 2 the range of separation has shrunk considerably. This change in the relative sizes of the separation and pooling regions will be discussed more fully below; for our present purposes we note only that in these regions the presence of an agency has a significant effect on the committee's prior actions and the floor's interpretation of them.

The middle two regions, numbers 3 and 4, present an intermediary case. Here, X_A falls in the range $[\frac{R}{2}, R]$, and the informational content of the committee's bill will determine whether or not the agency receives delegated powers. If the committee and floor play a pooling equilibrium, then the floor will know only that ω lies within the $[-R, R]$ interval, in which case the agency's ideal point is close enough that the floor prefers to delegate authority. If the signaling equilibrium is of the separating variety, then the floor can adjust the status quo so that ω will fall within the $[-\frac{R}{2}, \frac{R}{2}]$ range, and the agency will receive no discretionary authority.

One further comment about this equilibrium diagram is in order. The floor is best off under separating equilibria, so the optimal set of committees from the floor's point of view are those in Regions 2, 4, and 6 from the diagram. This means that any committee in the specified regions is as good as any other. But this range of optimal committees shrinks the closer the preferences of the floor and the president are. So we have the somewhat surprising prediction that fewer committee outliers will be observed under unified as opposed to divided government. As explained below, the reason is that floor players are wary of committees and executive actors with preferences that are too similar, as a sort of iron triangle can develop in which the committee refuses to divulge information so that the corresponding agency is given greater discretion.

Influence of Agency on Committee Actions

The equilibria presented in Figure 4.3 provide a stylized description of policy making under separate powers, when Congress has the option of delegating some authority to the executive. Before we draw general conclusions from these results, we pause for a moment to examine the impact that the presence of the agency has on committee-floor interactions and, conversely, the influence of legislative organization on the control of delegated authority. Concerning the former, Regions 1 and 2 mirror the baseline case without an agency, where the floor makes policy itself, so the vertical lines at $X_C = -\frac{R}{2}$ and $X_C = \frac{R}{2}$ mark the boundaries within which the committee would separate if the possibility of delegation to the executive were absent. What accounts for the fact that the range of separation becomes smaller in all subsequent regions?

The answer is twofold. First, recall that the logic of committee signaling depends on whether, given a separating equilibrium, either party would have incentives to change their actions. As it turns out, the possibility of delegation makes it more attractive for committees to hide (or misrepresent) their knowledge of ω.[14] This means, as pointed out, that the separating equilibrium breaks down and we are left with the pooling equilibrium by default. The presence of an agency, therefore, makes it more difficult for the committee to credibly transmit information to the floor by alleviating some of the negative effects of misinformation. The new boundary between the areas for which the committee can and cannot separate for negative values of X_C is shown in the figure starting at the point X_C^-, forming the dividing line between Regions 5 and 6 for negative values of X_C.[15]

Second, the presence of an agency affects the committee's incentives to communicate information to the floor. At first glance, this statement is difficult to understand; any other considerations lacking, the more information the committee conveys to the floor player in its bill *b*, the better off *both* players are, due to their risk aversion. So committees in previous costless signaling games always preferred separating equilibria whenever they could be sustained. Here, on the other hand, committee signals will affect not only the floor's information about the state of the world but also how much discretion is delegated to the agency. If a committee reveals little information to the floor player, then the response may be to imbue agencies with greater discretionary authority, which agencies can then use to move outcomes closer to their ideal point. If committees and agencies share similar policy goals, then the committee might be better off concealing information in the short run so that agencies can have greater latitude to make policy in the long run.

Committees will therefore have incentives to shift policy making to executive agencies for purely informational reasons, even in the absence of any costs of acquiring information themselves. These agencies will be able to incorporate their information into final policy outcomes more fully than committees could, so, paradoxically, committees may prefer

---

[14]The mathematics behind this are given in Appendix A. Intuitively, after an incorrect report by the committee, leading the floor to set $\hat{p}$ and *d* erroneously, the agency will use all its discretionary authority to bring outcomes back toward its ideal point. This partially offsets the negative distributional effects of the committee's misstatement and so gives the committee more incentives to mislead the floor in the first place.

[15]A corresponding line on the other side of the floor also exists, but its impact is subsumed by the effects described in the following paragraph.

to be less informative so that the policy process as a whole becomes more informed.[16] This finding emphasizes the fact that committee decision making, and legislative organization more generally, should not be studied in a vacuum; they exist in the shadow of delegation to the executive, and the committee's expectations about the anticipated delegation regime will influence committee members' actions earlier on.

Another angle from which to view these effects is to ask what would happen if committees, rather than obtaining their information about ω free, had to pay some fixed cost. Then we might ask what impact the presence of an agency has on committee incentives to specialize in their issue areas. Figure 4.4 shows the answer in topographical form: the lighter areas of the graph represent combinations of committee and agency ideal points for which the committee would pay more for information with an agency present than without; the gray areas are those where the incentives are the same; and the darker areas indicate combinations for which the committee has less incentives to gather information than before.

As can be seen, the darker areas are considerably larger than the lighter ones, so in general agencies inhibit rather than promote information acquisition in committees. Notice, too, that the light areas solely comprise combinations where the committee's ideal point is opposed to the agency's ($X_C < 0$ and $X_A > 0$). This highlights the complex relationship between committees and agencies in the production of policy. Agencies compete with committees in the market for influence over policy, but they can also obtain information at a low cost, thereby complementing the committee's own expertise. As the figure shows, for committees with policy preferences opposed to those of the executive, the substitution effect dominates, but when the policy goals of the committee and the agency are similar, they can tacitly cooperate to bias policy against the preferences of the (relatively uninformed) floor player.

Influence of Oversight on Agency Actions

Just as the presence of an agency affects committee actions, so, too, does the fact of politically motivated oversight limit the ability of politicians to control agencies. Notice from the discussion above that for a number of values of ω – specifically, when it falls in the range $[-R, -R + X_A]$ –

---

[16]The reasoning behind this hinges on the fact that agencies can make final policy decisions whereas committees must always have their suggestions ratified by the floor. This means that some committee expertise will be dissipated due to friction with the floor while agency information will not. Thus, these effects would exist even if we did not assume that committees and agencies have differential access to information. See Epstein and O'Halloran (1999) for a proof of this proposition.

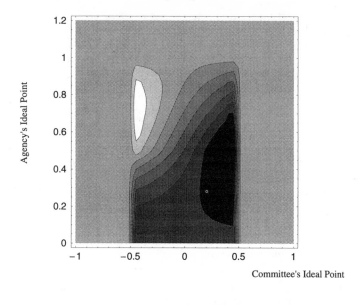

Agency Gives Committee
Greater Incentives to
Gather Information

Agency Gives Committee
Less Incentives to
Gather Information

Figure 4.4. The Impact of an Agency on Committees' Incentive to Gather Information

outcomes are less than $X_F = 0$. It is clear that both the floor player and the agency would prefer to adjust policy in this circumstance, for they could both be made better off if outcomes were in the $[0, X_A]$ range. In parlance, these outcomes are *Pareto inferior*. Were the agencies to be given more discretion, these outcomes could be avoided, but legislators do not have incentives to do so because this would result in even greater distributive losses for other values of ω. This result is in line with Moe's (1989, 276–7) contention that "agencies will be burdened with structures fully intended to cause their failure"; as long as politicians want to control bureaucrats as well as take advantage of their expertise, the output of bureaucratic policy making at times will be socially inefficient, hindered by restrictive procedures and politically motivated oversight.

At a deeper level, this result is due to the incomplete nature of contracts between Congress and the bureaucracy, an essential element of our transaction cost politics approach outlined in the previous chapter. Congress may prefer to make the value of *d* depend on the realized value of ω, say, by giving the agency greater discretion for extreme values of ω and less for moderate values. But then the agency would have incentives simply to claim that ω was in fact extreme, Congress could not verify the accuracy of this statement, and the agency would expropriate greater levels of discretion than Congress intended, much as heads of certain countries declare states of emergency in order to invoke extraordinary powers to impose curfews, intervene in the economy, curtail civil liberties, and so on.

To put it another way, our assumption that agency discretion cannot be made to depend on the realized state of the world makes our model one of incomplete contracting: There exists a variable (ω) that will affect the value of the contract to both parties; this variable is unknown at the time of the original contract but will be realized in the future; and the actual value of ω is either nonobservable by one party (Congress) or it is nonverifiable in the sense that a court cannot objectively determine its value, so that the original contract cannot be made contingent on ω.

Furthermore, the agency faces a time consistency problem, since it cannot credibly commit to any one set of policies depending on the value of ω. For instance, if the agency could promise to enact regulations to yield the expected policy outcome in the present game $X_A (1 - \frac{X_A}{R})$, that is), then Pareto inferior outcomes could be avoided and both players would be made better off by the reduction in uncertainty. Since the agency cannot credibly commit to such a course of action, however, it will be constrained *ex ante* by administrative procedures that may lead to *ex post* inefficient outcomes. In these circumstances, then, one party or another will have some residual discretion over what actions to take once the state of the world is revealed; when Congress delegates, this discretion will rest with the executive, so legislators are vulnerable to a political hold-up problem.

Limits on the Political Control of Agencies

Our assumption of incomplete contracts means that congressional control over executive agencies will necessarily be imperfect. This contrasts with some previous discussions, such as McCubbins and Schwartz (1984, 174–5), who imply that oversight and administrative procedures force agencies to enact legislators' preferred policies:

It is convenient for Congress to adopt broad legislative mandates and give substantial rule-making authority to the bureaucracy. The problem with doing so, of course, is that the bureaucracy might not pursue Congress's goals. But citizens and interest groups can be counted on to sound an alarm in most cases in which the bureaucracy has arguably violated Congress's goals. Then Congress can intervene to rectify the violation. Congress has not necessarily relinquished legislative responsibility to anyone else. It has just found a more efficient way to legislate.

Similar arguments are found in the works of other congressional dominance theorists, such as Fiorina (1982) and Weingast and Moran (1983). To suppose that Congress can costlessly delegate to agencies is to assume away the principal–agent problem: It arises, but is then solved through the design of incentives and governance structures.

If this were the case, though, Congress might as well delegate all issue areas to the executive, secure in the knowledge that it can dictate policy outcomes as well as if it made policy itself. The fact that Congress does not do so is one indication that control over agencies is imperfect; also, the theoretical investigations examined in Chapter 2 argue that administrative procedures might mitigate but not completely solve the principal–agent problems inherent in delegation to the executive. We therefore part company somewhat with the strong versions of the congressional dominance thesis; we believe that administrative procedures matter, but that Congress cannot perfectly align the incentives of bureaucrats with its own interests given the disparity of information between the two branches. Furthermore, insofar as legislators value agency expertise, it is not clear that Congress should even want to try. After all, if final outcomes will be brought back to legislators' ideal points no matter what, this might dampen the incentives that agencies have to gather specialized information. In short, legislators may not be able to distinguish "fire alarms" from "false alarms" without investing so much energy in expertise that they defeat the original purpose of delegation.

Our approach implies that legislators delegate to agencies in those areas where legislative policy making is least attractive relative to policy making in the executive branch. Therefore, agency losses will be inevitable, both in terms of shifting policy toward the executive's ideal point and in terms of Pareto inferior outcomes. This argument highlights the dangers of formulating a theory of oversight divorced from a theory of delegation. If policies that are decided in the executive are not chosen at random, if they represent areas in which congressional policy making is most prone to failure, and if contracts between the branches are necessarily incomplete, then it would be contradictory to assume that congressional oversight and control will be perfect.

General Propositions

Finally, we analyze our equilibrium to determine how our key variable of interest – the floor's decision to delegate discretionary authority – changes with movements in the committee's ideal point, the agency's ideal point, and the degree of uncertainty in the environment. Note two features of Figure 4.3. First, for any fixed value of X_A, as the committee's ideal point X_C draws nearer the floor's ideal point X_F, the equilibrium delegation decision either remains unchanged (for high and low values of X_A), or it switches from agency policy making to committees. Therefore, on average, the closer the committee's preferences to those of the floor, the more likely it is that policy will be made by specific, detailed legislation rather than by delegation to administrative agencies.

Second, given any fixed value of X_C, for smaller and smaller values of X_A, the equilibrium eventually flips to $\mathcal{D} = 1$; that is, to one of delegation. So, on average, the closer the president's (and hence the agency's) preferences to those of Congress, the more likely it is that policy will be made through delegation. We summarize these findings in our first two propositions:

Proposition 1: The closer the preferences of the committee to those of the median floor voter, the less likely Congress is to delegate authority to the executive.

Proposition 2: The closer the preferences of the president to those of the median floor voter, the more likely Congress is to delegate authority to the executive.

Recall that legislators' utility is measured in a policy space relative to the value of R, the range of values that ω can take on. Therefore, the size of R measures the importance of informational concerns; when R is large, legislators will care more about making well-formed policy, and when it is small they will care more about getting the right benefits to the right constituents. One natural question to ask, then, is what happens to the equilibria in Figure 4.3 as the value of R increases?

The answer is shown in Figure 4.5, which illustrates how the equilibrium ranges in Figure 4.3 change as R gets larger and larger. As the plots show, Regions 5 and 6 in Figure 4.3 (for which $\mathcal{D} = 1$) expand with R, until they take over almost the entire graph. As the value of R increases, the equilibrium for any fixed values of X_C and X_A will eventually fall into the zone of delegation. Thus, as the world becomes more and more complex, agency policy making becomes more attractive relative to committee action alone.

Proposition 3: The more uncertainty associated with a policy area, the more likely Congress is to delegate authority to the executive.

TESTABLE PREDICTIONS

We now translate these propositions into testable hypotheses concerning the effects that congressional–executive relations, legislative organiza-

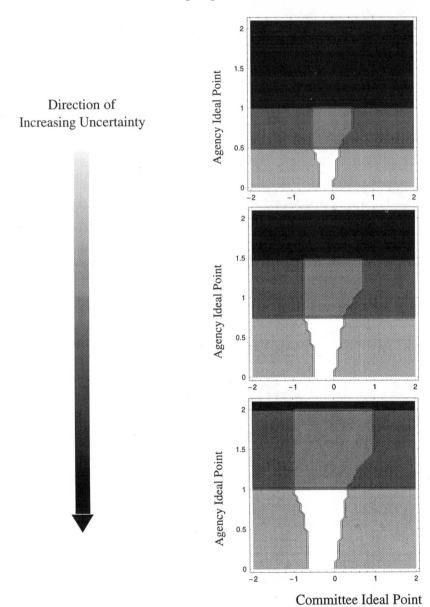

Direction of
Increasing Uncertainty

Committee Ideal Point

Figure 4.5. Changes in Equilibrium as Uncertainty Increases

tion, and issue-area characteristics will have on where policy is made – that is, how delegation and discretion change as X_C, X_P, R, and other real-world variables change. This section details our predictions, which are summarized in Table 4.1; some hypotheses follow directly from the model, while others combine our results with maintained hypotheses drawn from previous studies.

Congressional–Executive Relations

Divided Government

The first major proposition following from our model is that, as the level of legislative–executive conflict over policy increases, delegation to the executive becomes less attractive. If we take partisan affiliation as a rough proxy for policy preferences, then we would expect Congress to delegate more discretion during times of unified government than under divided partisan control of government.

This prediction allows us to address the recent debate over whether or not divided government has any policy-relevant consequences. Some observers (Cutler 1988; Sundquist 1988) adopt the view, now standard in popular discourse, that divided government leads to deadlock, stalemate, and ineffective government. They take the recent trend toward split partisan control of the legislative and executive branches as an indication that American politics has entered a new phase where parties can no longer serve to unify across branches of government and policy movement has become nearly impossible to achieve.

On the other hand, some commentators assert that the policy impact of divided government has been overstated. Krehbiel (1996) points out that our constitutional system of government has many impediments to policy making, so divided government per se may have little impact on the volume of legislation passed. Fiorina (1992) notes that if neither party wants to take the blame for a lack of policy movement, then divided government may actually facilitate coordination and cooperation in passing legislation, as arguably happened in 1996 prior to the national elections. And, most comprehensively, Mayhew (1991) surveys important postwar legislation and concludes that the level of legislative activity has not been significantly different under divided and unified governments.

Our analysis begins with Mayhew's (1991) list of important legislation, but we examine these laws from a different perspective. If our theory is correct, then the policy impact of divided government may occur not in the *quantity* of legislation passed, but in its *quality*. In particular, we assert that divided government will be associated with

Table 4.1. *Empirical Predictions*

No.	Hypothesis	Dependent Variable(s)	Independent Variable(s)
Congressional-Executive Relations: x_P			
1	Divided Government and Delegation	Discretion	Divided Government
2	Roll Call Votes and Delegation	Probability of Voting for Delegation	Party, Party*Divided Gov't
3	Agency Type and Delegation	Agency Independence, Discretion	Divided Gov't, Agency Independence
Legislative Organization: x_C			
4	Committee Composition	Committee Preferences	Congressional-Executive Conflict
5	Committee Outliers and Delegation	Discretion	Comm. Preferences, Comm. Preferences * Divided Government
6	Legislative Parties and Delegation	Discretion	Party Cohesion
7	Parliamentary Procedures and Delegation	Discretion	Multiple Referrals, Restrictive Rules
Issue Areas and Delegation: R			
8	Issue Areas and Delegation	Discretion	Issue Area Type
9	Issue Areas and Committees	Discretion	Oversight Hearings, Scope of Committee Jurisdiction

more direct legislation by Congress and less delegation. If executive agents are ceded less discretionary authority under divided government, then we may observe "procedural gridlock," under which bureaucrats have less authority to change policy, find themselves under greater scrutiny from outside actors, and in general have less leeway to make coherent, well-considered policy.

Conflict between the branches can be measured in a number of ways: a simple measure of divided and unified government; a more nuanced measure based on the percentage of seats held by the party opposing the president; and an even more sensitive measure in which the president is assigned an ideal point based on the positions he announces on congressional roll calls. Each of these possibilities will be explored in the data analysis in Chapter 6. We then state:

Hypothesis 1: Divided Government and Delegation
    Less discretionary authority will be delegated to the executive during times of divided government.

Individual Voting on Delegation

Members of Congress express their preferences about delegation not only in the legislation they pass but also in the roll-call votes taken over that legislation. If partisan conflict affects behavior at the individual level as well as at the aggregate, then we should observe legislators from the same party as the president favoring greater discretion, and legislators from the opposite side of the aisle, less. In other words, majority party members during unified government and minority party members during divided government should support greater delegation, while their counterparts should oppose it.

A similar study has been undertaken by Bensel (1980), who equates lower degrees of executive branch discretion with a "rule of law" standard and examines roll-call votes from bills passed in 1965–6, 1971, 1975, and 1977. Bensel concludes that legislators are more likely to support a rule-of-law standard if they are: (1) from the party opposite that of the president; (2) Republicans, consistent with the GOP's anti–big government orientation; and (3) rank-and-file members, as opposed to party and committee leaders.[17] Our work extends Bensel's data set over the postwar period and narrows its focus to major pieces of legislation, to see if his findings hold in a broader policy context. We also examine the impact of committee and party leadership on members' voting patterns on delegation.

Hypothesis 2: Roll-Call Votes and Delegation
    Legislators from the president's party will vote in support of delegation, while legislators from the other party will vote against it.

Agency Type

Another set of predictions pertains to the type of agency receiving delegated authority. For our purposes, agencies come in five different flavors:

---

[17]Bensel also argues that this standard is fundamentally incompatible with traditional notions of responsible party government, as new parties gaining office have less latitude to change public policy given the explicit rule-making authority delegated in previous administrations.

those located in the executive office of the president (EOP), cabinet-level agencies, independent agencies, independent regulatory commissions, and government corporations. As one moves from the former to the latter, these executive bureaus are more and more insulated from political control by the president. For instance, nearly all actors in the EOP serve at the president's pleasure; heads of cabinet-level agencies can be appointed with the advice and consent of the Senate and dismissed by the president alone; and members of independent commissions serve for fixed terms and cannot be removed. Agency type also has an impact on the budgetary process by which agencies request funding: independent agencies submit their budgets directly to Congress; while agencies in the normal cabinet hierarchies must first submit their proposals to the Office of Management and Budget, which then modifies agency requests and merges them into the president's overall budget plan.

The type of agency receiving delegated authority, then, is itself an important lever of political control, as is the possibility of circumventing the executive branch altogether by delegating to state or local governments or to the judiciary.[18] What factors influence legislators' choices regarding the structure of delegation? As executive agencies become more independent, it has been emphasized, the president has relatively less control over the agency's preferences, but at the cost of greater uncertainty over outcomes. Thus, the locational decision can be seen as a trade-off of bias toward the president's preferences, on the one hand, and variance in outcomes, on the other.[19]

We can incorporate this possibility into our model by assuming that when Congress delegates, it can specify not only the baseline policy $\hat{p}$ and discretion d, but also the level of agency independence. Furthermore, the preferences of more independent agencies are closer to those of Congress on average, but they have a higher variance than when the president alone controls the agency. In this variant of our model, as the president's preferences diverge from legislators', Congress will shift decision-making authority away from cabinet-level departments under presidential control and toward independent agencies. Since divided government is associated with less delegation, we also obtain the somewhat

[18]This strategic control over bureaucratic structure has been emphasized, e.g., by Moe (1989). On the importance of agency type and congressional goals, see also Wilson (1989, 239–41).

[19]As discussed in Chapter 2, this is similar to the view expressed by Fiorina (1986), who characterizes the problem in terms of delegation to biased agencies as opposed to direct legislation, which is then interpreted by a series of luck-of-the-draw court decisions. While we agree that courts may have some leeway when interpreting statutory provisions, we believe that this leeway decreases rather than increases when Congress explicitly states legislative intent by writing detailed, specific laws.

surprising prediction that more-independent agencies will receive less discretionary authority.[20] Overall, then, we state:

Hypothesis 3: Agency Type and Delegation

During times of divided government, Congress will delegate more often to independent agencies and non-executive branch actors.

Legislative Organization

Contrary Outliers

One of the central debates in the current legislative organization literature revolves around the preferences of committees vis-à-vis the floor. As explained in Chapter 2, distributive theories predict homogeneous outliers, or unrepresentative committees, while informational theories predict that committees will be representative of the floor as a whole. Given the importance of committees in the legislative process and the different views that competing theories of legislative organization take toward them, it is not surprising that the committee outlier debate has become so contentious. The empirical evidence so far is mixed, though, with neither alternative receiving clear-cut support.[21]

Our theory predicts that a range of committee medians will serve the floor's purposes equally well, but this range contracts as the policy preferences of the executive move closer to those of the median congressional voter. Therefore, in contrast to theories that claim that committees should either normally be outliers or should have medians identical to the floor median, our approach predicts that the range of committee medians should vary predictably over time, contracting during times of unified as opposed to divided government. So committee composition will be influenced by the degree of congressional–executive conflict in a rather counterintuitive manner.

Along these same lines, committees play roles, not only in the original drafting of legislation, but also in overseeing authority delegated to the executive. In this capacity, as shown in Epstein and O'Halloran (1995), the floor prefers oversight by actors with preferences biased against those of the executive agencies that they oversee.[22] In a system of separate powers, then, committee preferences should move counter to those of

---

[20]See Appendix A for the details of these calculations.

[21]See Krehbiel (1990), Cox and McCubbins (1993), Londregan and Snyder (1994), and Sinclair (1995).

[22]In Epstein and O'Halloran (1995), these intermediary actors are interest groups; here, we put committees in the role of bureaucratic overseers. For a similar result on the benefits of biased advice, see Calvert (1985).

the executive; that is, committees should be composed of contrary outliers.

Hypothesis 4: Committee Composition
(*a*) The range of committee medians should narrow during times of unified government.
(*b*) Committee medians will move opposite to changes in the preferences of the executive.

Outliers and Delegation

The next set of testable predictions revolves around the proposition that the closer the preferences of the median floor voter and the committee, the less likely Congress is to delegate power to the executive branch. The most direct test of this proposition uses the policy differences between committees and the floor as an explanatory variable for delegation to executive agencies, so that outlying committees will be associated with greater delegation.[23]

A second, less obvious prediction from our model is that the impact of committee outliers on discretion should lessen as the preferences of Congress and the executive diverge. The details behind this prediction are provided in Appendix A; intuitively, the idea is that at higher levels of interbranch conflict agencies would not receive much discretion in any case, so the influence of outlying committees is muted. Therefore, we have predictions about both the impact of committee outliers on discretion and their interaction with divided government.

Hypothesis 5: Committee Outliers and Delegation
(*a*) The more the committee considering legislation is a preference outlier, the more likely Congress is to delegate authority to the executive branch.
(*b*) The magnitude of committee outliers' impact on discretion will decline as interbranch conflict increases.

Legislative Parties

Standard roll call-based measures of legislators' ideal points may not capture perfectly the policy conflict between floor and committee members. If floor or party majorities can devise institutions that correctly

---

[23]Note that this proposition holds true even after accounting for the effects given in Hypothesis 4 above, which states that committee medians will move opposite to changes in the president's preferences. Even if legislators select the optimal committee medians, that is, equilibrium discretion will still fall as committees move further away from the floor.

structure the incentives of committee members, then even apparently outlying committees may produce policy more beneficial to legislators' reelection chances than policy made in the executive branch. In particular, party theorists (viz., Banks and Calvert 1992; Cox and McCubbins 1993) argue that strong congressional parties act like legislative cartels, alleviating coordination problems by aligning the incentives of committee and floor members through the selective provision of rewards and punishments.

Using these party theories as maintained hypotheses, we should observe less delegation to the executive branch when legislative parties are strong, all else being equal. Strong parties, in turn, are viewed as an artifact of homogeneous intraparty preferences. That is, when members of the majority party agree on major policy issues, they will be more willing to delegate authority to party leaders, who will in turn use their enhanced powers to push through the party's legislative agenda. This notion is the basis of Rohde's (1991) theory of "conditional party government"; it also has roots in Cooper and Brady's (1981) analysis of House leadership from Cannon to Rayburn. So homogeneous preferences within the majority party should be associated with more effective legislative policy making, leading Congress to delegate relatively less authority.

Hypothesis 6: Legislative Parties and Delegation
   The more cohesive the majority party in Congress is, the less authority will be delegated to the executive.

Parliamentary Procedures

Another possible institutional mechanism for increasing the relative benefits of the legislative process is the use of parliamentary procedures, including the multiple referral of bills and restrictive rules. Regarding the former, since 1977 the Speaker of the House has had the right to refer bills to more than one committee, under three possible procedures: joint referral, where the entire bill is sent to more than one committee at the same time; split referral, where different sections of the bill are sent to separate committees; and sequential referral, where the entire bill is considered by certain committees in a specified order. Multiple referrals may also be accompanied by time limits for each committee at the discretion of the Speaker.

Analyses of multiple referrals (Bach and Smith 1988; Davidson, Oleszek, and Kephart 1988; Collie and Cooper 1989; Bawn 1996) demonstrate that they are used disproportionately on important, complex legislation, offering the floor two advantages. First, multiple referrals force rival committees to compete with each other, vying to influence floor voters.[24] So they, in essence, create one large committee with preferences, on average, closer to those of the floor. Second, they combine the expertise of multiple committees, reducing the uncertainty associated with legislative action. Using the conclusions from these previous studies as maintained hypotheses, multiple referrals should make the legislative process more effective from the floor's point of view and thus lead to less delegation.

Similarly, restrictive rules are a much studied device by which the floor tries to streamline the consideration of complex and contentious legislation. Different approaches advance different rationales for the adoption of restrictive amendment procedures: to insulate committee jurisdictions from outside meddling; to encourage committee members' investment in expertise; or to protect the majority party agenda and the intraparty logrolls contained within legislation. No matter what their genesis, restrictive rules are agreed to indicate a harmony of interests between the floor and committees, and so they should also be associated with less authority delegated to the executive.

Hypothesis 7: Parliamentary Procedures and Delegation
(*a*) The amount of discretion delegated to the executive will decrease for multiply referred bills.
(*b*) The amount of discretion delegated to the executive will decrease for bills that receive restrictive amendment procedures.

Issue-Area Effects

Complexity and Delegation

One of the most interesting implications of our model, and the hardest to test, concerns the differences between issue areas characterized mainly by distributive concerns as opposed to those characterized by expertise. According to our theory, where the policy area is complex, making the link between policies and outcomes more uncertain, legislators will prefer bureaucratic policy making; if these concerns are minimal, though, policy making through committees gives Congress greater control over the distribution of benefits to constituents.

The amount of uncertainty surrounding an issue is difficult to measure in any direct way, so we take a twofold approach to the problem. First,

---

[24]Much as tournaments among agents can ameliorate problems of slippage and shirking in principal–agent relations, so multiple referrals can help control problems with outlier committees. The tournament literature is now a well-established subset of general principal–agent theory. See, e.g., Lazear and Rosen (1981) and Holmström (1982).

84

several previous authors have attempted to classify public laws according to a number of different schemes: some by the type of issue area involved (agriculture, defense, trade); some by the interest groups affected by the policy (taxpayers, corporations, the airline industry); and some by the scope of regulatory activity (national, local, or industry-specific).[25] Such schemes will be discussed at greater length in Chapter 8. We take several of these classifications and examine if any natural pattern emerges regarding informational intensity and delegation.

Hypothesis 8: Issue Areas and Delegation
   More authority will be delegated to the executive in informationally intense issue areas.

Issue Areas and Committees

Second, we measure the complexity of an issue area by the characteristics of the committee or committees that reported a given bill. One measure of committee-based expertise is the average number of hearings held by that committee per Congress, the hypothesis being that committees dealing with more complex issue areas will hold a larger number of hearings. That is, members who serve on committees dealing with technically and politically complex issues use a variety of means to gather information about the problem at hand, one of which is holding hearings.[26] Another measure of the complexity of a committee's policy domain is the scope of its jurisdiction; the greater the number of areas covered by a given committee, the greater the demands on legislative expertise.

Hypothesis 9: Issue Areas and Committees
   Bills reported by committees with informationally intense policy jurisdictions will delegate greater discretionary authority to the executive.

The chapters that follow will explore the data to be used in our analysis and test these three sets of predictions for congressional–executive relations, legislative organization, and issue-area characteristics, respectively. We first detail our various data sets, including a comprehensive survey of delegation and constraints in major postwar legislation. We then use these data, along with various other data sets on roll calls over delegation, committee assignments, and others, to test the propositions stated above.

---

[25]See Huntington (1971), Froman (1967), Salisbury (1969), and Ripley and Franklin (1984, 21–2) for discussions.
[26]See Fenno (1973) and Krehbiel (1991) for discussions of information gathering and committee expertise.

5

Data and Postwar Trends

When confronted with the difficulty in making whole numbers fit measurements which imperfect human beings, using imperfect sense organs, make with imperfect instruments in an imperfect and changing world, the practical man was long content to go on adding fresh divisions to his scale of measurement.

Lancelot Hogben, *Mathematics for the Millions*[1]

It is clear that a number of data sets will be necessary to test the nine propositions laid out in the previous chapter: roll-call votes, committee membership, issue areas, and so on. We set aside this chapter, though, to examine the one data set unique to the present study, namely, a measure of executive discretion. Our theory provides us with two starting points in this task. First, as our model centers on the passage of legislation, our proper unit of analysis is a law. Second, discretion in our model is composed of both delegation and constraints – the former giving power to the executive and the latter circumscribing its limits.

In constructing our discretion index, we are forced, to some extent, to rely on individual judgment. But to minimize subjectivity, we devised a set of systematic coding rules and procedures for each element of the data set. In this chapter and its accompanying appendixes, we describe our sample of laws, detail how we code and construct our key variable of interest, and present some summary statistics and trends in executive discretion over time.

DATA SAMPLE

Our sample of laws is based on Mayhew's (1991) list of important legislation in the postwar era, contained in his book *Divided We Gov-*

---

[1]Hogben (1983, 40).

ern. Mayhew's purpose in compiling this list was different than our current enterprise: He sought to show that the number of important pieces of legislation enacted during times of divided partisan control of government does not differ from those enacted under unified government. We shall return to the specific theme of divided government in Chapter 6. For our present purposes, what counts is that Mayhew devised a methodology for identifying important pieces of legislation, which will serve as our sample of laws to be analyzed.

Mayhew defined important legislation in a two-step – or as he calls it, a "two-sweep" – process. The first sweep of legislation includes those bills reported in the year-end roundups of both the *New York Times* and *Washington Post.* This sweep captures contemporary judgments about the productivity of national government and identifies those pieces of legislation that were thought to be of historic significance. The second sweep captures those laws that historians and political observers, in hindsight, identify as being of lasting importance. This second sweep covered laws only through the early 1980s, as laws passed more recently would not yet be included in the secondary sources that Mayhew relied on for posterior judgments.

Mayhew's data set includes 267 enactments over the 1947 to 1990 period, of which 64 were chosen in sweep one alone, 56 came from sweep two alone, and 147 were identified in both sweeps. Starting from this number, we arrived at our final sample in a series of steps, as shown in Figure 5.1. First, the seven sweep-one laws passed in the 102d Congress were added to the data set, bringing the total up to 274. From this list, we eliminated the twelve entries that were either treaties or constitutional amendments; these categories of enactments do not follow the normal legislative process and therefore do not fall within the purview of our theory. This pares the list down to a total of 262 entries.

To understand the next set of adjustments, it is important to explain the differences between Mayhew's substantive focus and ours. Mayhew was concerned with what he termed "enactments," which can be roughly described as important activities undertaken by the national government. In a few cases, these enactments do not line up one-for-one with pieces of legislation. On the one hand, Mayhew's list includes eight instances where the enactment that he considered important "piggy-backed" on another piece of legislation. For instance, the Economic Stabilization Act of 1970 was actually passed as part of the Defense Production Act (PL 91–379). In six of these eight cases, we simply counted the final bill as the important piece of legislation and coded it accordingly. In two of these cases, though, Mayhew counts both the original measure *and* the final law as separate enactments: the Social Security Increase of 1969 was rolled into the Tax Reform Act of 1969 (PL 91–172), and what

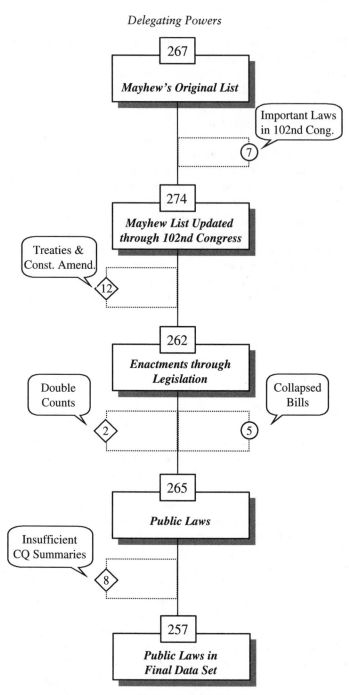

Figure 5.1. Data Road Map

began as an independent Child Care bill was eventually passed as Title
V of the Omnibus Budget Reconciliation Act of 1990 (PL 101–508).
Whereas Mayhew treats each of these measures as separate enactments,
we code them as a single bill and count them just once in our data set.[2]
We therefore lose two items in our list relative to Mayhew's through
these double counts.

On the other hand, in two cases Mayhew combines separate laws and
counts them as a single enactment. This happened in 1963, when two
mental health bills dealing with research and treatment centers (PL 88–
156 and PL 88–164) were combined into one enactment, and in 1978,
when five energy bills (PL 95–617 to 95–621) were all rolled into the
Carter "comprehensive energy package." We counted each of these col-
lapsed bills as separate entries in our list of laws, thus adding five items
relative to Mayhew. Overall, then, we began with 265 major public laws
from 1947 through 1992.

Last, from this list we removed eight bills that had insufficient *Congressional Quarterly (CQ)* summaries.[3] As described below, these summaries formed the basis for our coding of delegation, constraints, and
discretion, so when *CQ* offered little detail or an incomplete listing of a
bill's provisions, we could not code it consistently with the other bills.
This brings the final number down to 257 bills to code for discretion;
these bills are listed in Appendix B.

It is important to emphasize at this point that our investigation is in
fact limited to major legislation. We do this, not because we believe that
our results hold only for significant legislation, but because the struggles
over who controls policy will be most pronounced when the stakes are
high. And with the rise of omnibus legislation, focus on major bills
becomes even less problematic, as many significant enactments are combined into a single measure. On the other hand, we do not doubt that
the patterns we find in our data will be modified somewhat by the
inclusion of less important legislation, and therefore our findings should
be understood to be circumscribed accordingly.

---

[2]After all, it is not clear that the Child Care bill could have passed on its own
without being combined with the provisions in the Budget Reconciliation Act.

[3]These were: (1) The Federal Insecticide, Fungicide, and Rodenticide Act (PL 80–
104); (2) National Security Act of 1947 (PL 80–253); (3) The Portal to Portal Act of
1947 (PL 80–49); (4) Greece-Turkish Aid Act of 1947 (PL 80–75); (5) Food Additive
Amendments of 1958 (PL 85–929); (6) Foreign Assistance Act of 1973 (PL 93–189);
(7) Omnibus Budget Reconciliation Act of 1981 (PL 97–35); and (8) Emergency Jobs
Appropriations Act of 1983 (PL 98–8). These bills were, however, included in the
roll-call analysis described in Chapter 6.

DELEGATION RATIO

The key variable in our model is the amount of discretionary authority delegated to executive branch agencies. In Chapter 4, we modeled the setting of discretion as a two-step process, where legislators first decide whether or not to delegate ($\mathcal{D} = 0$ or 1) and, if they delegate, how much discretion (d) to cede the executive. Thus, we measure the delegation decision as a dichotomous variable equal to 1 if Congress delegates any discretionary authority and 0 otherwise, and we measure discretion as a continuous variable ranging from 0 (no delegation) to 1 (complete delegation), so that delegating no authority is equivalent to delegating but giving the executive no discretion.

As yet, few studies have attempted to operationalize a measure of executive discretion. The works that come closest are Aberbach (1990), who measures congressional oversight of the bureaucracy, and O'Halloran (1994), who examines changes over time in the constraints placed on executive authority in trade policy. Neither, however, creates a direct, general measure of bureaucratic discretion across issue areas. To tackle this problem, we create a new discretion index (d), which has two components: the delegation ratio (r) and relative constraints (c).

The easiest way to understand the construction of these indices is to examine the coding sheets used to gather them, a sample of which has been reproduced as Appendix C. The top section shows summary information for the bill being coded: the year and Congress in which it was passed, its public law (PL) number, the final bill passed, the law's official title, and a brief description of the act. Moving down, the bill was next coded as to whether or not it delegated any discretionary authority to the executive, on a Yes/No basis – as discussed above, this is the delegation decision $\mathcal{D}$ from our model. We defer the discussion of this variable for a moment, and return to it below.

Major Provisions

The next step in the analysis is to identify the total number of provisions in the bill. To obtain this information – and the remaining variables on the sheet as well – we relied on *Congressional Quarterly*'s legislative summaries. Beginning in the late 1940s, *Congressional Quarterly Almanac* listed the key provisions of major legislation enacted during each year. In fact, all of the laws in our sample were among those *Congressional Quarterly* considered important enough to include in its year-end summaries. This is not too surprising; after all, Mayhew's list is based on judgments about important enactments as defined by the *Washington Post* and *New York Times*, and being of that same genre, *Congressional*

Quarterly was also likely to have identified these laws as newsworthy. The advantages of using CQ summaries to code legislation are two-fold. First, the key elements of each law are extracted, separating the major provisions from the minor aspects of the statute. Second, and most important, CQ summaries provide a consistent format from which to code legislation over time and across issue areas, which is necessary in order to conduct the detailed contextual analysis required to test our theory.

The Major Provisions variable, then, was coded as the number of provisions in the CQ summary of a given law, where a provision was defined as an item (denoted by a new paragraph, bullet, or list) that provided substantive details about the legislation. This counting proce-dure was usually straightforward, but to decide borderline cases we devised a set of uniform coding rules.[4] The 1979 Trade Act displayed on the sample coding sheet, for example, contained 59 major provisions. As shown in Table 5.1, which contains summary statistics for this and all other variables detailed in this chapter, the average number of major provisions in our sample was 45, with a minimum of 1 and a maximum of 674 in the 1990 Clean Air Act.

Delegation Provisions

We now arrive at the heart of measuring delegation: For every bill, each major provision was read and coded to determine whether or not it delegated authority. Delegation for these purposes is the granting of substantive policy discretion by Congress to some other governmental body, including the executive branch, courts, states, or local govern-ments. Some examples of delegation include: (1) discretionary rule-making authority; (2) the authorization of a program that allows the agency some discretionary authority; (3) the creation of a board or commission with authority to regulate some aspect of economic activity; (4) granting an agency authority to modify or change decision-making criteria; (5) allowing an agency to allocate moneys or benefits where they determine the sum and/or possible recipients of those benefits; (6) allow-ing the agency to waive or exempt constituents from certain rules or

---

[4]These rules, as well as the other coding rules and procedures used to construct our data sets, are provided in Appendix D. A question arises as to how accurately *Congressional Quarterly* summarizes the key provisions of an act. As an independent check on CQ reporting, we randomly selected several laws and noted whether the CQ summaries covered the major titles of the law; in all cases, they did. Second, from the 93d Congress on, the Library of Congress Information Service (LOCIS) provides digests of the major provisions of public laws enacted. Again, in all cases the CQ summaries included as least as much detail as the LOCIS briefs.

Table 5.1. *Summary Statistics*

Variable	Mean	Std. Dev.	Min	Max
Delegation Measures				
Major Provisions	44.96	66.56	1	674
Delegation Provisions	12.80	19.67	0	213
Executive Delegations	11.51	17.51	0	187
Constraint Measures				
Appointment Limits	0.32	0.46	0	1
Time Limits	0.50	0.50	0	1
Spending Limits	0.50	0.50	0	1
Legislative Action	0.12	0.33	0	1
Executive Action	0.11	0.32	0	1
Legislative Veto	0.13	0.34	0	1
Reporting Requirements	0.55	0.50	0	1
Consultation Requirements	0.29	0.45	0	1
Public Hearings	0.12	0.33	0	1
Appeals Procedures	0.26	0.44	0	1
Rule-Making Requirements	0.79	0.41	0	1
Exemptions	0.46	0.50	0	1
Compensations	0.16	0.37	0	1
Direct Oversight	0.07	0.26	0	1
Calculated Variables				
Delegation Ratio	28.42%	20.62%	0	100%
Total Constraints	4.40	2.64	0	12
Constraint Ratio	31.03%	18.80%	0	85%
Relative Constraints	9.68%	8.92%	0	50%
Total Discretion	**18.31%**	**16.09%**	**0**	**100%**

Note: N = 257.

procedures; and (7) extensions of decision-making authority that would otherwise expire.[5] Provisions that merely authorized funds for an existing program, required reports or publication of information, or the hiring of staff or personnel were not counted as delegation.[6]

---

[5] Again, complete coding rules are provided in Appendix D.

[6] In some cases, the language of the summaries was insufficient to determine if the provision afforded substantive authority to the agency. In these cases, we located the provision referenced in the CQ legislative summaries in the appropriate section of the *Statutes-at-Large*. From the text of the law, we determined whether substantive authority was indeed delegated.

If no substantive authority was delegated in any provision, then we consider a law to be an example of direct legislation. For instance, we count the 1958 act that granted statehood to Alaska and the Social Security Amendments of 1961 as instances of direct legislation with no delegation, even though the former allowed the federal government to temporarily continue management of Alaskan fish and wildlife conservation, and the latter delegated to the executive branch the decision of how to notify recipients of their increased benefits – these delegations did not substantively alter the final policy enacted. On the other hand, the Mutual Defense Assistance Act of 1949, which gave the president sole authority to distribute up to $125 million in foreign aid, and the National Aeronautics and Space Act of 1958, which created NASA and charged it with devising a program for space exploration, are clear cases where substantive authority was delegated.

The Delegation Provisions variable thus counts the total number of provisions in the given bill that delegated authority to some other governmental actor. The coding sheet in Appendix C shows that, in the given trade act, 24 provisions delegated authority. Overall, an average of 12.8 provisions in each bill delegated authority, ranging from a minimum of 0 (19 bills delegated no authority to any other governmental body) to a maximum of 213.

Executive Delegation

The main focus of our analysis is the delegation of authority from Congress to the executive branch. Accordingly, the Executive Delegation variable counts the number of provisions granting authority to the executive, as opposed to the courts, states, or local governments. This information then served as the basis for coding the Delegation Yes/No variable above: Delegation was set to 1 (Yes) if the number of executive delegations was greater than zero, and it was set to 0 (No) otherwise. This, again, is consistent with the definition of the $\mathcal{D}$ variable in our theoretical model of delegation, indicating whether Congress gives any discretion to the executive.

From the total number of provisions contained in a law and the number of provisions that delegate substantive authority to the executive, we calculated the delegation ratio as:

$$r = \frac{Provisions\ with\ Executive\ Delegation}{Total\ Provisions}.$$

93

For instance, the CQ summary of the Trade Agreements Act of 1979 listed 59 major provisions, of which 24 delegated authority, all to the executive branch. So the delegation ratio for this law would be 24/59, or about 41 percent. The delegation ratio, then, measures the proportion of a law's major provisions that delegated substantive authority to the executive branch.

As a first check on the plausibility of our measure of delegation, we identified those bills that contain no executive delegations; that is, those bills for which $\mathcal{D} = 0$. Table 5.2 provides the year, Congress, public law number, and title for the 25 bills that met this criterion (this includes the 19 bills that delegated no authority at all, plus 6 bills that delegated only to non–executive branch actors). The table reveals some noteworthy results. Some entries, such as the Consumer Goods Pricing Act of 1975 and the Birthday of Martin Luther King, Jr., had only one major provision with no delegation: The former prohibited state laws allowing manufacture–dealer price fixing, while the latter established a national holiday. Some laws were cases of rare legislation that did not involve executive authority, such as the granting of Alaskan statehood, the Public Health Cigarette Smoking Act of 1969 (banning cigarette advertising on television), the Civil Rights Restoration Act of 1987 (which overruled the 1984 *Grove City* Supreme Court ruling), and the granting of reparations to Japanese-Americans who were relocated during World War II.

Others bills, though, were more substantive and contained a fair number of provisions, including the Internal Revenue Code of 1954, the Tax Reduction Act of 1975, and the Economic Recovery Tax Act of 1981, with 71, 40, and 80 major provisions, respectively. These bills pertain to tax and fiscal policy, areas in which Congress has traditionally been reluctant to cede power to the executive. Similarly for the Social Security increases, changes in the minimum wage, and other money bills on the list: These are all areas where the usual mode is for Congress to write specific, detailed legislation that leaves the executive little room for interpretation when enacting the law.

This pattern is reinforced when we examine the laws with the lowest delegation ratios for which $\mathcal{D} = 1$, shown in panel (a) of Table 5.3. These laws were not enacted through direct legislation, but nonetheless they delegated very little authority to the executive. Again, the vast majority are tax bills and associated fiscal measures, except for one civil rights act (again overruling a Supreme Court decision), and a transportation bill (another policy area where Congress concentrates on getting the right benefits to the right constituents).

Panel (b) of Table 5.3 shows the acts with the highest delegation ratios. These laws are obviously quite different in nature from those above. High-delegation laws tend to concern issues of defense and for-

Table 5.2. *Acts with No Executive Delegation ($\mathcal{D} = 0$)*

Year	Congress	PL Num.	Title
1948	80	80-471	Revenue Act of 1948
1950	81	81-734	Social Security Act Amendments of 1950
1950	81	81-814	Revenue Act of 1950
1950	81	81-909	Excess Profits Tax Act of 1950
1952	82	82-590	Social Security Increase of 1952
1953	83	83-31	Submerged Lands Act
1954	83	83-591	Internal Revenue Code of 1954
1954	83	83-761	Social Security Amendments of 1954
1955	84	84-381	Minimum Wage Increase of 1955
1958	85	85-508	Alaska Admission into Union
1961	87	87-30	Fair Labor Standards Amendment of 1961
1963	88	88-38	Equal Pay Act of 1963
1965	89	89-44	Excise Tax Reduction Act of 1965
1968	90	90-364	Revenue and Expenditure Control Act of 1968
1970	91	91-222	Public Health Cigarette Smoking Act of 1969
1972	92	92-336	Public Debt Limitation--Extension
1972	92	92-512	State and Local Fiscal Assistance Act of 1972
1973	93	93-233	Social Security Benefits--Increase
1975	94	94-12	Tax Reduction Act of 1975
1975	94	94-145	Consumer Goods Pricing Act of 1975
1981	97	97-34	Economic Recovery Tax Act of 1981
1983	98	98-144	Public Holiday--Birthday of Martin Luther King, Jr.
1988	100	100-259	The Civil Rights Restoration Act of 1987
1988	100	100-383	Wartime Relocation of Civilians
1989	101	101-157	Fair Labor Standards Amendments of 1989

eign policy (the Defense Production Act of 1970, the National Aeronautics and Space Act of 1958, and the Selective Service Amendments Act of 1969); environmental policy (the Water Quality Act of 1965, the Air Quality Act of 1967, and the Clean Air Amendments of 1970); and health and general social policy (the Maternal and Child Health and Mental Retardation Act of 1963, the Health Research Facilities Amendments of 1965, and the McKinney Homeless Assistance Act of 1987). Traditionally, Congress has willingly granted the executive great leeway to set policy in these areas, as the results of ill-formed policy are often drastic and the political advantages of well-formulated policy are not nearly as evident – they have only a political downside. We shall return

Table 5.3. *Acts with Lowest and Highest Delegation Ratio*

Acts with Least Delegation where $\mathcal{D}=1$

Year	Congress	PL Num.	Title	Delegation Ratio
1986	99	99-514	Tax Reform Act of 1986	0.005
1976	94	94-455	Tax Reform Act of 1976	0.010
1951	82	82-183	Revenue Act of 1951	0.018
1978	95	95-600	Revenue Act of 1978	0.020
1969	91	91-172	Tax Reform Act of 1969	0.022
1983	98	98-21	Social Security Amendments of 1983	0.023
1964	88	88-272	Revenue Act of 1964	0.024
1982	97	97-424	Surface Transportation Assistance Act of 1982	0.028
1985	99	99-177	Balanced Budget and Emergency Deficit Control Act of 1985	0.037
1976	94	94-553	Copyrights Act	0.042
1991	102	102-166	Civil Rights Act of 1991	0.042
1984	98	98-369	Deficit Reduction Act of 1984	0.045
1978	95	95-618	Energy Tax Act of 1978	0.051
1965	89	89-97	Social Security Amendments of 1965	0.052

(a)

Acts with Most Delegation

Year	Congress	PL Num.	Title	Delegation Ratio
1987	100	100-77	McKinney Homeless Assistance Act of 1987	0.62
1970	91	91-379	Defense Production Act—Amendments— Economic Stabilization	0.63
1955	84	84-86	Reciprocal Trade Act Extended of 1955	0.64
1965	89	89-234	Water Quality Act of 1965	0.64
1966	89	89-675	Clean Air Act Amendments of 1966	0.67
1967	90	90-148	Air Quality Act of 1967	0.68
1974	93	93-618	Trade Act of 1974	0.69
1970	91	91-604	Clean Air Amendments of 1970	0.71
1963	88	88-156	Maternal and Child Health and Mental Retardation Planning Amendments of 1963	0.75
1958	85	85-568	National Aeronautics and Space Act of 1958	0.79
1958	85	85-864	National Defense Education Act of 1958	0.82
1961	87	87-41	Inter-American Program- Appropriation	1.00
1963	88	88-164	Mental Retardation Facilities and Community Health Centers Construction Act of 1963	1.00
1965	89	89-115	Health Research Facilities Amendments of 1965	1.00
1969	91	91-124	Selective Service Amendments Act of 1969	1.00

(b)

to a more thorough examination of issue-area questions in Chapter 8; here we note that these patterns provide some support for our scheme of coding delegation.[7]

[7]We also checked the relationship between the delegation ratio and the number of major provisions in a bill, to make sure that our measure was not an artifact of *CQ's*

Panel (a) of Figure 5.2 shows the distribution of delegation ratios across all bills with a normal curve overlaid; the average delegation ratio is 28.4 percent. As seen in the graph, the distribution is more or less normal, but with a spike at 0. This pattern usually indicates a "pegging" phenomenon: A number of observations with a delegation ratio of 0 (that is, $\mathcal{D} = 0$) would actually be negative but for the restriction that Congress can give the executive no less than zero discretion. This again indicates that our analysis might reasonably predict the decision to delegate or not first, and then, given delegation, how much discretionary authority to cede the executive. For comparison, panel (b) of Figure 5.2 shows the distribution of delegation ratios for only those bills with $\mathcal{D} = 1$.

Agencies Receiving Authority

We next identified all actors receiving delegated authority mentioned in the *CQ* summaries, such as states, the courts, and federal or state agencies. Using various editions of the *United States Government Manual*, we also identified the location of these actors in one of the following eight categories: (1) the Executive Office of the President (which includes the president himself); (2) Cabinet Departments; (3) Independent Regulatory Agencies (agencies outside of the cabinet hierarchy); (4) Independent Commissions (whose members serve for fixed terms and cannot be removed by the president); (5) Government Corporations; (6) Judicial Actors; (7) State-Level Actors; or (8) Local Actors. Examples of these locations and the fraction of laws in our data set in which they were observed are detailed in Table 5.4. For instance, nearly 81 percent of all laws delegated authority to at least one cabinet department, 8.2 percent delegated to a government corporation, 16 percent to judicial actors, and just over 13 percent to local governmental actors.

Agencies Created

The last component of delegation to be determined is if any of the agencies or commissions receiving authority were newly created by the act. In most cases, the language of the *CQ* summaries made it clear when a new agency or program was being established. In cases where it was not so obvious, we again checked with the text of the law and the *Government Manuals* to determine when the agency came into existence.

---

reporting more (or fewer) delegations in larger bills. The correlation between the two is negative and statistically insignificant.

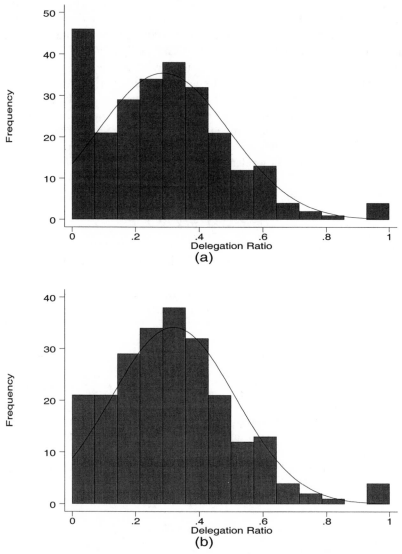

Figure 5.2. Histogram of Delegation Ratio, with and without Zero-Delegation Laws

In our trade policy example, nine different entities received delegated authority, none of which were newly created by the act. In total, 52.1 percent of the laws in our sample created at least one new agency, board, or commission.

Table 5.4. *Agency Locations and Percentage of Laws Containing Each Category*

Location	Examples	% of Laws Mentioning
EXECUTIVE OFFICE OF THE PRESIDENT	United States Trade Representative	40.8%
CABINET DEPARTMENTS	Department of Agriculture	80.9
INDEPENDENT REGULATORY AGENCIES	Federal Emergency Management Agency	38.1
INDEPENDENT COMMISSIONS	International Trade Commission	16.0
GOVERNMENT CORPORATIONS	AMTRAK	8.2
JUDICIAL ACTORS	Federal District Courts	16.0
STATE LEVEL ACTOR	State Utility Commissions	31.1
LOCAL ACTOR	Local School Boards	13.2

CONSTRAINTS

The delegation ratio, then, measures the amount of authority delegated in each law. However, this is only half the story in measuring executive discretion. The legislative oversight literature reviewed in Chapter 2 emphasizes the importance of administrative procedures – the numerous hoops and hurdles that bureaucrats face when exercising delegated authority – in regulating bureaucrats' actions. Therefore, the second component of executive discretion is the procedural constraints that Congress employs to limit the executive's policy leeway. For example, if Congress grants the executive the power to enter into international trade agreements but then makes these agreements subject to congressional approval (as in current fast-track procedures), then one would be hard-pressed to argue that this delegation of authority is equivalent to when Congress delegates without such a constraint. Similarly, we would not want to classify in the same way laws that might allow the Environmental Protection Agency to regulate "in the public interest" with those that allow the agency to alter emissions standards subject to specified criteria, and only after notifying the appropriate congressional committees, holding public hearings, and obtaining presidential approval for its determination.

Coding Administrative Procedures

To obtain our list of administrative procedures, we canvassed the congressional oversight literature – relying in particular on the works by Stewart (1975), Cass and Diver (1987), McCubbins, Noll, and Weingast (1987; 1989), Oleszek (1989), Strauss (1989), Aberbach (1990), and O'Halloran (1994) – for examples of procedural mechanisms that Congress writes into legislation to constrain the bureaucracy. After reading through the legislation in our data set, we added a few more categories, finally settling on a list of fourteen procedural constraints.

Table 5.5 enumerates our categories and provides a brief description of each, and Appendix D provides a detailed discussion of our coding rules along with examples. Summary statistics for all categories are shown in Table 5.1, with the means of each category indicating the percentage of bills that contain at least one instance of that type of administrative procedure. For instance, rule-making requirements appeared in nearly 80 percent of the laws in our sample; reporting requirements and spending limits in about half; and legislative action, executive action, and a legislative veto were included in just above 10 percent.

Of the procedural constraints, the legislative veto probably merits special attention, as it is widely believed that the 1983 *Chadha* case eliminated the legislative veto as an instrument of congressional control over the bureaucracy.[8] In fact, this is a misperception. *Chadha* only nullified legislative vetoes that did not satisfy bicameral presentment – those that rely on concurrent resolutions or one-house disapproval procedures – and Congress has continued to include legislative veto provisions in legislation enacted after *Chadha*. As Louis Fisher writes:

In response to the Court's ruling, Congress repealed some legislative vetoes and replaced them with joint resolutions, which satisfy the [Supreme Court's] ruling because joint resolutions must be passed by both houses and be presented to the president. However, Congress has also continued to enact legislative vetoes to handle certain situations. From June 23, 1983 to the end of the 99th Congress, 102 legislative vetoes (generally the committee-veto variety) have been enacted into law in twenty-four different statutes. Some of these legislative vetoes were about to be enacted at the time of the Court's decision. Others have been introduced, reported, and enacted long after Congress became aware of the Court's ruling.[9]

Thus, the constitutional and political status of the legislative veto remains somewhat murky, in part due to the fact that it would be hard for

[8] *Immigration and Naturalization Service v. Chadha*, 462 U.S. 919 (1983).
[9] Quoted in Oleszek (1989, 267–8).

Table 5.5. *Categories of Constraints*

CATEGORY	DESCRIPTION
APPOINTMENT POWER LIMITS	Are there any constraints on executive appointment powers that go beyond the advice and consent of the Senate?
TIME LIMITS	Are there sunset limits on delegation? That is, does any delegated authority expire after a certain fixed time period?
SPENDING LIMITS	Does the act define a maximum amount that the agency can allocate to any activity or set of activities, either stated explicitly or in a formula?
LEGISLATIVE ACTION REQUIRED	Do agency determinations require the action (approval) of Congress to take effect?
EXECUTIVE ACTION REQUIRED	Do agency determinations require the action (approval) of another agency or the president to take effect?
LEGISLATIVE VETO	Does Congress retain a unilateral ex post veto over the enactment of an agency regulation?
REPORTING REQUIREMENTS	Are any specific reporting requirements imposed on agency rulemaking?
CONSULTATION REQUIREMENTS	Are consultations with any other actor, either public or private, required prior to final agency actions?
PUBLIC HEARINGS	Are public hearings explicitly required?
APPEALS PROCEDURES	Is there a procedure stated in the act for a party adversely affected by agency actions to appeal the agency's decision?
RULE-MAKING REQUIREMENTS	Do explicit mandates require rulemaking or adjudicatory processes to be carried out in a certain manner (beyond the requirements of the APA)?
EXEMPTIONS	Is any particular group, product, or affected interest exempt from any aspect of regulation for a given period of time?
COMPENSATIONS	Are any groups, industries, or states given a specific compensation? In particular, does the act mention any group as receiving either additional time to adjust to the new regulations, or some concession because of the costs that may be imposed?
DIRECT OVERSIGHT	Is there a procedure defined in the implementing legislation by which a non-agency actor reviews the agency's activities—i.e., a GAO audit of the agency?

any one individual to prove that they had been injured – and therefore have legal standing – as a result of Congress's employing a veto in any particular case. In fact, in our sample only 12.4 percent of the pre-*Chadha* laws contained a legislative veto, as compared to 17.5 percent of the post-*Chadha* laws.

Constructing the Constraints Index

For each law in our data set, then, we recorded which categories of administrative procedures appeared at least once. A law could therefore contain as few as zero or as many as fourteen constraints. In the 1979 Trade Agreements Act, for instance, we found seven categories of constraints. As indicated on the sample coding sheet in Appendix C, provision number 52 (out of 59) imposed time limits on the president by limiting his authority to negotiate nontariff barrier (NTB) agreements to eight years. Also, provision number 4 required legislative action, in the form of fast-track procedures, before any agreement could take effect. The act also specified reporting requirements, consultation requirements, appeals procedures, rule-making requirements, and exemptions, as detailed on the coding sheet.

Our next step was to construct a single measure or index from these categories of constraints. The standard statistical tool employed to construct such an index is factor analysis, which attempts to explain the original data (in our case, the constraints in each bill) using only a small number of *factors* in the linear equation:

$$y_{ij} = z_{i1}b_{1j} + z_{i2}b_{2j} + \ldots + z_{iq}b_{qj} + e_{ij},$$

where y_{ij} is the value of the ith observation on the jth variable, z_{ik} is the ith observation on the kth common factor, b_{kj} is the set of linear coefficients called the factor loadings, and e_{ij}, similar to a residual, is known as the jth variable's unique factor. In this equation, q is the number of factors that significantly explain the larger set of variables, also called the *dimensionality* of the phenomenon being studied. For instance, it might be possible that constraints are a two-dimensional phenomenon, with one type occurring most often during unified government and the other during divided government, or some being used more commonly by Democrats than by Republicans. In determining which factors are significant, one examines their eigenvalues; a large decline in eigenvalues, if one exists, separates the significant from the insignificant factors.

As it turned out, we had a very simple case. First of all, as Figure 5.3 shows, the eigenvalue of the first factor was much larger than any of the other factors, indicating that the estimated factor numbers two and higher were statistical noise, and constraints can be represented by a single dimension. This interpretation is bolstered by the maximum likelihood estimations reported at the bottom of Table 5.6, which provides likelihood-ratio tests of the number of factors in the model versus (1) no factors and (2) more than one factor. Both tests yield significant χ^2 coefficients, suggesting that exactly one factor should be used.

Furthermore, as Table 5.6 shows, all fourteen categories loaded al-

102

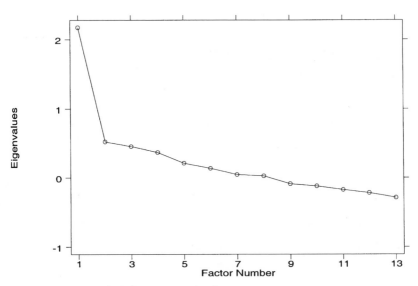

Figure 5.3. Eigenvalues from Factor Analysis

most equally on the first factor – that is, the range of the coefficients was rather small, clustering around a mean factor score of 0.39 with a standard deviation of 0.069. As a robustness check, we also estimated the model using multiple correlation analysis (MCA), a variant of factor analysis that is appropriate for dichotomous data.[10] We again found that the loadings were nearly equal across categories of constraints. We therefore constructed our constraint index by weighing all categories of administrative procedures equally, forming the *constraint ratio*, f_i, as the number of constraints observed in a given bill, over 14, the total number of possible constraints:

$$f_i = \frac{Categories\ of\ Constraints\ in\ a\ Law}{Total\ Categories}.$$

For the sample trade law, the constraint ratio is just 7/14, or 0.5.

The distribution of constraint ratios across bills is illustrated in panel (a) of Figure 5.4. Most bills had five constraints or less, with the distribution falling off gradually after that. As with the delegation ratio, it is useful to examine this distribution for only those bills with $\mathcal{D} = 1$, as laws that delegate no authority are likely to contain few constraints as

---

[10]MCA approximates the results of a factor analysis using tetrachoric correlations rather than the traditional Pearson's *r* coefficient. For details, see Krzanowski (1988, chap. 14).

103

Table 5.6. *Factor Loadings and Uniqueness*

Variable	Factor Loadings	MCA Loadings
Appointment Power Limits	0.446	0.352
Time Limits	0.388	0.307
Spending Limits	0.350	0.279
Legislative Action Required	0.351	0.415
Executive Action Required	0.381	0.477
Legislative Veto	0.381	0.452
Reporting Requirements	0.544	0.395
Consultation Requirements	0.469	0.390
Public Hearings	0.309	0.371
Appeals Procedures	0.424	0.369
Rule-Making Requirements	0.422	0.408
Exemptions	0.263	0.216
Compensations	0.290	0.329
Direct Oversight	0.358	0.544

Note: Maximum Likelihood tests for number of factors.
Test: 1 vs. no factors. χ^2 (14) = 275.01, Prob > χ^2 = 0.0000
Test: 1 vs. more factors. χ^2 (77) = 170.82, Prob > χ^2 = 0.0000

well. Panel (b) of the figure shows the new distribution, and, indeed, it is much more single-peaked than its predecessor.

Calculating Relative Constraints

For purposes that will be explained more fully below, we next define *relative constraints* (c_i) as the product of the constraint ratio and the delegation ratio:

$$c_i = f_i^* r_i.$$

Relative constraints thus scale the constraint index by the amount of delegation in a law. For a law with a delegation ratio of 0.4, for instance,

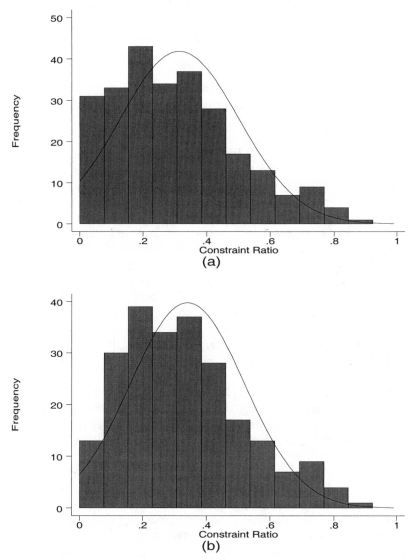

Figure 5.4. Histogram of Constraint Ratio, with and without Zero-Delegation Laws

the maximum possible value of c_i will be 0.4 as well. And by construction, when the delegation ratio is 0 ($\mathcal{D} = 0$), c_i will also be 0. Relative constraints will be important in our construction of the discretion measure, to which we now turn.

TOTAL DISCRETION

Relation between Delegation and Constraints

Having now measured both delegation and constraints for each law in our data set, we examine the bivariate relationship between the two. Before doing so, though, we pause to consider the potential implications of our different possible findings. One possibility, of course, is that there will be no systematic relationship, in which case we would conclude that the amount of authority that Congress delegates and the administrative procedures attached to that delegation are unrelated. Second, those who see delegation as an abdication of legislative responsibilities (i.e., Lowi 1969) might predict a negative relation between delegation and constraints, since by assumption legislators wish to remove themselves as far as possible from these unpopular issue areas. Third, those who emphasize the possibility that legislators take an active interest in overseeing the executive branch might predict, like McCubbins (1985), that the more Congress delegates the more it will constrain, suggesting a positive correlation.

Figure 5.5 shows a scatter plot of the delegation ratio and the constraint ratio, with box plots (indicating median values, interquartile ranges, and bootstrapped 90 percent confidence intervals) and rug plots (with a hash mark denoting each data point) along the top and right axes. Inspection of the plot reveals that observations with a delegation ratio of one and those with more than ten categories of constraints are univariate outliers, although no data points are simultaneous outliers on both dimensions.

The graph also includes a simple regression line of constraints on delegation, the slope of which is positive and statistically significant, indicating that in fact those laws that delegated more authority to the executive relative to the scope of the law also tended to impose more constraints on the use of this delegated authority.[11] Thus, it appears not to be true that when Congress delegates it tries to distance itself from the given policy area as much as possible; rather, Congress tries to

[11]The estimated OLS regression, with standard errors in parentheses, is:
$$f_l = 0.25 + 0.23 * r_i$$
$$(0.02) \quad (0.06)$$

106

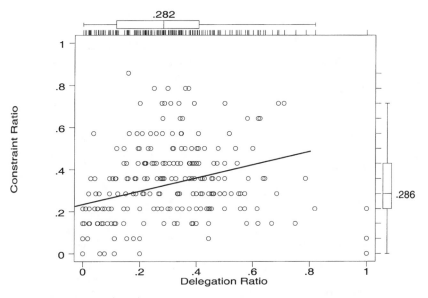

Figure 5.5. Scatterplot of Delegation Ratio and Constraint Ratio

control executive discretion through the imposition of procedural constraints. Note as well that there is considerable variation around the regression line: Some laws delegate little and impose a number of constraints, while others delegate a considerable amount of authority and impose few constraints (the bivariate correlation is only 0.255).

It is instructive at this point to subdivide this relationship between delegation and constraints into its component parts. An examination of Table 5.7, showing the correlations between the delegation ratio and the different categories of constraints, indicates that higher levels of delegation are associated with fewer constraints only in the categories of direct oversight (a slight decline) and exemptions (a more significant drop-off). All other categories tend to increase as delegation increases, especially consultation requirements, rule-making requirements, spending limits, appointment power limits, and time limits.

Calculating Discretion

We now turn to measuring total executive discretion, the key variable in our model, which combines both delegation and constraints. Since discretion is positively associated with delegation and negatively associated with constraints, the most obvious construction of our discretion index would be a simple difference between the delegation ratio and the con-

107

Table 5.7. *Correlations of Constraints with Delegation Ratio and Year*

Constraint Category	Delegation Ratio	Year
Appointment Power Limits	0.225	0.126
Time Limits	0.189	0.081
Spending Limits	0.227	0.059
Legislative Action Required	0.058	0.146
Executive Action Required	0.168	0.067
Legislative Veto	0.033	0.110
Reporting Requirements	0.097	0.242
Consultation Requirements	0.268	0.053
Public Hearings	0.144	0.014
Appeals Procedures	0.034	0.196
Rule-Making Requirements	0.233	0.017
Exemptions	-0.154	0.407
Compensations	0.058	0.181
Direct Oversight	-0.017	0.169

straint ratio: $d_i = r_i - f_i$. However, this operationalization immediately runs into the problem of producing negative values of executive discretion. The reason for this is clear; when Congress delegates a little and adds many constraints, the difference between the ratios will become negative.

This observation, in turn, suggests that constraints should be considered in proportion to the amount of authority delegated. The clearest way to visualize this problem is by analogy with a cup of water. Let the cup start empty, and think of the delegation ratio as the percentage of the cup that is originally filled with water. Then the constraint ratio is the proportion of that water removed from the cup – a constraint ratio of 0.5 means that half of the water is removed. Therefore, the constraints placed on a high-delegation bill will have greater policy impact than constraints associated with a bill that delegates very little. To complete the analogy, discretion is then the proportion of the cup left filled with water after the constraints have been removed.

In terms of our measures, we want to subtract from the delegation ratio r_i the product of the delegation ratio and the constraint ratio $r_i^* f_i$. But this latter term is just the relative constraints measure c_i given above. Thus, we define discretion as delegation minus relative constraints:

$$d_i = r_i - c_i.$$

In our sample trade law, discretion is $d_i = 0.41 - (0.41^*0.5) = 20.5\%$. Defining discretion in this way accomplishes three goals: It avoids negative values of discretion, it translates delegation and constraints into common units that can then be compared, and it provides a continuous measure of discretion that falls between zero and one. Histograms of the discretion index, with and without the zero-delegation laws, are provided in Figure 5.6; again, the latter is more single-peaked than the former.

Laws with Most and Least Discretion

Using this definition, we assigned a discretion index to all laws in our sample. By construction, all laws with a delegation ratio of 0 will also have a discretion index of 0, so laws that do not delegate give the executive no discretion. Table 5.8 shows those laws with the least discretion for which $\mathcal{D} = 1$, and those with the most discretion. As expected, the former list is almost identical to its counterpart in Table 5.3, with the notable inclusion of the Omnibus Budget Reconciliation Act of 1990, which had a sizable delegation ratio (0.16) but so many constraints (12) that its final discretion index was only $0.16 - [0.16^*(12/14)] = 0.023$.

More significant differences arise at higher levels of delegation; some acts that delegated significant authority were not at the top of the discretion list. For example, two trade acts – the Trade Agreements Act Extension of 1955 and the Trade Act of 1974 – were eliminated, as were the Clean Air Amendments of 1970, the Water Quality Act of 1965, and the Defense Production Act of 1970. The final list of top discretion bills, even more than the corresponding list for delegation, centers around issues of defense, social policy, and environmental regulation.

Translating our definition of discretion back into the original delegation-constraints diagram, Figure 5.7 overlays several iso-discretion lines, combinations of delegations and constraints that result in the same level

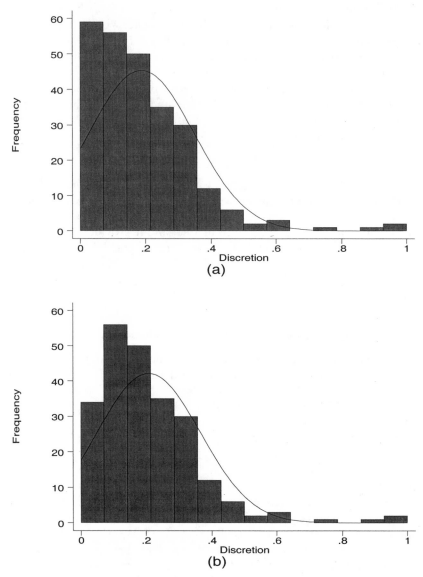

Figure 5.6. Histogram of Discretion Index, with and without Zero-Delegation Laws

Table 5.8. *Acts with Least and Most Total Discretion*

Acts with Least Discretion where $\mathcal{D}=1$

Year	Congress	PL Num.	Title	Discretion
1986	99	99-514	Tax Reform Act of 1986	0.004
1976	94	94-455	Tax Reform Act of 1976	0.008
1978	95	95-600	Revenue Act of 1978	0.014
1985	99	99-177	Public Debt Limit—Balanced Budget and Emergency Deficit Control Act of 1985	0.016
1951	82	82-183	Revenue Act of 1951	0.017
1983	98	98-21	Social Security Amendments of 1983	0.018
1982	97	97-424	Surface Transportation Assistance Act of 1982	0.018
1969	91	91-172	Tax Reform Act of 1969	0.019
1964	88	88-272	Revenue Act of 1964	0.021
1990	101	101-508	Omnibus Budget Reconciliation Act of 1990	0.023
1991	102	102-166	Civil Rights Act of 1991	0.027
1984	98	98-369	Deficit Reduction Act of 1984	0.033
1976	94	94-553	Copyrights Act	0.033
1965	89	89-97	Social Security Amendments of 1965	0.041
1967	90	90-248	Social Security Amendments of 1967	0.041
1974	93	93-344	Congressional Budget and Impoundment Control Act of 1974	0.041

(a)

Acts with Most Discretion

Year	Congress	PL Num.	Title	Discretion
1978	95	95-619	National Energy Conservation Policy Act	0.48
1967	90	90-148	Air Quality Act of 1967	0.49
1970	91	91-224	Water and Environmental Quality Improvement Act of 1970	0.50
1958	85	85-568	National Aeronautics and Space Act of 1958	0.51
1987	100	100-77	McKinney Homeless Assistance Act of 1987	0.53
1966	89	89-675	Clean Air Act Amendments of 1966	0.57
1958	85	85-864	National Defense Education Act of 1958	0.64
1963	88	88-156	Maternal and Child Health and Mental Retardation Planning Amendments of 1963	0.64
1963	88	88-164	Mental Retardation Facilities and Community Health Centers Construction Act of 1963	0.79
1965	89	89-115	Health Research Facilities Amendments of 1965	0.93
1961	87	87-41	Inter-American Program--Appropriation	1.00
1969	91	91-124	Selective Service Amendments Act of 1969	1.00

(b)

of total discretion. As shown, these are curved, opening downward and to the right, in the direction of increasing discretion. Thus, our definition of discretion as the difference between delegation and relative constraints (c_i) produces curved iso-discretion lines, rather than the straight lines that would have resulted from using the constraint ratio (f_i) instead. One implication of our functional form, then, is that at low levels of delegation increasing the number of constraints has relatively little effect on discretion, while at higher levels of delegation the marginal impact of increasing constraints is much greater.

POSTWAR TRENDS IN EXECUTIVE DISCRETION

We shall use our discretion measure to test the hypotheses detailed in the previous chapter. First, though, we can use year-by-year trends in discretion to address some of the questions raised in Chapter 1 concerning the growth of the federal bureaucracy, the division of policy-making authority among the branches, and the ability of Congress to effectively oversee executive agencies. In particular, has the scope of government activity increased? If so, does this imply a shift of authority to the executive at Congress's expense? Or has congressional oversight kept pace with changes in executive authority?

The Growth in Government

To begin with, our data corroborate the move toward more detailed, omnibus legislation noted first in Schick (1980) and discussed further in Smith (1989), Wildavsky (1992), and Brady and Volden (1998), among others.[12] Our proxy for the content and complexity of legislation is the average number of major provisions per law and, as Figure 5.8 shows, the average number of major provisions has cycled over time, but with a rising trend. (To preserve the scale of the figure, the 101st and 102d Congresses, with averages of 258 and 77, respectively, have been omitted.) These findings accord well with other objective measures of the size of legislation; for instance, Ornstein, Mann, and Malbin (1994) find that the average number of pages per bill has increased significantly in the past two decades. Combined with the fact that federal authority in the postwar era has entered some new policy areas (housing, energy, and health care) and expanded in others (civil rights, trade, and the environment), these figures all point to the conclusion that the overall scope and complexity of federal government activity has significantly increased during the period studied.[13]

---

[12]"Omnibus legislation" is a term used to describe a bill composed of many parts, each of which could stand as separate legislation; as a result, omnibus bills tend to be more complex and wider in scope than more narrowly tailored measures. See Schneier and Gross (1993, 127–30).

[13]Scholarly reviews of expanding federal authority during this period can be found in Sundquist (1981) and Lowi (1988).

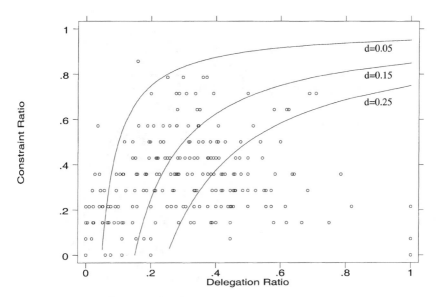

Figure 5.7. Iso-Discretion Lines

The Myth of Runaway Bureaucracy

Has this growth in the range of activities undertaken at the federal level been accompanied by an explosion in executive branch discretion? If so, then this would lend credence to the statement that the federal bureaucracy is now an independent "fourth branch" of government. The argument goes as follows: over time, as the scope of government activity has increased, the federal bureaucracy has played an increasingly active role in shaping public policy. Because of all the problems of oversight and control discussed in Chapter 2, this has led to an unrestrained bureaucracy setting policy without effective political supervision.[14] Therefore, the increased role of the federal government has resulted in an overall strengthening of executive power vis-à-vis Congress.

To examine these claims, Figure 5.9 charts average executive discretion by year. The most salient feature of this graph is its correspondence with conventional wisdom about overall postwar policy making. In the era from 1947 through 1960, the Truman and Eisenhower administra-

[14]This view is especially common among those who bemoan the lack of overt congressional oversight of the bureaucracy. See, in particular, Niskanen (1971), as well as Pearson (1975), Seidman (1975), Mitnick (1980), and Dodd and Schott (1986).

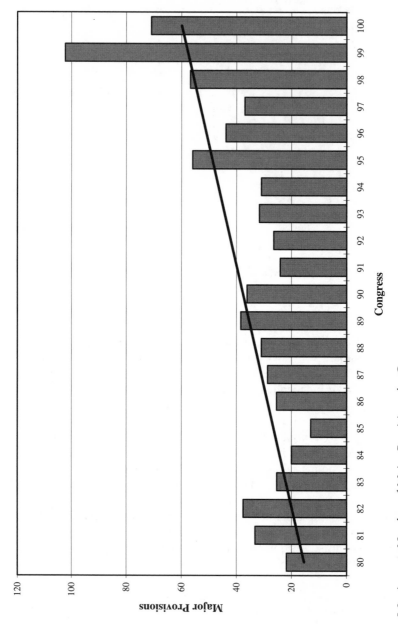

Figure 5.8. Average Number of Major Provisions, by Congress

tions, average discretion was close to its overall mean of 18.3 percent. The notable outlier occurs in 1953, the first year Eisenhower was in office – a year in which only one major piece of legislation was passed granting no discretion to the executive branch.[15] For the remainder of Eisenhower's term, though, a number of major pieces of Cold War legislation were enacted that tended to grant significant amounts of discretion to the president and other executive branch actors.

Following upon this, the 1960s were a time of greatly increased government activity. Beginning in the Kennedy administration, continuing through the Great Society programs, and on into the first few years of the Nixon administration, the average executive discretion rose to 25.5 percent.[16] This, of course, was the era referred to as the Second New Deal, during which major new policy initiatives were launched in the areas of civil rights, housing, the environment, education, and consumer protection, among others. The figure shows that these major policy initiatives not only legislated much new law, they also gave executive branch actors significant discretion in executing those laws. Small wonder, then, that scholars observing the national political scene at the end of this era (such as Lowi in 1969) perceived a growing trend toward increased executive discretion.

The 1970s saw a return to the pre-1960s pattern, however, as discretion during the Nixon, Ford, and Carter administrations was again close to the overall average (the Carter administration being distinguished by its relatively low level of discretion relative to other periods of unified government). The 1980s then saw a significant decline in average discretion: This was the era of divided government, giving rise to fears of a permanent Congress and policy gridlock. Indeed, Congress delegated very little discretionary authority to the executive in this period, especially during the early Reagan years. The two notable exceptions here are 1987, when Democrats retook control of the Senate and Jim Wright (D-TX) was Speaker of the House, and 1992, when election-year politics resulted in a significant amount of major legislation being passed.

Aggregating these year-to-year fluctuations, we can examine the overall trend in executive discretion in the postwar era. As illustrated in the figure, our data show an overall *decline* in the level of total discretion delegated to the executive. So, even though the number of major provi-

---

[15]This was the Submerged Lands Act (PL 83–31), which ratified the existing division of state and federal rights over the use of tidelands oil reserves.

[16]In fact, the highest average discretion for any year in our sample was during 1969, the first year of the Nixon administration. Closer inspection, though, shows that this is somewhat misleading. Only four major laws were enacted during this year, including the Selective Service Amendments Act (PL 91–124), a one-provision law that allowed the president to reinstitute the draft lottery system. Without this law, the average discretion level would have been 17.7%.

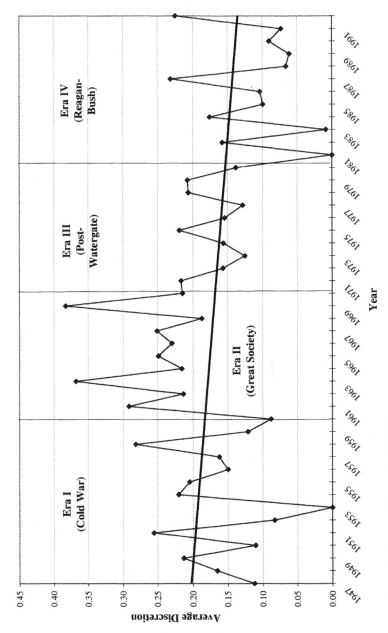

Figure 5.9. Average Discretion, by Year

sions in legislation – which we take as a proxy for the amount of government activity – has increased over time, the amount of discretionary authority given to the executive has declined on average since 1947. The fear of a runaway bureaucracy, then, appears from our data to be somewhat overblown. Or, to put it another way, the statement that the federal government as a whole is doing more is not equivalent to the statement that the executive branch in particular is exercising more discretion in setting policy.

Oversight through Procedural Constraints

Given our definition of discretion as the difference between the delegation ratio and relative constraints, two possible explanations exist for this combination of greater government activity and less discretion. One is that Congress is writing more-explicit legislation now than it did in the past (the delegation ratio is falling). If this were the case, then the increased scope of government activity would have come in the form of more-detailed statutes – more legislative input and less from the executive. But, as Figure 5.10 shows, the delegation ratio has remained more or less constant in the postwar era, again with a peak in the 1960s and a trough during the 1980s. Although the scope of federal government activity has increased over time, then, the amount of authority delegated to the executive, relative to the total amount of federal government activity, has not changed.

Having ruled out this possibility, the decline in executive discretion must come from changes in the constraints placed on delegated authority. Indeed, Figure 5.11 shows that, over time, the constraint ratio has risen significantly. In particular, an examination of Table 5.7 reveals that the use of exemptions, reporting requirements, appeals procedures, and compensations has increased over time; note that these categories rely mostly on third parties to constrain executive decision making.

In sum, our data paint the following picture of postwar policy making. First, we corroborate the trend noted by others toward greater overall government activity and omnibus legislation. We next ask what the implications of this increase are for the division of labor between Congress and the executive and find that this growth in government has not meant, on average, an explosion of the executive branch or a breakdown in Congress's oversight role. To the contrary, we find that average discretion has declined during this period.

Disaggregating this finding into its components, we observe that the delegation ratio has remained more or less constant throughout the period, so the relative roles of Congress and the executive in making policy has not changed. The decrease in discretion has instead come

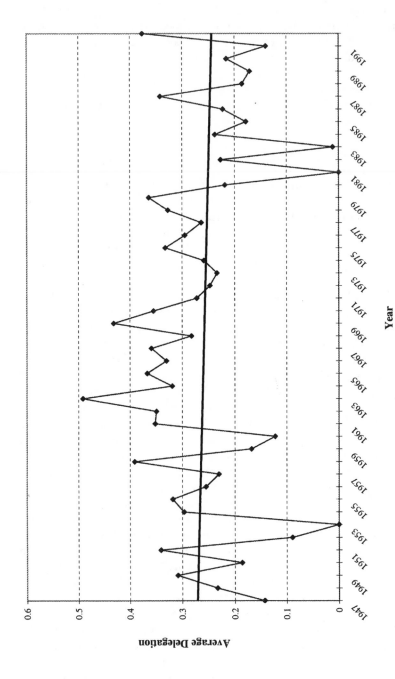

Figure 5.10. Average Delegation Ratio, by Year

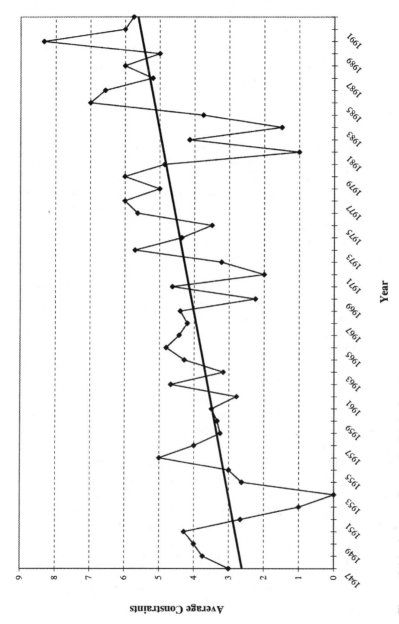

Figure 5.11. Average Constraint Ratio, by Year

from augmenting the constraints on executive authority, empowering courts and outside interests more in the process of overseeing executive branch authority – in other words, the politics is now in the procedures. From legislators' perspective, this finding makes a good deal of sense: As government activity widens in scope and becomes more complex, a fixed number of legislators will have a harder time overseeing executive branch activities. They will therefore enlist outside interest groups, the courts, and other executive actors as allies in the task of congressional oversight.

This last observation lends a new perspective to the current literature on interest groups and their influence on policy. In particular, a number of authors have noted the fragmentation of many formerly monolithic interests – agriculture and medical services, for instance – as well as the proliferation of what Salisbury (1990) calls "externality groups," such as Common Cause, environmental groups, and the various organizations under the Nader umbrella.[17] This has led to an explosion of the number of interest groups in Washington and the breakdown of formerly cozy iron triangle relationships into what Jones (1979) calls "at best, sloppy hexagons." Our findings suggest that, by increasing the number of procedural constraints on executive agencies, Congress is writing laws that allow interest groups more impact on policy, which in turn gives rational groups greater incentive to organize and come to Washington. The increasing number of lobby groups, by this account, is a creature of Congress's own creation. This view awaits more explicit confirmation, but it does indicate an important linkage between the structure of the interest-group system, the division of policy-making authority across the branches, and the administrative procedures that circumscribe agency actions.

Both our model in the previous chapter and the extant literature on interbranch relations highlight the crucial importance of executive discretion in understanding the nature of modern public policy. This chapter has defined for the first time a systematic measure of executive branch discretion across 257 pieces of important postwar legislation as the amount of authority delegated to executive branch actors in the implementation of legislation less the amount of procedural constraints that limit this authority. The last part of this chapter employed our discretion index to examine some basic postwar trends in delegation and constraints. The following chapters will use this variable to test the propositions arising from our model, relating discretion to congressional–executive policy conflict (Chapter 6), legislative organization (Chapter 7), and issue-area characteristics (Chapter 8).

---

[17]For an interesting in-depth look at Common Cause and its lobbying efforts on the MX missile and campaign finance reform, see Rothenberg (1992).

6

Delegation and Congressional–Executive Relations

Congress and the Presidency are like two gears, each whirling at its own rate of speed. It is not surprising that, on coming together, they often clash.

Polsby, *Congress and the Presidency*[1]

Congressional–executive relations have long been a favored stomping ground for institutional scholars. The dynamics established by the Article 1, Section 7 game have inspired ruminations on the roles that vetoes, presidential leadership and agenda setting, and interbranch bargaining play in the macropolicy production of the federal government. To this list, we add the observation that one crucial dimension of interbranch negotiations concerns the amount of leeway that Congress admits to the president in the execution of public laws. The model presented in Chapter 4 suggests that, as delegation becomes less attractive in terms of legislators' reelection concerns, Congress will substitute legislative policy making for agency policy making.

In the pages that follow, we test this basic proposition from a number of different angles. We examine whether (1) divided government leads to lower average levels of executive branch discretion; (2) individual members more often vote in favor of delegation to presidents of their own party as opposed to presidents of the opposite party; (3) actual or threatened vetoes increase executive discretion; (4) legislators rely more on federalism and judicial oversight to circumvent the executive during times of divided government; and (5) legislators give power to executive actors further from the president's direct control under divided government. Our findings have important implications for the debate over the policy impact of divided government, which we briefly summarize before turning to the empirical analysis.

[1]Polsby (1976, 198).

DIVIDED GOVERNMENT: THE DEBATE

Divided government has recently received considerable attention in both scholarly debate and popular discourse. Typically, critics claim that policy making under divided government is "a difficult, arduous process, characterized by conflict, delay, and indecision, and leading frequently to deadlock, inadequate and ineffective policies, or no policies at all."[2] Yet empirical evidence of divided government's impact on policy remains elusive. Indeed, after extensively analyzing the frequency of important legislation and congressional investigations from 1946 to 1990, Mayhew (1991, 179) concludes that "unified versus divided control has probably not made a notable difference during the postwar era." Are popular perceptions regarding divided government incorrect, or have empirical analyses failed to capture its real effects?

The arguments bemoaning the negative consequences of divided government are based on a long tradition in American political thought linking parties and the system of separate powers. The reasoning is as follows: Although initially opposed by the founding fathers, political parties developed as a necessary corollary to our constitutional system of separate powers and checks and balances. As recounted by Sundquist (1988, 614), "traditional theory identified political parties as the indispensable instrument that brought cohesion and unity, and hence effectiveness, to the government as a whole by linking the executive and legislative branches in a bond of common interest." Similarly, Key (1947, 667) states, "For the government to function, the obstructions of governmental mechanism must be overcome, and it is the party that casts a web, at times weak, at times strong, over the dispersed organs of government and gives them a semblance of unity."[3] American parties, though admittedly weak in comparison with their European counterparts, were seen as an essential unifying force given our fragmented governmental structure.

Yet parties can fulfill their coordinating role only when the same party controls both the legislative and executive branches. Up until the 1950s, the assumption that a single party would control the federal government seemed natural. Divided partisan control had been ephemeral, appearing mainly as a transition from unified control by one party to the other. In the fifty-eight years between 1897 and 1954, divided government existed only 14 percent of the time, with the longest single episode of divided control being only two years. But since the mid-1950s, this pattern has reversed itself, to the point where divided government is now the norm:

---

[2]Sundquist (1988, 629); see also Cutler (1988).

[3]For the traditional theory on responsible parties, see also Ford (1898), Schattschneider (1942), and APSA Committee on Political Parties (1950).

In the forty-four years from 1955 to 1998, partisan control of government was divided 68 percent of the time, including a twelve-year stretch from 1980 to 1992.[4] This shift from unified party government to coalitional government leads Sundquist (1988) to call for a new theory of political science in which parties no longer serve to unify across all branches of government.

Given this traditional theory of responsible party government, the negative consequences of divided control are obvious: deadlock, partisan squabbles, and incoherent public policy. For instance, Cutler (1989) lays the blame for large deficits at the doorstep of divided government. Kiewiet and McCubbins (1991, 182–4) provide evidence that congressional conflict with the Office of Management and Budget over the disbursement of appropriated funds increases during times of divided control. And Fiorina (1992) claims that divided government further erodes the accountability of government officials for policies adopted and outcomes realized during their tenure.[5]

Divided Government and Policy Production

Has the prolonged presence of divided control indeed undermined the fabric of our political system? Despite the fact that this negative assessment has been most prevalent in popular discussions of divided government, a strong argument can be made that divided control does not matter. One can have gridlock under unified government, as in the Carter years, and coherent policy does not necessarily depend on a strong party system. Fiorina (1992) further notes that in certain cases partisan competition has led to greater government activism, either through an interparty "bidding war" or because neither party wants to appear responsible for the failure of a popular policy initiative.

Most of the empirical analyses to date find little evidence that divided government has an appreciable impact on outcomes. Alt and Stewart (1990) use historical data to show that budget deficits (and surpluses) are uncorrelated with the presence of divided government. Lemieux and Stewart (1990) and Cameron, Cover, and Segal (1990) find little to indicate that the Senate's acceptance or rejection of Supreme Court appointments is affected by divided partisan control. Fiorina (1992) summarizes evidence that, in general, presidential appointments to executive branch offices are not rejected more often under divided government.

---

[4]Indeed, the brief period of unified government in the 103d Congress (1993–4) can now be seen as a transition from one form of *divided* government to another.

[5]For additional suggestive evidence of the effects of divided government on policy, see Cox and Kernell (1991). An interesting review of this literature is found in Brady (1993).

And King and Ragsdale (1988) conclude that treaties, conventions, and protocols are accepted by the Senate equally under unified and divided control.

The one positive finding, noted by Rohde and Simon (1985), is that presidents veto more legislation when at least one branch of Congress is controlled by the opposite party. Furthermore, divided control also seems to influence the president's legislative success in Congress. For instance, after controlling for any trend over time, analysis of *Congressional Quarterly*'s Presidential Success Scores from 1953 to 1992 shows that the president's efficacy in enacting controversial policy initiatives decreased by approximately 15 percent during times of divided control.[6]

This evidence, while a good starting point for further analysis, is rather indirect. Most of the correlations measured are not between divided government and policy outcomes, but rather between divided government and certain procedural actions. It could be, for instance, that treaties submitted to the Senate are watered down in times of divided government to obtain the necessary two-thirds support, or that executive branch appointments are less ideologically extreme. If the ultimate question is the impact of divided government on policy, then more direct measures of outcomes are necessary.

Toward this end, the most comprehensive study of divided government to date is that by Mayhew (1991) in his book *Divided We Govern*. Looking at 267 major statutes enacted between 1947 and 1990, he finds that "unified as opposed to divided control has not made an important difference in recent times in the incidence of . . . important legislation."[7] Figure 6.1, calculated from Mayhew's Table 4.1 (1991, 52–73), shows that the average number of pieces of legislation passed per Congress during unified government, 12.8, does not differ significantly from the number passed under divided government, 11.7. From this evidence, Mayhew argues that public policy generally responds to changes in external conditions and public opinion, and that the partisan affiliation of the actors occupying different seats in government has only a marginal impact on what legislation gets passed.

---

[6]The results were as follows:

$$\text{President Success} = \underset{(5.19)}{100.61} - \underset{(3.83)}{15.32}(\text{Divided}) - 0.468(\text{Year}),$$

explaining some 61 percent of the total variation in the data (t-statistics in parentheses). For further analysis of divided government's impact on presidential success scores, see Gibson (1994).

[7]Mayhew (1991, 4).

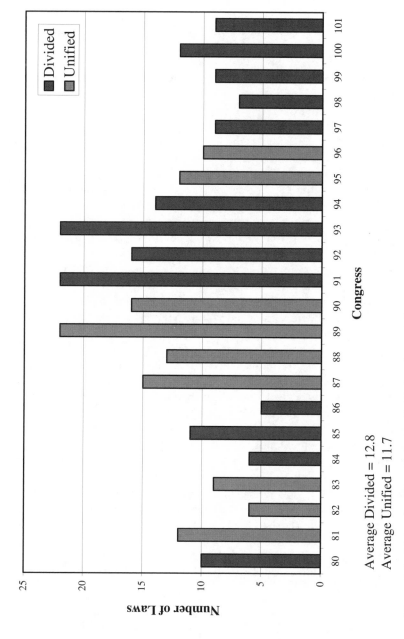

Figure 6.1. Major Acts Passed during Unified and Divided Government

The Sources of Policy Gridlock

Taking off from Mayhew's theme, two recent studies have also explored the effects of divided government on policy. Keith Krehbiel, in his book *Pivotal Politics: A Theory of U.S. Lawmaking,* and David Brady and Craig Volden, in their book *Revolving Gridlock,* combine a median voter model with the institutional arrangements of the filibuster and veto to understand when policy innovation is most likely and under what conditions we should observe policy gridlock.

Krehbiel (1998) argues that, given the procedures for passing policy (the Article I, Section 7 game), the key voters will not be the medians in each house, but rather the filibuster pivot, the veto pivot, and the president's own ideal point. This leads to the definition of a "gridlock region," which is defined as the set of status quo policies that cannot be overturned given policy preferences and supermajority institutions: The larger this interval, the harder it will be to pass new legislation.

For instance, assume that the line in Figure 6.2 represents a single left-right spectrum in some policy area. The median floor voter is denoted as M and is situated in the middle of the line. The two-thirds veto override member on the right is denoted V^+; the override voter on the left is V^-. The three-fifths filibuster player is F^+, and F^- represents its mirror image. We allow the president's preferred policy to vary from moderate to more extreme ranges, which we label 1, 2, and 3, respectively.

The set of gridlocked status quos depends on the relative position of the president's preferred policy. Figure 6.2 shows three sample values for the president's ideal point and the corresponding gridlock intervals. When the president's ideal point is in region 1, the filibuster voters on either side of the median circumscribe the interval. When the president's ideal point falls in range 2, the interval goes from F^- to P, and in range 3 the gridlock region extends from F^- to V^+, the two-thirds voter on the same side as the president.

The prediction that follows from this exercise is that, as the gridlock interval increases, policy movement becomes more difficult. The gridlock region, in turn, will usually be larger under divided government, but not necessarily – especially when the legislature is highly polarized.[8] Thus, it is the size of the gridlock region and not divided government *per se* that determines the likelihood that legislation will be enacted.

Brady and Volden (1998) apply a similar logic, arguing that the

---

[8] Assume, for example, that $V^- = 33$, $F^- = 40$, $M = 50$, $F^+ = 52$, and $V^+ = 67$, and let the president's ideal point at time 1 be $P_1 = 58$ and at time 2 be $P_2 = 39$. Then $|M - P_1| = 8$ and $|M - P_2| = 11$, so the president is further from the congressional median at time 2, but the gridlock regions are $G_1 = |58 - 40| = 18$, and $G_2 = |39 - 52| = 13$, so the gridlock region has become smaller.

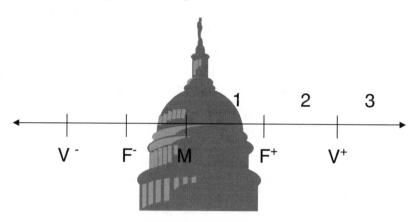

President's Ideal Point (P)	Gridlock Interval
Region 1: $M \leq P \leq F^+$	$[F^-, F^+]$
Region 2: $F^+ \leq P \leq V^+$	$[F^-, P]$
Region 3: $V^+ \leq P$	$[F^-, V^+]$

Figure 6.2. Gridlock Region

gridlock and policy stalemate of the last two decades is a manifestation of budget politics. Prior to 1981, they claim, Congress and the president could have their cake and eat it too, expanding social programs while keeping taxes low. But looming deficits meant that budget politics came to play an ever-increasing role in congressional politics. Conflicting interests can no longer be satisfied by increasing the deficit, and consequently Congress and the president face tough choices: Creating a new program or increasing spending in one area means cutting another. When interests are well organized and politically active on both sides of an issue, the usual result is policy stalemate and a persistence of the status quo.

Furthermore, innovations in the budget process, such as Gramm-Rudman-Hollings in 1985 and pay-as-you-go (PAYGO) in 1990, link budget and program decisions together such that increases in one area must necessarily cause decreases elsewhere. Combined with the need for supermajorities, this constraint has been the cause of gridlock for more than a decade, holding new policy innovations hostage to budgetary concerns. Given these institutional and procedural constraints, a change in the party of the president is not sufficient to bring about an end to gridlock; presidents of either party would face the same problems. So policy gridlock is the result of tighter fiscal constraints rather than divided government.

New Perspectives on Divided Government

Although these works have added to our understanding of divided government, most of the empirical analysis they offer deals either with congressional–executive relations directly or with the passage of major pieces of legislation. Insofar as some early attacks on gridlock intimated that it had resulted in too few laws being passed, this is a worthwhile enterprise. But the fact that divided government by itself is not significantly related to the quantity of legislative activity should not greatly surprise scholars of American political development. After all, it is well known that the U.S. government was designed to be conservative in the classic sense of the word; that is, conserving what the people have achieved for themselves by making policy change difficult. The Founders' original scheme has worked to perfection over the last two centuries and more: Policy change is mostly incremental with occasional bursts of activity, a system of punctuated equilibrium. Furthermore, the institutions of policy making that have arisen within our constitutional system – strong committees and supermajority procedures – have exacerbated this tendency. So one should not expect divided government in and of itself to have much more than a marginal impact on the volume of significant legislation.

The more realistic assertion is that divided government will influence the *content* of the policies that are passed, be they many or few in number. For instance, to say that important pieces of trade legislation have been passed in each postwar administration masks the fact that those laws enacted under divided government uniformly decrease the executive's authority to regulate international trade, while those passed during times of unified government expand that authority.[9] Similarly, Mayhew cites the Civil Rights Acts of 1957, 1960, 1964, and 1965 as major pieces of legislation. But the Acts of 1957 and 1960, passed under divided government, were limited in scope, while the Acts of 1964 and 1965, passed under unified government, gave executive agencies significant authority to regulate employment, housing, voter registration, and federal elections. The War Powers Resolution and the Budget and Impoundment Act, both passed near the end of Nixon's tenure, are major pieces of legislation, but their primary aim is to circumscribe the president's policy-making power in two important areas of public policy, and

---

[9]This point will be discussed at greater length later in this chapter.

it is clearly no accident that they were passed during a period of not only divided government but also interbranch tension of epic proportions.

Investigating the quality of public policy during times of unified and divided government is, in general, a difficult task. Our project looks at this issue from one particular angle, that of the amount of discretionary authority delegated to the executive, which we believe captures a number of issues having direct and significant policy implications. Executive agencies play a major role in deciding the details of federal policy, and they operate within a political environment shaped by executive and legislative preferences: Presidents appoint agency heads and other important personnel, while legislators design the rules by which agencies make policy. The argument is that divided control influences how Congress designs the institutions of delegation, and that these institutions in turn affect policy outcomes. Thus, in the modern administrative state, even if partisan conflict does not influence the number of laws enacted, it may still affect policy outcomes through delegation and executive branch implementation. The result of divided control over national political institutions, by this logic, may be "procedural gridlock," policy stalemate and inflexibility produced through the intermediating institutions of administrative procedures.

DISCRETION AND DIVIDED GOVERNMENT

Data and Estimation

We first examine the hypothesis that less authority will be delegated to the executive branch during divided as opposed to unified government, reanalyzing the Mayhew (1991) data set to predict executive branch discretion rather than the number of significant pieces of legislation enacted. Table 6.1 details the variables we employ in the analysis and provides descriptive statistics for each measure. Our dependent variable is the total amount of **discretion** delegated to the executive, as described in Chapter 5.

For our independent variables, we start with **divided** government, which is coded 0 whenever both chambers of Congress and the presidency are controlled by the same party, and 1 otherwise. The **seat share** measure is a more sensitive indicator of divided government, defined as the percentage of seats held by the party opposite the president less the percentage held by the president's party, averaged across the House and the Senate. For example, when the president's party holds 45 percent of the seats in both chambers and the opposition 55 percent, seat share equals 10 percent. The prediction is that as the percentage of seats held

129

Table 6.1. *Description of Variables and Summary Statistics*

Variable	Description	Mean	Std. Dev.	Min.	Max.
Discretion	The amount of authority that executive agencies have to move policy, as defined in Chapter 5.	0.18	0.16	0.00	1.00
Divided	1 if either House of Congress is controlled by the opposite party of the president; 0 otherwise.	0.55	0.50	0.00	1.00
Seat Share	Average net percent of House and Senate seats held by the party opposite the president.	-0.016	0.107	-0.18	0.15
Gridlock	Gridlock interval taking into account congressional filibuster and veto override procedures.	40.35	9.92	16.26	61.43
Start Term	1 if the first two years following a presidential election; 0 otherwise.	0.58	0.50	0.00	1.00
Activist	(Congress-86) for years 1961-68; (95-Congress) for years 1969-76; 0 otherwise.	1.33	1.51	0.00	4.00
Budget Surplus	U.S. federal budget surplus/deficit over total federal outlays.	-0.075	0.097	-0.26	0.40

Sources: Budget Surplus, *Economic Report of the President* (1997); other measures calculated by the authors. Gridlock region calculated using real ADA scores provided in Groseclose, Levitt, and Snyder (1997). N=257.

by the opposite party increases, Congress grants less discretionary authority to the executive.

We also include additional variables suggested by previous authors to capture congressional–executive conflict, beginning with the **gridlock interval**, which measures both interbranch conflict and polarization within the legislature. We calculated the gridlock interval using real ADA scores for the House, Senate, and president – that is, ADA scores corrected for movement in legislative preferences over time.[10] So for each year we measured the position of the president and each of the pivot points in the House and the Senate, and from this we calculated

[10]These scores were calculated in Groseclose, Levitt, and Snyder (1997). We are grateful to the authors for providing us with these data.

the gridlock region. The prediction is that as the gridlock region increases, Congress will delegate less discretionary authority to the president.[11]

From Mayhew's data, we borrow a **start term** variable that takes on the value 1 for the first two years after a presidential election and 0 otherwise. Mayhew asserted that this variable captures the honeymoon effect that usually follows presidential elections. Therefore we should expect to see more policy production, or in our case more discretion, when the executive has just entered office. We also included an **Activist** variable, which captures the public's demand for policy. Mayhew simply included a dummy variable for the years 1961 to 1976. We employ a more fine-grained version of this measure, which starts at 0, rises steadily one unit for each Congress between 1961 and 1968, and then declines steadily from 1969 to 1976.

Finally, Brady and Volden argue that during times of tighter fiscal constraints Congress is less able to arrive at a legislative compromise, and we should therefore see less policy movement. To account for this possibility we also controlled for the percent of the federal **budget surplus** as a share of total federal outlays, hypothesizing that Congress should grant the executive less discretion to set policy when the deficit is large.

The main prediction from our model is that executive discretion will be significantly higher during times of unified as opposed to divided government. As a first, direct approach to this question, we summarize the mean values of discretion and its components by divided government, as shown in Table 6.2. The table also indicates the difference between these mean values, the percentage difference, and significance as measured by a difference of means test.

It is clear, first of all, that Congress delegates less and constrains more under divided government. The average delegation ratio is 26.3 percent under divided government and 31.0 percent under unified, while the constraint ratio is 32.3 percent under divided government and 29.4

---

[11]Our calculations of the gridlock region rely on an elaboration of the model from Figure 6.2 above: With both a House and a Senate, assuming that the House median is interior to F^- and F^+ and P is greater than the Senate median, the gridlock interval will be bounded by F^- below and bounded above by the lesser of P and the greater of V_H^+ and V_S^+. For example, in 1977 we have: $F^- = 31.1$, $V_H^+ = 64.3$, $V_S^+ = 67.5$ and $P = 71.4$. So the gridlock interval is bounded by 31.1 and 67.5, giving it a length of 36.4. Appendix E provides all real ADA cut points and the gridlock region, as well as summaries of the other conflict measures.

Note that, his theoretical model to the contrary, Krehbiel (1998) does not actually use the gridlock variable in his empirical analysis. What he labels "change in gridlock interval" is actually the change in the seat-share measure from one Congress to the next, and so our results regarding this variable are not directly comparable to his.

Table 6.2. *Difference of Means Test of the Effect of Unified and Divided Government on Delegation, Discretion, and Constraints*

Variable	Divided	Unified	Difference	% Difference	Significant
Components of Discretion					
Delegation Ratio	0.263	0.310	-0.047	-17.9%	✔
Constraint Ratio	0.323	0.294	0.029	9.0%	
Relative Constraints	0.097	0.096	0.001	1.0%	
Discretion	0.162	0.209	-0.047	-29.0%	✔
Categories of Constraints					
Appointment Power Limits	0.34	0.29	0.05	15.11%	
Time Limits	0.54	0.46	0.07	13.89%	
Spending Limits	0.49	0.50	-0.01	-2.31%	
Legislative Action Required	0.13	0.11	0.02	15.51%	
Executive Action Required	0.14	0.08	0.06	44.43%	
Legislative Veto	0.16	0.10	0.07	40.95%	
Reporting Requirements	0.59	0.50	0.09	14.74%	
Consultation Requirements	0.26	0.33	-0.07	-26.82%	
Public Hearings	0.11	0.15	-0.04	-39.94%	
Appeals Procedures	0.28	0.23	0.05	16.65%	
Rule-Making Requirements	0.75	0.84	-0.10	-12.99%	✔
Exemptions	0.49	0.43	0.07	13.57%	
Compensations	0.20	0.12	0.08	38.26%	✔
Direct Oversight	·0.11	0.03	0.07	67.07%	✔

Note: Difference of means calculated from a two-sample t-test with equal variances. ✔denotes significance at the 10 percent level, two-tailed test. Total number of observations equals 257, with 115 laws passed under unified government and 142 under divided.

percent under unified. Interestingly, relative constraints are nearly identical under both regimes; this results from fewer constraints but greater delegation under unified government, and greater constraints on less delegation under divided.[12] Finally, a large and significant difference is apparent in the discretion afforded the executive branch when we move

[12]Recall that relative constraints are the product of the delegation ratio and the constraint ratio.

from unified to divided government. As shown in the table, this difference is 29 percent, significant at the 1 percent level. Thus, our most basic hypothesis is corroborated by these simple bivariate relations.

The bottom half of the table examines in greater detail the impact of divided government on the various categories of administrative procedures that Congress uses to circumscribe delegated authority. The relative frequency of most categories rises under divided government, in line with the observation that Congress constrains more during times of divided control. The only categories that decline are spending limits (almost identical), rule-making requirements (still very highly used under both regimes), consultation requirements, and public hearings. The use of all other categories rises during divided government, with the largest increases appearing in executive action required, legislative veto, appeals procedures, compensations, and especially direct oversight.

In general, administrative procedures constrain executive agencies by enfranchising four different types of actors into the regulatory process: other executive agencies, interest groups, the courts, and Congress itself. The table shows that a move from unified to divided government increases all constraints in the latter category: Legislative action required, legislative veto, reporting requirements, and direct oversight. Thus, while our findings support the arguments made in McCubbins, Noll, and Weingast (1987) that legislators constrain bureaucrats in such a way as to ensure the continued access of interest groups, they also indicate that legislators design procedures to make agencies directly accountable to Congress as well.

Figure 6.3 provides a quick summary of the bivariate relation between seat share and average discretion, with one data point for each Congress, unified government in bold, and divided government in italics. The regression line is downward-sloping and statistically significant, as our theory would predict, suggesting that discretion declines as the party opposite the president increases its control over the legislative branch. Notable overachievers in terms of discretion include Nixon's first term, the Kennedy/Johnson Congress, and the start of Eisenhower's second term. Underachievers include one Congress each for Reagan and Bush and Carter's entire tenure.

Regression Analysis

The next question is whether these patterns continue to be in evidence when other factors that might influence executive discretion are taken into account. As a prelude to the regression analysis, both here and in subsequent chapters, several diagnostics were performed on the data. Each model was checked for omitted variables using a Ramsey (1969) RESET test, and for heteroskedasticity using a Cook and Weisberg

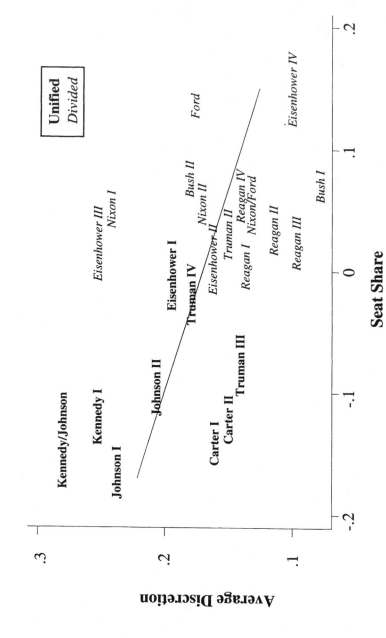

Figure 6.3. Discretion vs. Seat Share, by Congress

(1983) test. Post-regression analysis was performed to identify influential outliers via their Cook's distances.[13] As all models examined below tested positive for heteroskedasticity, they were estimated using robust regression. The possibility of a nonlinear model specification was also explored, to see if the degree of congressional control affected discretion more in some ranges than in others. However, examination of fitted-versus-residual plots and augmented component-plus-residual plots showed no evidence of nonlinearity.

Several alternative model specifications were analyzed, and the results are provided in Table 6.3. Each model included the controls for the beginning of a president's term, government surplus, and activist public moods. Of these variables, the beginning of a president's term – or the honeymoon effect – had no significant impact on discretion. The budget surplus variable had a positive and significant coefficient, indicating that during times of tighter fiscal constraints Congress is less willing to delegate. This finding in turn suggests that, with less federal money to go around, legislators do focus more intensely on getting direct benefits to favored constituents and less on programs that give the executive wide latitude over spending patterns. And the significant activist variable shows that the period including the Great Society and the Nixon administration was one, not only of high legislative productivity, but of an increased executive role in implementing policy as well. This seems natural: With more federal activity and a fixed amount of time and energy, Congress was forced to some degree to rely on the executive for implementation.

As for our key measures of interbranch conflict, the first set of results shown in Table 6.3 indicates that the divided government variable does indeed impact discretion. A move from unified to divided government decreases discretion by about 3.2 percent, an appreciable difference when compared to a mean of 18.3 percent for the entire sample. Our basic hypothesis is, therefore, supported by the data: Under divided government Congress does delegate less policy-making authority to the executive branch. Even after controlling for other variables that might account for government activity, divided government is a significant predictor of executive discretion.

The second model substitutes seat share as a measure of divided government. The regression results show that as the percentage of seats held by the party opposite the president increases, the amount of discretionary authority delegated to the president decreases, although, as Table

---

[13]Following Bollen and Jackman (1990), we eliminated observations with a Cook's distance of greater than $4/n$, where n is the sample size.

Table 6.3. *OLS and Tobit Estimates of the Effect of Congressional-Executive Conflict on Discretion*

Dependent Variable: Discretion

Model Var.	Robust OLS Estimates				Tobit Estimates			
	Model 1	Model 2	Model 3	Model 4	Model 1	Model 2	Model 3	Model 4
Divided	-0.032 (-2.01)**				-0.038 (-1.77)**			
Seat Share		-0.134 (-1.59)*				-0.22 (-1.94)**		
Gridlock			-0.0003 (-0.39)	-0.0006 (-0.71)			0.0007 (0.58)	0.0003 (0.32)
Gridlock * Divided				-0.001 (-2.05)**				-0.0009 (-1.60)*
Start Term	-0.009 (-0.57)	-0.013 (-0.81)	-0.009 (-0.58)	-0.006 (-0.38)	0.002 (0.11)	-0.003 (-0.15)	0.003 (0.15)	0.003 (0.16)
Budget Surplus	0.228 (1.98)**	0.253 (2.23)**	0.294 (2.61)**	0.241 (2.10)**	0.178 (1.53)*	0.178 (1.53)*	0.201 (1.73)**	0.177 (1.52)*
Activist	0.012 (2.17)**	0.011 (2.01)**	0.012 (2.09)**	0.012 (2.22)**	0.017 (2.41)**	0.016 (2.27)**	0.017 (2.25)**	0.017 (2.24)**
Constant	0.184 (9.01)**	0.167 (8.57)**	0.184 (4.93)**	0.205 (5.38)**	0.184 (7.32)**	0.163 (7.42)**	0.137 (2.86)**	0.166 (3.26)**
F_{n-k}^{k}	5.17**	4.76**	4.04**	4.19**				
χ_{k}^{2}					14.54**	15.18**	11.76**	14.31**
No. Obs.	244	244	244	244	257	257	257	257

Note: t-statistics in parentheses, one-tailed test; * $\alpha < .10$; ** $\alpha < .05$. OLS regressions omit observations with Cook's distances greater than $4/n$.

136

6.3 indicates, with the control variables added these results are significant only at the 10 percent level.

Column 3 of Table 6.3 introduces the gridlock interval into the analysis. As indicated, this measure has no direct effect on discretion. But when we interact gridlock with divided government, as shown in column 4, the size of the gridlock interval does have an appreciable effect. This finding suggests that under divided government the key pivot points – the two-thirds veto points and the three-fifths filibuster points – have the most impact on the design of policy-making institutions. This can be explained by realizing that the gridlock region is a measure of polarization *within* the Congress, as well as conflict *between* Congress and the president. Therefore, we might expect to see the gridlock region play a more prominent role in policy formation when interbranch conflict is high.

These results suggest that there may be something like a *presidential pull* being observed, in the terminology of Brady and Fiorina (1997). That is, during unified government presidents can construct an agenda, make compromises, and work with their party leaders to enact policy; therefore, polarization within the legislature has less of an impact on policy formation. During times of divided partisan control of government, on the other hand, this type of policy leadership will tend to break down, as the president will find it more difficult to push his legislative agenda through a Congress that does not share his concerns. The policy process will then revert to the familiar interbranch bargaining game where pivotal players matter and policy movement is made more difficult by divisions within the legislature.

As a final check on our analysis, recall from the discussion in Chapter 5 that the distribution of the discretion variable across observations displays a positive skew with a number of observations at zero. We remarked then that this might indicate a "pegging" effect; the data may be censored, as Congress can do no more (or less) than give the executive zero discretion in any given law. We therefore repeat the regression analysis above under the assumption that some observations might have been less than zero but for this censoring effect. We do this by reestimating models 1 through 4 of Table 6.3 using a Tobit regression in place of robust linear regression,[14] where one assumes that although the underlying variable y^* is distributed normally – $y^* \sim N(\mu, \sigma)$ –, the researcher observes only the variable y defined such that:

$$y = 0 \text{ if } y^* \leq 0;$$
$$y = y^* \text{ if } y^* > 0.$$

[14]See Chapter 22 of Greene (1993) for a summary of the Tobit model.

All observations greater than or equal to zero will then follow a truncated normal distribution, and an observation of y = 0 will be observed with probability:

$$\text{Prob}(y = 0) = \text{Prob}(y^* \leq 0);$$
$$= \Phi(-\mu/\sigma);$$
$$= 1 - \Phi(\mu/\sigma).$$

As shown in the right half of the table, our basic results were unchanged in this specification: Both divided government and the seat share measure had a negative and significant impact on executive branch discretion, with the magnitude of their impact rising somewhat. Since the truncation in the data is slight (only 25 out of 257 observations had zero delegation), this Tobit estimation should be seen as a check on our previous results, lending greater validity to our conclusion that Congress delegates less and constrains more under divided government.

Delegation and Trade Policy

Even if one accepts the fact that divided control of government leads Congress to cede less discretionary authority to executive branch actors, there remains the question of the degree to which all this has a real impact on outcomes, the bottom line of public policy. In general, of course, it is difficult to measure the policy consequences of any given law, and even more challenging to link these policy changes to executive branch discretion or lack thereof. However, in the particular area of trade policy we do have a good deal of evidence on the relation between divided government, and the structure of delegation, and at least one dimension of overall policy outcomes – the tariff rate – is directly measurable, making this a good testing ground for our theory.

To begin with, Table 6.4 lists the major postwar trade acts, whether the act was passed under unified or divided government, and the direction in which it changed executive discretion over trade policy.[15] As shown, a remarkably steady pattern emerges: Under unified government, discretion was increased; and under divided government, it was decreased. For instance, the 1955 Extension of the Reciprocal Trade Agreements Act included a national security clause that prohibited the president from reducing tariffs on commodities seen as vital to the nation's security. This clause was chiefly designed to protect the oil and steel industries, both key Democratic constituencies. Similarly, the 1988 Omnibus Trade and Competitiveness Act introduced "reverse fast-track"

---

[15]See O'Halloran (1994), Chapter 5, for a complete description of these acts and their impact on executive discretion.

procedures, whereby Congress could repeal the application of fast track to a given trade agreement if the president failed to notify Congress adequately. The only exceptions to this pattern came in 1951, when Congress first introduced the peril point provision, and in 1974, when Congress granted the Nixon administration the right to negotiate the reduction of nontariff barriers under the newly created fast-track procedures. However, this latter authority came only after a six-year hiatus in which the president had been given no trade negotiating authority at all, similar to the Republicans' present-day refusal to extend fast-track negotiating authority to the Clinton administration.

One can further examine whether these changes in discretion had an appreciable impact on tariff levels over the same time period, assuming that the president, having a national constituency, will be less susceptible to protectionist demands than will members of Congress, so that greater discretion should be associated with lower tariff levels. This question was investigated in Epstein and O'Halloran (1996), in which changes in the tariff were regressed on changes in discretion, inflation, unemployment, and GNP. The coefficient on discretion was negative and significant, as predicted, with an increase in executive discretion leading to a 2.4 percent drop in the tariff rate, all else being equal. In this one concrete case, then, the mechanisms suggested by our theory affect not only the procedural latitude given to executive branch actors, but final policy outcomes as well.

ROLL CALLS OVER DELEGATION

The previous section showed that aggregate patterns of discretion respond to congressional–executive conflict in a predictable way: During times of high partisan conflict, less discretionary authority was delegated to the president. In this section, we ask if individual members' voting behavior reflects similar partisan divisions. In particular, are members of the same party as the president more likely to vote to increase the president's discretion than members of the opposite party?

Roll-Call Vote Data

We examined all the roll calls associated with the passage of the 265 laws in our data set on the floor of the House of Representatives.[16] This includes roll-call votes on rules, amendments, procedural motions, final

---

[16]Here we include the 257 laws for which discretion data were available, plus the eight laws with insufficient *Congressional Quarterly* summaries, as illustrated in Figure 5.1.

Table 6.4. *Major U.S. Trade Legislation, Divided Government, and Delegation, 1948–1992*

Legislation	Administration	Divided/Unified	Delegation
1948 Extension of the RTAA	Truman	*Divided*	*Decreased*
1949 Extension of the RTAA	Truman	**Unified**	**Increased**
1951 Extension of the RTAA	Truman	**Unified**	*Decreased*
1953 Extension of the RTAA	Eisenhower	**Unified**	**Increased**
1954 Extension of the RTAA	Eisenhower	**Unified**	**Increased**
1955 Extension of the RTAA	Eisenhower	*Divided*	*Decreased*
1958 Extension of the RTAA	Eisenhower	*Divided*	*Decreased*
1962 Trade Expansion Act	Kennedy	**Unified**	**Increased**
1974 Trade Reform Act	Nixon	*Divided*	**Increased**
1979 Trade Agreements Act	Carter	**Unified**	**Increased**
1984 Trade and Tariff Act	Reagan	*Divided*	*Decreased*
1988 Omnibus Trade and Competitiveness Act	Reagan	*Divided*	*Decreased*

passage, conference reports, and veto overrides. The House recorded a roll-call vote on all but sixteen of the laws, giving us a total sample of 249 bills, and on these bills there were a total of 1,314 recorded roll-call votes.

We next coded each roll call to see if the vote was over delegation or not. Again, as in the formal model, we define discretion as the latitude that an agency has to move policy away from the status quo. Similar to the task undertaken in Chapter 5, where we coded for the specific administrative procedures associated with the executive's use of delegated authority, executive discretion can be circumscribed in a number of ways: setting spending limits, specifying impermissible actions, or limiting the range by which an agency can set policy. Our purpose here is not to spell out in detail the particular mechanisms for limiting agency discretion, but rather to identify those measures on which members sought to alter the terms of delegation by either increasing or decreasing executive authority.

We should note that Bensel (1980) performed a similar task, analyzing legislative motions in the House of Representatives for the years 1965–6 (Johnson), 1971 (Nixon), 1975 (Ford), and 1977 (Carter), in order to ascertain in which situations legislators voted according to a "rule of law" standard, meaning laws that are implemented uniformly and with as little room for executive discretion as possible. As Bensel (1980, 736–7) states:

> The restoration of a rule of law would require a general increase in statutory articulation: the extent to which statutory language limits bureaucratic discretion by stipulating specific and objective standards, rules and penalties and provides for responsible agency performance. . . . The construction of an ideal rule of law standard . . . would imply the absolute minimization of bureaucratic discretion.

Similar to Bensel's enterprise, much of our analysis focuses on legal definitions, specifications of regulatory authority, types of delegated power, and the administrative structure of decision making. Unlike Bensel, however, we do not focus solely on statutory articulation – conformity to the rule of law standard – but rather the authority granted to executive agencies and the limits placed on the exercise of this authority. Where Bensel investigated what he calls the rule of law, we are looking at delegation, and the two concepts do not exactly coincide. For example, delegating decision-making authority to multiple agencies in the executive branch is one way of limiting the control an agency has over a policy area, and as such it decreases discretion even though it does not conform to Bensel's rule-of-law criteria. Similarly, shared federal – state responsibility for administering programs mitigates executive discretion even though it violates a strict rule-of-law standard.

The procedure we adopted is as follows. First, for each roll call in our data set, we read the corresponding *Congressional Quarterly Weekly Report* brief to determine if the motion was over delegation.[17] If not, then the roll call was eliminated from the data set. This left us with 479 roll-call votes over delegation. The next step was to determine if the motion increased or decreased discretion. Most motions fell into six general categories: (1) a rule for considering a bill; (2) passage of the bill; (3) an amendment to the bill; (4) a motion to recommit with instructions; (5) a conference report; and (6) a veto override. To code each roll call, we first determined the relevant alternative to the motion being considered. For example, if the vote was on an amendment, the alternative was the unamended bill. If the vote was on final passage or a veto override, the appropriate reference was existing law. If the vote was on a conference report, then the relevant status quo was the version of the bill passed by the House.[18] Given a motion and its relevant alternative,

---

[17]In most cases, it was clear when the motion under consideration sought to limit discretion. If in doubt, we referred to the *Congressional Quarterly* legislative summaries surrounding the passage of the bill. If still in doubt, we went to the *Congressional Record* and read the debates surrounding the motion's passage.

[18]Appendix F details the full coding rules used in the analysis, and Table F.1 discusses each alternative motion, the relevant status quo, and the sources used to code the motion.

we determined which gave the executive greater discretionary authority. If the motion under consideration would have increased discretion, then the roll call was coded as Increase; if the motion decreased discretion, the vote was coded as Decrease. Of the 479 roll calls over delegation, 266 sought to raise the executive's discretion and 213 sought to lower the executive's discretion.[19]

Finally, we recorded each member's individual vote on these roll calls, giving us a total sample of 187,385 member votes to be analyzed.[20] We also included member-specific information, such as whether the member was on the committee that reported the bill, held leadership positions within the chamber and on the committee, had seniority, and her/his partisan affiliation. In addition, we recorded the president's position on each roll call: favor, oppose, or no announced position. These data are summarized in Table 6.5.

Individual Voting over Delegation

The prediction that arises from our model is that members will support delegation to the executive more when the president belongs to the same party. To operationalize this hypothesis, we first constructed a new variable called **Pro-delegation Vote**, which is equal to 1 if a member voted Aye on a proposition to raise the executive's discretionary authority, or Nay on a vote to lower discretion, and 0 otherwise.

Distributions of this variable disaggregated by party and administration are shown in Figure 6.4. The horizontal axis in each graph indicates the proportion of votes in which an individual member supported greater delegation. The vertical axis shows the proportion of members with a given pro-delegation voting score. The distribution marked with crosses indicates Democrats; the circles denote Republicans. These graphs provide a useful way to compare partisan support for executive delegation across administrations. During the Truman administration, for instance, Republicans generally voted against measures that increased executive discretion, with the modal Republican voting in favor of increased discretion only about 25 percent of the time. Democrats, on the

---

[19]As a check on our classification, we examined the average Poole-Rosenthal first-dimension coordinates for those votes classified Increase and Decrease. Consistent with the hypothesis that greater delegation is a more liberal position than less delegation, the average Nominate score for Increase votes was -0.28, while the average for Decrease votes was 0.35.

[20]These votes were compiled from the ICPSR roll-call data set, as updated by Poole and Rosenthal (1997) in their analysis of historic roll-call voting patterns in the House of Representatives. We are grateful to the authors for making their data publicly available. In the analysis, we examined only Yea and Nay votes, leaving out announced, paired, or present votes.

Table 6.5. *Descriptive Statistics for Roll-Call Voting Analysis*

Variable	Description	Mean	Std. Dev.	Min	Max
Raise Discretion	1 if the measure would increase executive discretion; 0 if the measure would decrease executive discretion.	0.55	0.49	0.00	1.00
Vote	1 if the member voted Aye; 0 if the member voted Nay.	66.19%	47.30%	0	1
Pro-Delegation Vote	1 if Vote = Raise Discretion; 0 otherwise.	58.49%	49.27%	0	1
President's Position	1 if the president supported the position of greater delegation; 0 if the president had no announced position; -1 if the president supported the position of less delegation.	21.37%	64.33%	-1	1
Member Party	1 for Republicans; 0 for Democrats.	39.6%	48.9%	0	1
President Party	1 if the president is a Republican; 0 otherwise.	56.0%	49.6%	0	1
President Same	1 if the Member Party = President Party; 0 otherwise.	50.9%	49.9%	0	1
On Committee	1 if the member was on the committee that reported the bill; 0 otherwise.	11.2%	31.5%	0	1
*Committee Leader**	11-13: committee chair; 21-24: ranking minority member; 0 otherwise.	0.68	3.33	0	24
*Party Leader**	31-51 for Speaker, Majority leader, and Majority Whip; 61-71 for Minority leader, and Minority Whip; 0 otherwise.	0.60	5.74	0	71
Seniority	Total number of terms served in the House of Representatives.	5.34	4.05	1	26

*Note: Codes for party and committee leaders are taken from Nelson (1993).

other hand, were much more disposed to grant the executive greater discretion, with a mode of close to 80 percent support.

These nine graphs exhibit a clear partisan pattern in voting over delegation. When Republicans held the presidency, the Democrat and

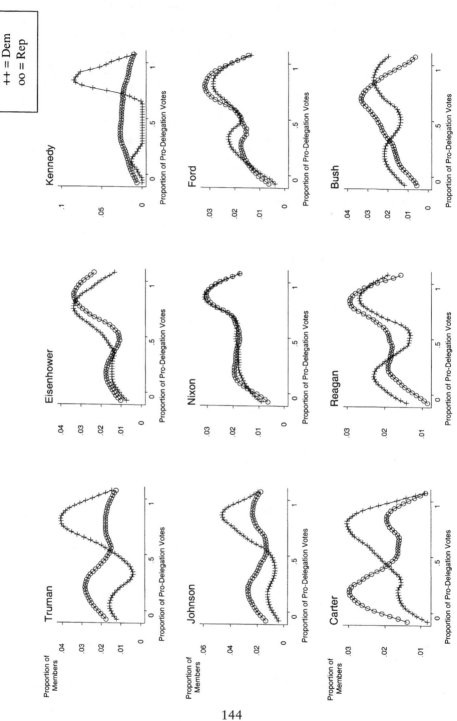

Figure 6.4. Support for Delegation, by Party and Administration

Republican distributions look nearly identical, both parties supporting delegation at about the same rate. But when Democrats were in the White House, the Democrat distribution is considerably more supportive of delegation than the Republican distribution. This indicates that during times of unified government – the Truman, Kennedy, Johnson, and Carter administrations – voting patterns over delegation polarized, with Democrats quite willing on average to give discretionary authority to executive branch actors, and the Republicans rather wary of delegating such power. Thus, a simple interbranch policy conflict approach predicts well these aggregate patterns of voting over delegation.

The president's announced stance on each roll-call vote was used to create a **President's position** variable, which took on the value of 1 if the president supported a measure to increase discretion or opposed a measure to decrease authority, −1 in the opposite cases, and 0 if the president had no announced position. Not surprisingly, presidents in general supported greater executive discretion. Of the roll calls on which they took positions, Democratic presidents supported an increase in discretion on 97 occasions and a decrease in discretion on only 24. For Republican presidents, the corresponding figures are 64 instances of support and 35 of opposition. Thus, presidents of both parties tend to support greater executive autonomy in policy making, Democrats even more so than Republicans.

These data were further analyzed to see how well partisan characteristics predicted individual votes over delegation. The probit estimates shown in the first column of Table 6.6 reveal that Democrats more frequently support delegation than do Republicans, and that all members were more likely to vote for propositions supported by the president (and vote against those that he opposed). The first of these findings accords well with conventional wisdom that Democrats prefer bigger government (insofar as the expansion of federal authority usually means giving more discretion to the executive branch), while the second must be interpreted with some care. It may indicate that presidents do sway members' voting decisions by taking a preannounced position, but it may also indicate that presidents are careful to announce a position one way or the other only when they have a reasonable chance of success, thus avoiding embarrassing legislative defeats whenever possible.

The table also shows that more senior members tend to vote against delegation. Again two interpretations come to mind. The first is that members become more attached to the institution over time and guard its policy-making prerogatives more jealously against executive incursions, whereas junior members focus more on passing policy, even if it means handing over some discretionary authority to the executive branch. The other possibility is that this behavior is endogenous: The best way to ensure continued reelection is to make sure that Congress retains control

145

Table 6.6. *Probit Estimates of Individual Roll-Call Voting over Delegation*

Model Var.	Dependent Variable: Pro-Delegation Vote				
	Model 1	Model 2	Model 3	Model 4	Model 5
Member Party	-0.20 (-32.94)**	-0.13 (-20.26)**	-0.20 (-33.25)**	-0.20 (-31.67)**	-0.20 (-33.09)**
President Position	0.20 (43.05)**	-0.13 (-19.83)**	0.20 (43.18)**	0.20 (43.07)**	0.20 (43.07)**
Seniority	-0.002 (-3.29)**	-0.003 (-4.18)**	-0.002 (-3.15)**	-0.004 (-4.40)**	-0.004 (-4.30)**
President Same	0.21 (36.06)**	0.07 (11.69)**	0.20 (32.48)**	0.21 (35.99)**	0.21 (34.96)**
President Same* President's Position		0.66 (69.71)**			
On Committee and President Same=1			0.10 (7.09)**		
On Committee and President Same=0			-0.0005 (-0.04)		
Majority Committee Leader				0.074 (3.62)**	
Minority Committee Leader				-0.006 (-0.24)	
Majority Party Leader				0.17 (3.86)**	
Minority Party Leader				-0.03 (-0.60)	
Committee Leader and President Same=1					0.04 (1.69)**
Committee Leader and President Same=0					0.04 (1.92)**
Party Leader and President Same=1					0.12 (2.77)**
Party Leader and President Same=0					0.01 (0.35)
Constant	0.16 (25.09)**	0.20 (31.04**)	0.16 (24.14)**	0.16 (24.88)**	0.16 (25.10)**
χ_k^2	4070**	9003**	4121**	4099**	4084**

Note: t-statistics in parentheses, one-tailed test; * $\alpha < .10$; ** $\alpha < .05$. N = 187,385

over as many policy levers as possible, and the members who understand this better are those who stay around long enough to accrue seniority.

In addition, even after controlling for these effects, members do support delegation more to presidents of their own party. Our basic hypothesis that interbranch conflict affects members' votes over delegation is thus supported; legislators are more willing to cede to presidents institutional power when they share similar policy goals. This finding is supported even more strongly in column 2, where an interactive term is added between the president's position and the variable indicating whether or not the president is of the same party. The coefficient on this term is positive and significant, suggesting that partisan divisions intensify on those roll calls for which the president has announced a position beforehand. This finding has several explanations. One is that on pieces of legislation important enough for the president to take a position, party members rally in his support. Alternatively, the president may strategically take positions on issues that are controversial and divide the political parties.

Evaluating the substantive impact these variables have on members' voting behavior, we find that in Model 1 the member's party, president's position, and president of the same party variables all have roughly equal effects on the probability that a member will support delegation.[21] Using the standard normal distribution from the probit estimates, a one standard deviation change in any of these variables changes the likelihood of support for delegation by about 4 to 5 percent, holding all other variables at their means. On the other hand, the seniority variable had only a modest effect on a member's decision to delegate, with a one standard deviation increase in a member's seniority decreasing the probability of a pro-delegation vote by only 0.3 percent.

We next investigate the relation between whether a member was on the committee that reported a given bill and that member's roll-call votes over delegation. Model 3 shows that committee members of the same party as the president support greater delegation, while the coefficient on committee members from the opposite party is insignificant. At first blush, these results may seem to run counter to our view that executive branch discretion is a substitute for committee decision making. But recall from Chapter 4 that our theoretical model predicts that members with preferences near those of the president prefer the agency to have large amounts of discretion in order to take advantage of bureaucratic expertise. Indeed, part of the equilibrium configuration of messages and actions has the committee *withholding* information from the floor in certain instances so that, in equilibrium, agencies will have greater discretion to set policy. This result highlights the tacit collusion or iron triangle type of behavior that may at times take place between agencies and the committees that oversee them. Therefore, committee members who share the same policy goals as the executive branch would be expected to favor greater agency discretion.

---

[21]The standardized coefficients on theses variables are −0.198, 0.261, and 0.213, respectively.

Models 4 and 5 examine the impact of party and committee leadership on support for delegation. The former shows that both majority-party committee and party leaders support delegation more than minority-party leaders, while the latter shows increased support from committee leaders and from congressional party leaders of the same party as the president. Given the rather confusing nature of these results, we took a closer look at leadership support for delegation in Table 6.7, which separates out party and committee leaders' support for delegation by party and administration.

The data in the table reveal some interesting patterns. For Democrats as a party, overall trends in support follow clearly partisan divisions. The order of presidents from the most supported to the least are *Kennedy, Johnson, Truman*, Eisenhower, Ford, Nixon, Bush, *Carter*, and Reagan, Carter being the one obvious outlier (Democratic presidents are in italics). Relative to these scores, Democratic party leaders consistently demonstrate higher support levels. Since Democrats were the majority party for all but two Congresses in this period, this could indicate institutional incentives attached to majority-party leadership. These incentives may reflect, as Bensel (1980) suggests, implicit collusion with the executive to share power over important decisions. Or alternatively, it may reflect party leaders' task of building coalitions to pass legislation, meaning that they have less room to be partisan, particularistic, or protective of congressional prerogatives.

Democratic committee leaders, on the other hand, are sometimes more and at other times less supportive of delegation when compared to the average Democratic floor voter. Inspection of the table shows that committee leaders were less supportive in the Truman, Eisenhower, and Johnson administrations and more supportive in all others. The fact that three of the first four administrations appear as periods of lower committee support suggests that a time trend may be at work. Committee leaders were more protective of congressional institutional goals during the 1950s and 1960s, which were by all accounts the high-water mark of committee power in the twentieth century. As the barricades of seniority were slowly eroded through the congressional reforms of the 1970s, and as the internal rifts of the Democratic party eased with the conversion of conservative Southern districts to the Republican party, these members acted less like *committee* leaders and more like committee *leaders* – they protected their individual policy areas less and spent more energy trying to pass legislation.

On the Republican side, similar partisan patterns emerge with respect to aggregate party voting. From most to least support for delegation, the ordering is Eisenhower, Ford, Nixon, Reagan, Bush, *Johnson, Kennedy,* and *Truman,* with *Carter* again bringing up the rear. That is, Republican

Table 6.7. *Roll-Call Support for Delegation by Party, Leadership Status, and Administration*

	Democrats			Republicans		
Administration	*Party Leaders*	*Committee Leaders*	*All Members*	*Party Leaders*	*Committee Leaders*	*All Members*
Truman	68.75%	58.09%	63.43%	40.00%	41.71%	45.94%
Eisenhower	64.18	57.07	61.10	66.67	58.14	64.63
Kennedy	90.90	82.77	80.76	57.14	47.77	51.26
Johnson	74.15	66.41	70.74	50.00	51.20	51.74
Nixon	60.49	59.09	58.51	61.35	62.00	58.86
Ford	74.07	63.94	59.55	66.04	63.88	60.44
Carter	60.28	60.68	56.52	35.29	49.26	43.79
Reagan	55.77	56.41	55.03	55.44	61.19	58.09
Bush	60.65	59.07	56.78	56.36	51.88	55.22

members uniformly supported Republican presidents at higher rates than they supported Democratic presidents.

With Republican committee and party leaders, the patterns are less clear-cut. In all likelihood, this is due to the Republicans' minority status in the House throughout most of the postwar period. For committee leaders, no obvious patterns at all appear in the data. Party leaders, though, generally follow a more consistent partisan tack than do rank-and-file members. They were more supportive of Bush, Eisenhower, Ford, and Nixon than the average Republican floor member, and less supportive of Truman, Johnson, and Carter. The only deviations from this pattern come with Kennedy, who was opposed more by the average Republican member than by Republican leadership, and Reagan, who was more supported by the rank and file.

Party Voting over Delegation

We next examine the roll-call data from a slightly different angle, taking each roll call and determining the percentage of Democrats and Republicans voting Aye. All else being equal, we expect that members from the same party as the president will be more likely to support measures that delegate than will members of the opposite party. If the partisan voting hypothesis is correct, then we should observe the following four patterns in overall partisan voting:

1. Democrats will vote to lower discretion more when Republicans as opposed to Democrats control the presidency;

2. Democrats will vote to raise discretion more when Democrats as opposed to Republicans control the presidency;
3. Republicans will vote to lower discretion more when Democrats as opposed to Republicans control the presidency; and
4. Republicans will vote to raise discretion more when Republicans as opposed to Democrats control the presidency.

In short, members will vote to increase the discretionary power of presidents from the same party and decrease the power of presidents from the opposite party.

We tested these hypotheses by dividing the sample into eight possible cases, broken down by party of the president, congressional party, and whether the vote was to raise or lower executive discretion, as illustrated in Figure 6.5. The four hypotheses above can be translated into the following predictions: The value (percentage) in Case 3 will be greater than Case 1, Case 2 greater than Case 4, Case 5 greater than Case 7, and Case 8 greater than Case 6.

Table 6.8 summarizes the percentage of members voting Aye in each of the eight cases. For instance, on roll calls to raise discretion, House Democrats voted Aye 81 percent of the time when a Democrat controlled the White House and 69 percent of the time when a Republican was in office. The bottom half of Table 6.8 reports the results of F-tests on each of the four hypotheses stated above. In three of the four cases, the difference in voting patterns was in accordance with our predictions and statistically significant. In the one case that was not significant – Case 3 versus Case 1 – the difference was in the hypothesized direction; it seems that Democrats are loath to vote against executive discretion no matter who occupies the White House. Thus, the patterns that emerge at the individual level reappear in aggregate party voting: Members support delegation to presidents of their own party more than to presidents of the opposite party.

VETOES AND DELEGATION

We next examine the impact of the presidential veto on discretion. The Constitution lays out a framework for legislative–executive bargaining through the possible or threatened use of a veto. From our model, presidents always prefer more discretion to less, so the prediction is that we should expect to see less executive leeway in bills that are passed over vetoes than otherwise.

This is a straightforward question, but unfortunately the data at hand allow us only scant opportunity to test it directly. For the 257 laws

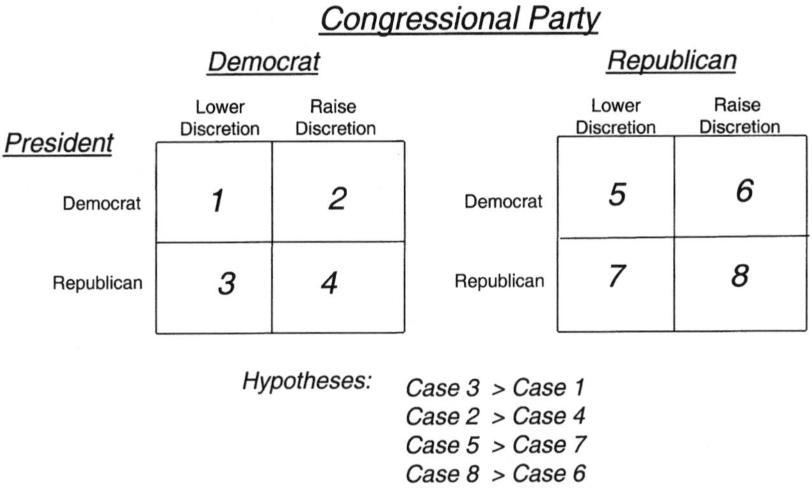

Congressional Party

Figure 6.5. Voting over Discretion, by Congressional Party and Party of the President

under consideration, only twelve were passed over a presidential veto. To these, we therefore added the fifteen additional laws that had veto threats issued against them at some stage of the legislative process. Thus we analyzed a total of twenty-seven laws that sparked presidential opposition on the level of a veto or a veto threat. Undoubtedly, this is a rather small number on which to base definitive conclusions, but it does allow us to look at some basic patterns in the data.

Table 6.9 shows average total discretion by veto type. Laws not passed over vetoes or veto threats gave the executive higher average discretion, with a mean total discretion of 21.1 percent under unified government and 16.8 percent under divided. Laws passed over a veto or veto threat, however, showed a marked difference in the amount of discretion delegated to the executive: an average of 16.4 percent under unified government and 12.7 percent under divided. Summarizing these effects, a difference-of-means test indicates that laws enacted over a veto or veto threat granted the executive significantly less discretionary authority than those that were not.

THE STRUCTURE OF DELEGATION: TO WHOM DO
YOU DELEGATE?

We next test our theory of structural choice, where the claim is that divided government should lead Congress to move decision-making au-

Table 6.8. *Percentage of House Members Voting in Favor of a Roll Call by Party, Party of the President, and Whether to Raise or Lower Discretion*

	Congress			
	Democrat		**Republican**	
President	**Lower**	**Raise**	**Lower**	**Raise**
Democrat	53%	81%	71%	65%
	(1)	(2)	(5)	(6)
Republican	57%	69%	60%	73%
	(3)	(4)	(7)	(8)

Note: N = 479;
Cases from Figure 6.5 referenced in parentheses.

Partisan Voting over Discretion

Alternative Hypotheses

Hypothesis	**F-statistic**	$P > F_{n-k}^{k}$
Case 3 – Case 1 = 0	1.16	0.246
Case 2 – Case 4 = 0	11.35	0.0008
Case 5 – Case 7 = 0	6.55	0.011
Case 8 – Case 6 = 0	5.91	0.015

Table 6.9. *Average Executive Discretion for Laws Enacted over Presidential Vetoes, by Unified and Divided Government*

	Veto Override or Threat	
Partisan Conflict	**No**	**Yes**
Unified	21.1%	16.4%
	(110)	(5)
Divided	16.8%	12.7%
	(120)	(22)
N	230	27

Note: number of observations in parentheses.

thority to spheres further from presidential control. Political actors, it has been emphasized, carefully calibrate the means by which policy-making power is ceded to the executive branch. As Moe (1989, 268) writes:

Structural choices have important consequences for the content and direction of policy, and political actors know it. When they make choices about structure, they are implicitly making choices about policy. And precisely because this is so, issues of structure are inevitably caught up in the larger political struggle. Any notion that political actors might confine their attention to policymaking and turn organizational design over to neutral criteria or efficiency experts denies the realties of politics.

One method by which delegated authority is circumscribed lies in the administrative procedures that constrain executive branch actions; these types of constraints are captured in our data set as one component of overall discretion. But structural choices also include the particular actors to whom authority is delegated: cabinet departments, independent agencies, or state-level actors. Legislators must first decide whether to give authority to the executive or to the states – this is the *federalism* question. And if authority will be located in the executive branch, Congress must choose the type of executive actor to receive the delegated authority – this is the *locational* question. Both are crucial threshold decisions in the delegation of regulatory authority.

These issues of strategic institutional design have been investigated in two recent studies. Kafka (1996) places Moe's logic of structural choice within a Lowi-Wilson framework. He assumes that legislators control independent commissions, while the president influences executive bureaus. Therefore, policies with particularized benefits will be delegated to independent agencies, whereas policies with diffuse benefits will be administered by agencies of the more traditional executive department form.

Horn (1995) identifies two competing costs in the choice of regulatory structure: commitment costs and agency costs (in the sense of losses from principal–agent problems). In order to extract rents from interest groups, the argument goes, legislators would like the policy bargains that they agree upon to be durable. They therefore favor delegation to more independent agencies when the paramount concern is to insulate policy from political meddling, say, by future legislators who may have different policy objectives. On the other hand, these executive actors are associated with higher agency costs because they will be more difficult to oversee and control. It follows that in situations where the most important implementation concern is to make agencies hew to congressional intent, more politically responsive cabinet-type agencies will be chosen.

To these essentially distributive approaches to structural choice we add the observation that, whatever the reason for choosing independent agencies over more politically responsive executive departments, the trend toward independent commissions should increase the higher the level of policy conflict between Congress and the executive. Assume, for instance, that moving from independent agencies to cabinet agencies reduces the variance associated with policy outcomes, at the cost of greater presidential control. During times of divided government, then, congressional preferences over the structure of delegation will shift, so that more authority will be given to executive actors further from the president's political reach, or Congress will delegate to the states and bypass the executive altogether.[22]

TESTING FOR STRATEGIC DELEGATION

To investigate this claim, we identified the agencies mentioned in the *Congressional Quarterly* legislative summaries for each of our 257 public laws. Each of these recipients of delegated authority was then classified according to the following scheme. First, state and local government agencies were identified, along with the courts, as non-executive branch actors.[23] All executive branch actors were then classified into one of the following five categories, using contemporaneous *U.S. Government Manuals* as a reference:

1. Executive Office of the President;
2. Cabinet Departments;
3. Independent Agencies;
4. Independent Regulatory Commissions;
5. Government Corporations.

Table 6.10 provides the frequencies of these observations by category, along with their frequencies under divided and unified government. On average, each law identified about four different executive branch actors to receive authority, for a total of 961 agency-law observations. The table shows that cabinet departments were the most frequent recipients of delegated authority, comprising close to 60 percent of all observations. Government corporations were the least used; only 2.6 percent of the time did Congress delegate authority to these independent entities. The table also shows some indication of strategic delegation: The first two categories, EOP and cabinet departments, are used relatively more

[22]The relation between this logic and our formal model is discussed in Chapter 4.

[23]In some instances, authority was given to actors under congressional control, as when the Speaker of the House was allowed to appoint members to a commission, or when estimates from the Congressional Budget Office were used as a benchmark when implementing policy. These were not counted as delegations of authority, since in our model delegation is equated with policy authority residing outside of Congress.

often under unified government, while independent agencies and commissions are used more often under divided control.[24]

These categories are listed in decreasing order of presidential control, which is to say increasing order of independence. The executive office of the president, including for instance the Office of the United States Trade Representative, the National Security Council, and the Council of Economic Advisors, contains the president's personal staff as well as his closest advisors. The cabinet departments, such as Agriculture, Defense, and Labor, have more-elaborate hierarchical structures, but the president appoints all agency and division heads with the consent of the Senate and can remove them at will. Moreover, their budgets are submitted to Congress as part of the president's overall budget plan.

Independent agencies, by contrast, can submit their own budgets directly to Congress. Examples in this category include the Central Intelligence Agency and the Environmental Protection Agency. Heads of independent regulatory commissions – such as the Federal Trade Commission and the Interstate Commerce Commission – are appointed by the president, but they serve for fixed terms. And government corporations, including Amtrak and the Post Office, get a proportion of their budget from market operations as opposed to direct federal government transfers.

We emphasize, though, that the politics of structural choice is not necessarily one of presidential versus congressional control of agencies. Independent agencies may be exactly that – independent from both legislative scrutiny and executive interference. The correct view, as noted above, is one of bias versus variance: Congress chooses between the biased but relatively certain policy outcomes that result from delegation to presidentially influenced actors, and less biased but more uncertain outcomes that result from delegation to independent agencies.

As an example of the greater uncertainty associated with delegating authority to independent commissions, consider the 1997 confrontation between the Clinton administration and the Federal Maritime Commission over the imposition of trade sanctions on Japanese ships. The commission's action was precipitated by a long-running dispute between the United States and Japan over the expensive fees and restrictions imposed on U.S. shipping fleets operating in Japanese ports. Events were unfolding at a leisurely diplomatic pace when suddenly the small, almost unknown Maritime Commission entered the fray by ordering the Coast Guard to bar Japanese cargo ships from U.S. ports. The commission threatened to impose sanctions after Japanese shipping companies, on

---

[24]A χ^2 test on Table 6.10 yielded a Pearson $\chi^2(4)$ statistic of 9.11, with an associated probability of 0.058. The magnitude and direction of this effect will be estimated more precisely below.

Table 6.10. *Discretion and Bureaucratic Structure (Percentage of Laws Delegating Authority to an Agency Type by Divided and Unified Government)*

Recipients of Delegated Authority	Unified	Divided	All
Executive Office of the President	53	73	126
	(13.4%)	(12.9%)	(13.1%)
Cabinet Departments	254	319	573
	(64.3)	(56.4)	(59.6)
Independent Agencies	61	123	184
	(15.4)	(21.7)	(19.2)
Independent Regulatory Commissions	17	36	53
	(4.3)	(6.4)	(5.4)
Government Corporations	10	15	25
	(2.5)	(2.7)	(2.6)
Totals	**395**	**566**	**961**
	(100%)	**(100%)**	**(100%)**

Note: Percentage of observations for each agency location in parentheses.

order from their government, refused to pay $4 million in fines that had been imposed in an effort to relax Japanese port rules.

The commission's actions sent top administration officials scrambling, as they sought to work out an agreement with the Japanese that would persuade the Federal Maritime Commission to forgo the embargo. In the end, a compromise was reached between the Clinton administration and Japanese officials, averting the spectacle of Coast Guard cutters hunting down Japanese freighters, at least for the time being.[25] This episode illustrates how even the most obscure independent commissions can have profound effects on government policy and the potential uncertainty raised by their autonomy.

Non-Executive Delegations

For our purposes here, two questions guide our inquiry. First, does divided government influence delegation to non-executive actors; and second, does divided government influence where within the executive branch authority is delegated? To answer the first question, for each law in our database we counted the percentage of provisions that delegated authority to actors outside of the executive branch, including state agen-

[25]For a discussion of these events, see Steven Lee Myer, "An Obscure Maritime Panel Gets Tough," *New York Times*, October 18, 1997, and David Sanger, "Japan Nears Pact with U.S. on Threat to Bar Its Ships from U.S. Ports," *New York Times*, October 18, 1997.

cies, local authorities, and the courts. For instance, the 1990 Clean Air Act contained a total of 213 provisions that delegated authority, of which 26 delegated to non-executive actors. So the non-executive delegation ratio for this law is 12.2 percent.

During times of divided government, 3.5 percent of the provisions, on average, delegate authority to bodies other than the federal bureaucracy, compared to 2.1 percent when the same party controls both Congress and the presidency, a difference of 1.4 percent, which a difference-of-means test shows to be significant at the 5 percent level. This evidence supports our hypothesis; non-executive actors do receive a greater percentage of delegations during divided government.

On the other hand, there is an alternative explanation for these findings. Divided government during the period studied was almost entirely due to a Democratic Congress and a Republican president. Republicans as a party oppose large federal government in favor of devolving power to the states. Thus, a model that predicts that the greater control Republicans have, the greater delegation to non-executive actors, would perform essentially just as well as ours. These findings, then, while supportive of our theory, should be taken as provisional.

Spheres of Presidential Control

The next question to address is where in the executive branch hierarchy will authority reside? In many ways, we can think of the president's influence as consisting of a set of concentric circles. As authority is delegated to the layers further from the president's core group of cabinet heads and EOP staff, presidential influence also wanes and becomes more diffuse. If this is true, then the logic of our model would predict that as congressional–executive conflict increases we should see Congress delegating authority to agencies less directly controlled by the president.

We employ ordered probit analysis to estimate the relation between divided government and agency independence, since the location of delegated authority can take on one of five inherently ordered values, with the EOP being the least independent and government corporations the most. The data in Table 6.10, however, show only the frequency with which each category occurred under divided and unified control. If certain categories were used in laws that delegated little overall authority, then we should count them less heavily in our analysis. Therefore, each agency observation was weighted by the amount of discretionary authority delegated in the given law.

Furthermore, the hypothesized patterns of delegation might show up most clearly in those instances where a new agency was created, as it is in those circumstances where legislators have the most leeway over the placement of delegated authority. Therefore, we also conducted the analysis separately for all newly created agencies (these accounted for 202 out of our 961 observations). Finally, we employed two measures of interbranch conflict: divided government and the seat-share measure discussed above.

The results of the estimation, shown in Table 6.11, generally support our hypothesis. Models 1 and 2 test the proposition using only the two measures of interbranch conflict. The table shows that, as one moves from unified to divided government, and as the percentage of seats held by members of Congress of the opposite party from that of the president increases, Congress tends to move authority away from the president's direct control and to the outer layers of the concentric circles of presidential influence. This statement continues to hold even when we control for other factors that may affect policy making, such as the beginning of a presidential term, policy activism, and the size of the federal deficit. As shown in the right half of the table, these effects become more pronounced when one examines only those newly created agencies. These results have significant substantive implications as well: For instance, the probability of delegating to an EOP actor rises over 20 percent due to a switch from divided to unified government, and the probability of delegating to an independent commission falls from 13 to 7 percent.

If we combine this finding – that divided government is associated with authority being delegated to spheres further from the president's control – with the earlier finding that divided control leads Congress to delegate less discretionary authority in general, we arrive at the implication that more independent agencies receive less discretionary authority than those more directly under presidential control. Indeed, this is the case in our data: A negative and statistically significant relation exists between the discretion measure and the five-category measure of location. If we further decompose this relationship into its constituent parts, we find that, while the amount of authority delegated to agencies is relatively constant as one moves from one category to the next, more and more administrative procedural constraints are placed on the use of this authority. This is consistent with the mean-variance trade-off discussed above; since more independent agencies are difficult for either Congress or the president to control, legislators circumscribe their actions both by direct constraints on agencies and by enfranchising outside actors to help oversee them.

It is also interesting to examine the number of agencies receiving delegated authority under unified as opposed to divided government. One might imagine that Congress would be more eager to distribute executive authority across agencies under divided government, thereby establishing interagency competition over policy production. Indeed, the

Table 6.11. *Ordered Probit Estimates of Agency Location for All Laws*

	All Agencies				New Agency Created			
	Model 1	Model 2	Model 3	Model 4	Model 1	Model 2	Model 3	Model 4
Divided	0.15		0.11		0.22		0.19	
	(2.09)**		(1.56)*		(1.42)*		(1.19)	
Seat Share		0.86		0.66		1.66		1.69
		(2.51)**		(1.81)**		(2.23)**		(2.14)**
Start Term			-0.072	-0.05			0.16	0.21
			(-0.98)	(-0.74)			(0.99)	(1.23)
Activist			-0.01	-0.01			0.074	0.09
			(-0.33)	(-0.20)			(1.47)*	(1.68)**
Budget Surplus			-0.61	-0.59			-2.29	-2.13
			(-1.53)*	(-1.47)*			(-2.29)**	(-2.12)**
μ_1	-0.96	-0.63	-0.99	-0.73	-1.46	-0.81	-1.13	-0.42
μ_2	0.70	1.03	0.67	0.93	0.25	0.091	0.60	1.33
μ_3	1.58	1.91	1.56	1.82	1.00	1.67	1.38	2.11
μ_4	2.02	2.36	2.00	2.27	1.74	2.42	2.13	2.87
χ^2_k	4.39**	6.29**	8.82*	9.66**	2.02	5.00**	8.44*	11.62**
Num. Obs.	961	961	961	961	202	202	202	202

Note: z-scores in parentheses, one tailed test; * $\alpha < .10$; ** $\alpha < .05$.

average number of agencies receiving delegated authority under divided government is 4.38, as compared with 3.91 under unified. This difference becomes even more marked if we examine the more relevant statistic of number of agencies per unit of discretion, which is 58.89 under divided and 29.55 under unified. Thus, Congress does play agencies off against each other more under divided government, despite the reductions in efficiency and centralized control that this might entail.

Example: Social Security

The recent debate over the Social Security Administration will help to illustrate the politics of structural choice. A cornerstone of Franklin Roosevelt's New Deal, Social Security was initially administered by an independent board, which was replaced in 1946 by the Social Security Administration (SSA). It continued as an independent agency until 1953 when the Republican-controlled Congress supported Eisenhower's move to consolidate the social services under the newly created Department of Health, Education and Welfare, which subsequently became Health and Human Services (HHS), thereby lodging the SSA firmly within the cabinet department hierarchy.

On August 15, 1995, all this changed when the Social Security Administration was extracted from its place in the Department of Health and Human Services and became an independent agency once again. The reshuffling of administrative personnel was not simply a card trick; it was accompanied by real changes in the daily operations of the agency. Previously, the administrative head had been designated by the secretary of HHS and could be removed by the president. Under the new arrangement, the commissioner of the SSA was to be appointed by the president with Senate confirmation and was then to serve for a fixed six-year term. Also, the agency's budget was no longer one of many items in the HHS department requests; rather, the reorganization required that the president send two budgets for the agency to Congress each year: the president's final request as well as the agency's original proposal to the White House.

The move to create an independent agency was the brainchild of Senator Patrick Moynihan (D-NY). In an effort to aid pensioners and strengthen the Social Security program, Moynihan had argued for years that the SSA should be made independent as a way to "heighten its visibility and isolate it somewhat from the political party that controlled the White House, giving it more autonomy to direct and protect the Social Security Trust Fund, which paid social security benefits."[26] Three

[26]*Congressional Quarterly Almanac* (Washington, D.C.: Congressional Quarterly Press, 1993), 381.

bills to this effect, though, had died in the Senate after passing the House in 1986, 1989, and 1992. The Clinton administration initially opposed the reorganization of the SSA, as had the Reagan and Bush administrations before it, maintaining that Social Security was best left under the purview of HHS. Secretary of HHS Donna Shalala, like her GOP predecessors, argued that making SSA an independent agency would "seriously dilute the attention and support it will receive at the highest level of our government."[27]

Nonetheless, Moynihan garnered sufficient support to pass the bill by voice vote in the Senate, picking up some support from Republicans (who no longer had the GOP White House position to defend) without losing Democratic backing. Likewise, the House considered the bill under expedited procedures and passed the measure by a vote of 413–0. The question, however, is why was Moynihan successful in 1995 when he had failed thrice before?

The answer comes from the logic of interbranch conflict. All presidents have incentives to retain control over Social Security, one of the country's most popular social programs, so that their policy preferences can be represented as more conservative along this dimension than those of either the House or the Senate. Democrats in general support an independent SSA, as a means of curtailing political influence over an important social program. Republicans had no such policy motivations, and while a president of their own party occupied the White House they were content with the status quo. In other words, any attempt to make the agency independent would be vetoed by the president, and this veto could not be overridden, thus precluding policy movement.

Once a Democrat gained control of the White House, however, the situation took a new twist. Congressional Democrats maintained their stance in favor of independence, but now they were joined by the Republicans, eager to impair presidential influence over social security once a Democrat controlled the White House. This paved the way for Moynihan's measure to sail through with large, veto-proof majorities in both houses. In sum, legislative and executive preferences over the SSA polarized, leading Congress to move the agency further from executive control.

IMPLICATIONS OF DIVIDED GOVERNMENT FOR PUBLIC POLICY

Our model of transaction cost politics predicts that, as the preferences of Congress and the president diverge, legislators will delegate less dis-

[27]Ibid.

cretionary authority to executive branch actors. This chapter tested the implications of this hypothesis in five different ways. We examined the direct effect of divided government on discretion at the aggregate level, individual roll-call voting patterns, the impact of vetoes on discretion, divided government and delegation to non-executive branch actors, and the strategic design of institutions by giving power to executive branch actors further from the president's control. In each case, the empirical analysis supported our hypotheses.

These findings lend greater credibility to our approach to the policy-making process, but they also have important implications for the divided-government debate. First, we are able to systematically test theories of strategic institutional design, which have been proposed in the literature but only subject to verification by case studies. Second, we found that, contrary to the findings of Mayhew (1991) and others, divided government does have significant impacts upon policy. These effects are not felt in the quantity of legislation passed, but they are reflected in the quality of these laws. More-constrained executive branch agencies under divided government have less leeway to set policy, are less able to incorporate their expertise into regulations, are subject to more oversight by interest groups, the courts, and congressional committees; and are therefore in greater danger of falling prey to "procedural gridlock."

In other words, our system of separate powers influences not only policy made through the normal legislative channels but delegated policy making as well. We know that bicameralism, strong committees, supermajority requirements, and the possibility of a presidential veto make difficult the passage of new legislation, forcing a series of compromises at each stage and making rapid or radical policy change difficult if not impossible. This chapter shows that the same logic also holds with policy made via authority delegated to executive agencies: When the concordance of preferences between the branches is high, agencies will be given a relatively free hand in the fashioning of regulations, but interbranch conflict over policy will lead to agencies being burdened with restrictive administrative procedures, again requiring the assent of numerous actors – both within the government and without – to effectuate policy movement.

7

Delegation and Legislative Organization

The legislature and the executive are not so much parallel as they are interdependent. . . . This conclusion, drawn from an examination of the actual relationships existing within the two branches, emphasizes the disadvantages for purposes of understanding the political process of accepting too literally the formal separation of legislature from the executive.

David Truman, *The Governmental Process*[1]

We now turn to the second set of hypotheses that emerge from our model, those regarding legislative organization and congressional delegation. Our intent is to place the study of legislative organization, and in particular the committee system, within the larger framework of the U.S. governmental process and to explore how the possibility of delegating authority to the executive alters legislators' incentives, behavior, and policy choices. The key prediction analyzed here is that, since congressional policy making and delegation are substitutes, albeit imperfect ones, inefficiencies in the legislative process should lead rational legislators to rely less on committees and to shift more discretionary authority to executive agencies.

We begin our analysis by first reviewing the different theories of legislative organization, concluding that Congress's most distinctive feature – its system of strong committees – must derive not from legislators' desire for informational or distributive benefits, but from incentives created by the larger constitutional system, including separate powers. We then test this theory in three ways: (1) by relating the presence or absence of committee outliers to interbranch conflict; (2) by exploring the impact of committee–floor conflict on Congress's decision to delegate; and (3) by examining the ways in which parliamentary devices like restrictive

[1]Truman (1951, 437).

rules and multiple referrals affect agency discretion. We conclude with a summary of our results concerning committees, parties, and legislative organization in a system of separate powers.

PERSPECTIVES ON LEGISLATIVE ORGANIZATION

In the past decade, the study of legislative organization has become a battleground for congressional scholarship. Three competing theories have emerged from this debate – the distributive, informational, and party approaches – each having its own view of individual motivations and subsequent predictions for (1) how legislators organize themselves; (2) the types of procedures invoked in passing legislation; and (3) the results of this collective choice process. Ultimately, this debate is an argument over where power resides in Congress: in congressional committees, on the House floor, or in the majority-party caucus.

A Tale of Three Theories

According to the distributive theory, the major problem that members face, given single-member districts and generally weak parties, is distributing benefits to their constituents. But acting alone, legislators cannot secure these advantages, as a majority is needed to pass legislation on the floor. Congress solves this collective action problem by investing power in issue-specific committees via the following procedure: Members request and are generally granted seats on committees that directly affect their constituents; committees thus tend to be composed of homogeneous high demanders, where all members of the committee share similar policy goals and want high spending in their policy area; members' continued position on a committee is ensured by a well-established seniority system; and committee members' influence over policy domains is protected by procedural controls, including gatekeeping powers, restrictive rules, and control over conference committees.[2] In sum, the distributive theory of legislative organization predicts that committees are unrepresentative of the floor, that committee bills are considered under privileged parliamentary procedures and are rarely amended, and that final policy is composed of universalistic logrolls. Congressional committees are the glue that binds legislative logrolls together, and as such power in Congress resides in committees.

Informational approaches to legislative organization argue that the major problem members face is passing reasonable policy in an uncertain

[2]See, e.g., Mayhew (1974), Shepsle (1978), and Weingast and Marshall (1988).

world. To overcome this problem, legislators turn to committees to help mitigate informational asymmetries.[3] Committees are composed of experts in a particular policy area whose preferences may not all align on the same side of the policy debate. There is a tendency for floor members to be wary of granting committees privileged procedures, so open rules are the order of the day; floor members grant restrictive or closed rules only when the resulting informational gains outweigh possible distributive losses. The floor also controls conference committees, by appointing non–committee members, by instructing the committee to take certain actions, and by refusing to enact a conference report not to its liking. Ultimately, power in Congress resides with the median floor voter, and on average committees will be representative of the parent chamber; restrictive rules will be rare; and final policy will be majoritarian, reflecting the median floor voter's preferences.

Partisan theories of legislative organization argue that the major problem confronting legislators is working together collectively to ensure reelection. Unorganized groups of legislators might overproduce particularistic benefits (pork barrel legislation) and underproduce collective benefits (major policy legislation) in an electorally inefficient fashion.[4] To solve this coordination problem, the majority-party caucus delegates authority to party leaders, who in turn promote the collective interests of party members. Majority-party control, in turn, is maintained through the committee system: first, through the selection process where the appointment powers of the Committee on Committees are used to advance those more loyal to the party leadership; second, through agenda control by using the Speaker's scheduling powers and restrictive rules to further partisan purposes; and third, by tilting party and staff committee ratios in the majority party's favor. According to this view, majority-party committee delegations are representative of the party caucus, restrictive rules are common, and final policy is partisan, reflecting the median majority-party member's preferences and built around intraparty logrolls.

Limits of Existing Theories

These three approaches all begin with a specification of members' core reelection needs and some collective action problem they face in achieving these aims, such as majority cycling on distributive issues, informational asymmetries, or team production problems within parties. Each

[3]See Gilligan and Krehbiel (1987; 1989) and Krehbiel (1991).
[4]See Rohde (1991), Cox and McCubbins (1993), Aldrich (1995), and Sinclair (1995).

then derives an explanation of how the present set of institutional arrangements, including strong committees, satisfies these needs by solving the particular problem at hand.

Note, first, that although these approaches have sometimes been portrayed as mutually exclusive, it is not clear that they need to be competing rather than complementary: Legislators may encounter a series of collective problems in their quest for reelection, each of which is alleviated to some extent by the committee system. Insofar as different policies have different politics, each theory of legislative organization may explain certain aspects of the policy-making process well within its separate sphere.

Second, and more central to our present concerns, it is clear that even if these theories capture important aspects of the congressional policy-making process, as stated they must be incomplete. Legislators in all political systems have both informational and distributive needs, as both are necessary for reelection. And incentives for acting as a party team are not unique to U.S. legislators. But legislators elsewhere have not chosen to organize themselves in the same way; the U.S. Congress stands apart in the degree to which it relies on committees for fashioning the fine points of legislation. Conversely, a quick glance at most democracies shows that the influence wielded by legislative parties varies across countries, from weak and unorganized as in the United States to highly centralized and resource-rich as in Great Britain.

It cannot be, then, that basic legislative needs alone dictate the specific institutional structures that we find in Congress. The details of legislative organization must consequently derive to some degree from the larger political system in which they are embedded, including the electoral system of single-member plurality winner districts, bicameralism, and – our focus – the separation-of-powers system. Once viewed from this perspective, the question becomes, not whether committees solve informational, distributive, or partisan dilemmas, but rather why in the U.S. Congress these dilemmas are solved through committees rather than through some alternative institutional arrangement. That is, the question is not why congressional committees are *powerful*, but why *committees* are powerful.

Legislative Organization under Separate Powers

The answer suggested by our approach is that Congress needs committees to offset executive branch agencies, both so that legislators can have their own source of expertise on complex issues and to direct resources to favored constituents. This counterpoise between committees and agencies works in two directions. On the one hand, committees check

166

agencies through the oversight process and by advancing their own solutions to policy problems, allowing specific legislation to substitute for agencies' regulations. On the other hand, agencies provide Congress with an alternative source of policy making, thus breaking the monopoly power that committees would otherwise command over the production of legislation. This system serves Congress well as a whole: Committees and agencies must compete to some degree for policy influence, albeit at the cost of some redundancy and duplication of effort, and this competition works to the advantage of relatively uninformed floor members.[5]

We contend, then, that legislative organization in the United States must be understood within its broader governmental context, one in which policy production does not begin and end within Congress itself. Rather, legislative committees do their work in the shadow of delegation to the executive branch. Under this view, Congress needs committees both to offset executive expertise and to direct resources to favored constituents. But these demands rise and fall with changes in interbranch tension. Working from this premise, in Chapter 4 we derived a series of predictions different from those in the existing legislative organization literature – some at odds, some complementary, but all derived from a richer set of institutional considerations and not at all obvious unless one begins with a system-wide perspective on legislative organization.

Our first prediction is that when committees are less informed about the details of policy than the executive agencies they will oversee, committee preferences need not coincide exactly with the floor median; rather, there is a range of committee medians that serve the floor's purposes equally well. But this range of acceptable committees will shrink as the preferences of Congress and the president become more similar. We therefore arrive at the surprising prediction that we should expect fewer committee outliers during times of unified government than under divided government.

Second, if committees are formed in part to oversee delegated authority, then the median floor voter will rationally tilt committee preferences to be biased against those of the executive. So in contrast to both the informational and the distributive views, we predict that committee pref-

---

[5]One might also ask why committees have been chosen as the legislative vehicles to counterbalance executive policy making rather than legislative parties, for instance. The answer derives mainly from our electoral system of single-member districts, which encourages the personal vote and separates, to some degree, members' individual electoral fortunes from those of the party at large. See Epstein, Brady, Kawato, and O'Halloran (1996) for an argument along these lines explaining the emergence of seniority-based committee systems in the United States and Japan as a result of the personal vote and the rise of careerism. See also Diermeier and Myerson (1997), who show that legislators have greater incentives to decentralize control the greater the number of veto players in the system, including presidential vetoes and bicameralism.

erences should vary predictably over time to serve as a counterweight to those of the president. Committees will therefore be composed of *contrary outliers.*

Third, we predict that, as the legislative process serves members' reelection needs less well, the median floor voter will choose to delegate more discretion to executive agencies; committee outliers should therefore be correlated with greater levels of executive discretion. Our theory also predicts that this relationship should be attenuated at higher levels of congressional–executive conflict, yielding explicit predictions concerning the interaction between committee outliers and divided government.

Fourth, our analysis can speak to the role of parties in legislative organization. We take as a maintained hypothesis that when the majority party is united, members will delegate authority to party leaders who can help align the preferences of committee and floor voters. But when the majority is fragmented, intraparty coalitions become more difficult to form and maintain and power devolves back toward the median voter. Therefore, less cohesive majority parties should also be associated with greater delegation to the executive.

Finally, we offer some evidence on the role of specific parliamentary devices in the construction of legislation. Although previous theories disagree on the exact reason for restrictive rules – protecting committee prerogatives, promoting committee specialization and expertise, or enacting a partisan agenda – all concur that such rules can help overcome legislators' collective dilemmas. And the multiple referral of bills has recently emerged as one means for controlling committee-based excesses. If these perspectives are correct, then the presence of any one of these procedural devices should ease the problems of collective legislative action and should therefore be correlated with less delegation to the executive branch.

COMMITTEE OUTLIERS IN A SYSTEM OF SEPARATE POWERS

Are Committees Preference Outliers?

We begin with our analysis of the impact of congressional–executive conflict on committee composition. The previous literature addressing the ideological makeup of committees can be divided into two major strands. The first speaks to the question of whether or not the policy preferences of committee members are broadly representative of the parent chamber as a whole. These studies identify some measure of individual preferences (or a set of such measures) and then determine whether or not committee preferences are statistically different from floor preferences. The second tradition uses the degree to which committees are preference outliers relative to the median floor voter to predict other variables of interest, such as the use of restrictive rules; we shall examine this theme in the following section.

Early studies in the former vein (Ray 1980; Weingast and Marshall 1988) examine a handful of committees and indicate some evidence for the prevalence of outliers. Krehbiel (1990) engages in a broader study, analyzing all committees in the 99th Congress and relying on both ADA scores and interest-group ratings as measures of preferences. A standard difference-of-means test of committee members versus non–committee members suggests that only a few committees emerge as statistical outliers. Krehbiel also compares the standard deviations of committees with that of the floor to search for bimodal outliers, again finding little support for the outliers thesis.

Cox and McCubbins (1993) repeat this experiment utilizing a Wilcoxian rank sum difference of medians test (instead of a difference-of-means test), examining all committees from the 86th through 97th Congresses. They employ a variety of preference measures (ACA and ADA ratings, conservative coalition scores, and Nominate scores), again finding few outliers, with the Agriculture, Education and Labor, and Armed Services Committees as regular exceptions. Cox and McCubbins also investigate differences in preferences between party contingents on committees and party caucuses and find more outliers, especially on nonprestige committees.

Most recently, Londregan and Snyder (1994) investigate all committees from the 82d through 98th Congresses using a sampling technique that treats observations of members' ideal points in each Congress (measured with Nominate scores) as random draws from a larger distribution, whose true mean is estimated from voting patterns across several Congresses. They then bootstrap standard errors for committee ideal points drawn from these distributions for each Congress, comparing both differences in means and medians. The authors find significantly more support for the outliers hypothesis, claiming that on average about one-third of the committees in each Congress should be classified as outliers.

The evidence on the number of outlying committees, then, is decidedly mixed, ranging from "very few" to "a healthy proportion." It seems clear that the distributive prediction that all committees should be outliers in their policy areas finds very little support, but the alternative thesis of no outliers may not be quite right either. These competing predictions are rather stark, though, largely due to their Congress-centered perspective on policy making: The theories generating them predict either that

169

committees should be representative or unrepresentative of the chamber as a whole.

Our approach starts instead with the premise that the systematic forces shaping committee composition, restrictive rule assignment, and ultimately the content of final legislation come not just from within Congress but from the larger political system as well. If our thesis is correct, then committee composition should not be constant over time, but rather change predictably in response to changes in congressional-executive policy conflict: Committee medians should move counter to changes in the policy preferences of the president, and fewer outliers should be observed during times of unified government.

Outliers in Postwar Standing Committees

We now test these predictions with data drawn from all postwar standing committees. As of the 102d Congress, twenty-two standing committees composed the legislative machinery of the House of Representatives.[6] Relying on the Garrison Nelson (1993) data set, we constructed a list of all committee assignments from the 80th to 102d Congresses.[7] We then combined these rosters with Poole and Rosenthal (1997) Nominate scores, which order members along a general liberal–conservative continuum, to calculate the median committee preferences as well as median party contingent preferences by committee and by Congress. This gave us a total of 478 committee–Congress observations.

From these data a number of variables were constructed. The first set of variables measure policy differences between committees and floor members. **Committee–floor difference** is defined as the median committee Nominate score less the median floor Nominate score. **Committee–party difference** is defined as the median Nominate score of the majority-party committee contingent less the median Nominate score of the majority-party caucus. Positive differences in both measures denote conservative outliers, while negative scores indicate liberal outliers. The absolute values of these two variables are labeled **committee–floor outlier** and **committee–party outlier,** respectively.

Similarly, preference differences between the president and the median

[6]Committees that changed name during this period were identified by their name as of the 102d Congress. Only one committee was abolished completely, the Internal Security Committee, which from the 80th to 90th Congresses was the Committee on Un-American Activities.

[7]These data were compiled while the authors were participants in the Harvard-MIT Research Training Group. We thank Charles Stewart for his assistance. All data were checked against the relevant volumes of the *Congressional Directory;* committee rosters used were those as of the beginning of each Congress.

floor member, labeled **president–floor difference,** were calculated using real ADA scores, while **president–party difference** is defined as the gap between the real ADA score of the president and the median majority party caucus member. These difference variables were coded consistently with the committee measures above, so that negative values indicate that the president is more liberal than the reference group and positive values indicate conservative outliers. Then **president–floor outlier** and **president–party outlier** are the absolute values of these two differences.

It is clear that the greater the variance of preferences within the chamber, the more likely it is that committee medians will vary from floor medians – a point emphasized by Londregan and Snyder (1994). Therefore, we shall include measures of **House polarization** and **party polarization** as control variables, calculated as the standard deviation of the Nominate scores within the House and majority party, respectively. We also include a measure of the **gridlock** region, as defined in Chapter 6, which takes into account both policy conflict between Congress and the executive and polarization within the legislature. Table 7.1 provides a list of summary statistics for all variables.

Results: Committees as Contrary Outliers

Contrary Outliers

The first hypothesis to be tested is that committee ideal points will tend to move counter to those of the president: More, conservative presidents beget more liberal committees, and vice versa. If this is correct, then the committee–floor difference variable should move opposite to president–floor difference. Model 1 from Table 7.2 tests this prediction in an ordinary least squares bivariate regression. As shown, the coefficient on president–floor difference is negative and significant, as predicted. Note also that the constant is negative and significant, indicating that throughout the period studied committees tended to have a liberal bias, which is not too surprising given Democratic control of the House throughout this period for all except the 80th and 83d Congresses.

Model 3 repeats this analysis using committee–party difference as the dependent variable and president–party difference as the independent variable. This model, then, tests to see whether majority-party contingents also tend to move counter to the preferences of the president. The negative and significant coefficient indicates that this is indeed the case. Note also that the constant here is positive, suggesting that party contingents are shaded toward the preferences of the median floor voter, a mirror image of the finding above that overall committee composition is tilted toward the majority party.

171

Table 7.1. *Description of Variables and Summary Statistics*

Variable	Description	Mean	Std. Dev.	Min	Max
Committee-Floor Difference	Median Committee Nominate Score – Median Floor Nominate Score	-0.02	0.12	-0.44	0.57
Committee-Party Difference	Median Majority Party Contingent Nominate Score – Median Party Caucus Nominate Score	0.01	0.10	-0.32	0.42
Committee-Floor Outlier	Absolute Value of Committee-Floor Difference	0.09	0.08	0	0.57
Committee-Party Outlier	Absolute Value of Committee-Party Difference	0.08	0.07	0.001	0.42
President-Floor Difference	President's Real ADA Score—Median House Real ADA Score	-2.50	39.48	-61.20	57.39
President-Party Difference	President's Real ADA Score—Median Majority Party Caucus ADA Score	20.86	42.16	-67.81	79.18
President-Floor Outlier	Absolute Value of President-Floor Difference	35.66	17.03	4.46	61.20
President-Party Outlier	Absolute Value of President-Party Difference	38.67	26.74	1.70	79.18
House Polarization	Standard Deviation of House Nominate Scores	0.33	0.04	0.27	0.47
Party Polarization	Standard Deviation of Majority Party Nominate Scores	0.22	0.03	0.15	0.27
Gridlock	Gridlock interval taking into account congressional filibuster and override procedures, averaged by Congress	39.52	7.39	23.55	59.72

Note: All data averaged by Congress. Total Observations = 478.
Sources: Nominate Scores from Poole and Rosenthal (1997); Real ADA scores from Groseclose, Levitt, and Snyder (1997); Gridlock calculated by the authors in Chapter 6.

To look a little more closely at these results, the data set was divided into two samples: those observations in which the president was a liberal outlier and those where the president was conservative relative to Congress. Rerunning our analysis on these two groups separately, the contrary outlier effect is most pronounced when the president is more conservative than the median House member. Once again, divided government seems to play a significant role in how legislators decide to organize themselves for collective action: Congressional committees react most consistently to conservative Republican presidents as opposed to more liberal Republicans. A time trend was also added to the model and proved to be insignificant, so our results reflect more than just an increasing trend toward policy conflict between Congress and the president. Thus our prediction of committees as contrary outliers is supported in the data.

We can test these findings against two competing models of legislative organization: the informational and party models. The former of these two predicts that committees should reflect the preferences of the median floor voter; the latter, that majority-party contingents are representative of the majority-party caucus. Were these hypotheses correct, the variables committee–floor difference and committee–party difference would be equal to zero, on average. A t-test of these predictions, however, shows that both can be rejected.[8] On the other hand, these differences, while statistically significant, are not so great as to lend much support to the distributive hypothesis that outliers are the norm, as their average values are considerably less than one standard deviation of either the committee–floor difference or committee–party difference variables.

Furthermore, the coefficients on the difference variables in our estimations are significant, as are the overall models, as shown by the F-statistics reported at the bottom of Table 7.2. Our specifications thus outperform simple models predicting that the difference between committee and floor preferences should be constant across all observations. This is not to imply that the former models tell us nothing about legislative organization – we shall argue below that they all contribute to understanding different types of policy making – but rather to state that extra leverage is gained by placing committees within the larger context of our separation of powers system.

---

[8]A null hypothesis that the committee–floor difference is equal to zero can be rejected at the 0.0003 significance level in a two-tailed test. Similarly, a null hypothesis that the committee–party difference is equal to zero can also be rejected at the 0.010 significance level in a two-tailed test.

Table 7.2. *Ordinary Least Squares Estimates Predicting Committee Outliers*

Dep. Var.	Committee-Floor Difference		Committee-Party Difference	
Indep. Var.	Model 1	Model 2	Model 3	Model 4
Constant	-0.020	-0.005	0.017	0.010
	(-3.77)**	(-0.27)	(3.20)**	(0.58)
President-Floor Difference	-0.0002	-0.0002		
	(-1.68)**	(-2.14)**		
President-Party Difference			-0.0002	-0.0002
			(-2.01)**	(-2.33)**
Prestige Committees				
Appropriations		-0.022		0.034
		(-0.80)		(1.44)
Budget		-0.044		-0.039
		(-1.26)		(-1.27)
Rules		-0.11		-0.033
		(-4.17)**		(-1.41)
Ways and Means		-0.042		-0.023
		(-1.54)		(-0.96)
Policy Committees				
Banking, Finance and Urban Affairs		-0.081		-0.062
		(-2.95)**		(-2.65)**
Education and Labor		-0.14		-0.12
		(-5.25)**		(-5.11)**
Energy and Commerce		0.013		-0.01
		(0.46)		(-0.41)
Foreign Affairs		-0.12		-0.07
		(-4.43)**		(-2.96)**
Government Operations		-0.07		-0.049
		(-2.68)**		(-2.10)**
Judiciary		-0.033		-0.047
		(-1.20)		(-2.01)**

(cont.)

Committee-Specific Effects

The regressions including committee-specific dummy variables are also quite revealing. By carefully selecting the reference group for this analysis, we can derive relative committee outliers. In Model 2 of Table 7.2, the omitted category is Public Works and Transportation, the committee whose median was closest to the overall floor median throughout the period studied. In Model 4, the omitted category is the House Administration Committee, whose majority-contingent median was closest to that of the majority-party caucus. Committees with positive coefficients, then, were conservative outliers relative to the composition of the House or majority party, and those with negative coefficients were liberal outliers.

The committees have also been divided into the four categories suggested by Bach and Smith (1988): prestige committees, policy committees, constituency committees, and other committees. The first category

Table 7.2. *(cont.)*

Dep. Var.	Committee-Floor Difference		Committee-Party Difference	
Indep. Var.	Model 1	Model 2	Model 3	Model 4
Constituency Committees				
Agriculture		0.088		0.14
		(3.22)**		(6.00)**
Armed Services		0.080		0.14
		(2.91)**		(5.97)**
Interior		0.010		-0.021
		(0.37)		(-0.92)
Internal Security		0.16		0.12
		(4.92)**		(4.48)**
Merchant Marine and Fisheries		0.005		0.003
		(0.19)		(0.15)
Public Works				0.029
				(1.23)
Science, Space, and Technology		0.016		0.045
		(0.55)		(1.81)*
Small Business		0.012		0.027
		(0.33)		(0.86)
Veterans' Affairs		0.059		0.11
		(2.15)**		(4.70)**
Other Committees				
District of Columbia		-0.051		0.026
		(-1.85)*		(1.10)
House Administration		-0.023		
		(-0.84)		
Post Office and Civil Service		-0.053		-0.045
		(-1.94)*		(-1.90)*
Standards of Official Conduct		0.17		0.06
		(5.35)**		(2.18)**
F_{n-k}^{k}	2.80*	13.59**	4.03**	15.87**

Note: t-statistics in parentheses; two-tailed test *<.10; **<.05. N = 478

includes Appropriations, Rules, Ways and Means, and Budget; members with assignments to any one of the first three of these committees cannot sit on any other committee simultaneously, except for the Budget Committee.[9] These committees consider a wealth of major legislation, including core taxing and spending issues, and are consistently the most highly sought after by House members for their ability to sway important policy.

Slightly less general, but nevertheless quite influential, are Bach and Smith's policy committees: Banking, Education and Labor, Energy and

[9] Membership of the Budget Committee is restricted to five each from Appropriations and Ways and Means and seventeen from other committees. No member can serve on the Budget Committee for more than six years in any ten-year period. For a discussion of these committees and their status within the House, see Smith and Deering (1990, 86–95).

Commerce, Foreign Affairs, Judiciary, and Government Operations. These committees tend to deal with more narrowly tailored issues, which nonetheless generate intense interest from all sides of the political spectrum. On the other hand, the constituency committees – Agriculture; Armed Services; Interior; Merchant Marine; Public Works, Science, Space; and Technology; Small Business; and Veterans' Affairs – all cater to specific policy areas in which one side (the constituency) is mobilized but usually faces no organized counterweight on the opposite side of the issue.

The patterns revealed in the outlier analysis from Models 2 and 4 are, in fact, quite striking. Of the four prestige committees, three (Appropriations, Budget, and Ways and Means) have insignificant coefficients, meaning that they are representative of the floor median. The only prestige committee with a significant coefficient is the Rules Committee, which is a liberal outlier in Model 2 but not Model 4; it is overall more liberal than the median floor voter, but its majority-party contingent is broadly representative of the party as a whole. This finding is in line with previous descriptions of the Rules Committee (including Bach and Smith's own account) as being tilted toward the preferences of the majority-party caucus. Otherwise, the preferences of all prestige committees mirror those of the floor, in line with the predictions of the informational approach that, in the most important policy matters, where committee expertise is essential, floor members gain the most utility from representative committees.

The policy committees, on the other hand, have a uniformly negative or liberal leaning. In four of these committees (Banking, Education and Labor, Foreign Affairs, and Government Operations) this leftward bias is significant in both models. For the Judiciary Committee the sign is also negative, but the coefficient is significant only in Model 4. And for Energy and Commerce the coefficient is positive in Model 2, negative in Model 4, and insignificant in both cases. The policy committees, like prestige committees, are all involved with the shaping of important legislation, although their policy jurisdictions are not quite as broad. Therefore, committee members will face pressures from interest groups on either side of an issue: pro-labor and pro-business for Education and Labor, fiscal conservatives and government activists on Banking, Finance and Urban Affairs, and so on. The liberal bias indicates that the Democrats, the majority party throughout most of our study, stacked these committees with partisans willing to pursue the party line in these policy battles.

The constituent committees show a similar pattern, but with a uniformly positive or conservative sway. Again in four committees – Agriculture, Armed Services, Internal Security, and Veterans Affairs – this conservative bias is consistently significant, while for Science, Space, and Technology it is significant in Model 4 only.[10] In all other cases but one, the sign is positive but not significant at the 10 percent level. The positive bias here may very likely reflect a tendency for certain types of legislators to self-select onto these committees: Members on the Agriculture Committee tend to come from more conservative midwestern and southern states, and similarly, members of the Armed Services, Internal Security, and Veterans' Affairs Committees tend to be pro-military. In both cases, the end result is that the members on the committee are supporters of the narrow constituency that the committee serves, favoring the distribution of benefits to those groups.

The bottom line is that, within a broader framework of legislative organization under separate powers, these results are more or less consistent with the informational, partisan, and distributive theories. Distributive committees are outliers in the direction of their area of distribution, policy committees have a partisan bent, and prestige committees, which require the highest levels of expertise, are representative of the median floor voter. These topics will be explored at greater length in Chapter 8. For now, we note that each of the three seemingly incompatible major theories of legislative organization seems to apply well within its own distinct sphere.

Reining-in Outliers

One counterintuitive prediction of our model is that we should observe more committee outliers under divided government than under unified government. The logic is that, during times of unified government, floor members worry that committees and agencies will work in cahoots with one another to the floor's detriment; this is the classic iron triangle story. To prevent this from occurring, rational floor voters will rein in committees, stacking them with members who are more representative of the floor median. The possibilities of interbranch collusion, then, affect floor preferences over committee composition.

Once stated, this seems like a reasonable prediction. Finding it in the data, however, may pose some difficulties, as party leaders have little leeway in practice to alter committee composition. Given the general norm of a seniority system, very few opportunities exist for changing committee medians from one Congress to the next, except in the case of membership turnover or transfers and strategic appointment of new committee members. Therefore, the effects predicted above will most

[10]As noted above, the Agriculture and Armed Services Committees also emerge as univariate outliers in previous analyses of committee composition.

likely be seen more as incremental responses to changes in congressional–executive conflict rather than abrupt departures from the previous
committee lineups.

Table 7.3 tests our prediction in several ways. The dependent variable
is committee–floor outlier, the absolute value of the committee–floor
difference variable used in Models 1 and 2 above. Absolute values are
used in the analysis to remain consistent with our theoretical model,
which is posed only in terms of congressional–executive conflict without
regard to the direction of these differences, similar to previous tests of
committee outliers. Model 1 examines a simple bivariate relation between this variable and president–floor outlier, the absolute difference
between the president's real ADA score and the median floor member's.
The results show that while the coefficient is in the predicted direction,
it does not pass muster on the significance test.

One reason for this, as Londregan and Snyder (1994) argue, is that
committee outliers should be measured relative to the degree of polarization within the legislature. With this in mind, Model 2 reestimates the
equation with the gridlock variable defined in Chapter 6, which includes
not only congressional–executive conflict but also dispersion of preferences within the legislature, and finds a significant and positive correlation. Model 3 reintroduces the president–floor outlier measure, but this
time controls for the degree of polarization in the majority party and,
similar to the gridlock measure, shows a positive and significant coefficient.[11] Therefore, the hypothesis that committees are more polarized
under higher levels of interbranch conflict receives some measure of
support from the data.

Model 4 from the table disaggregates these results by committee type,
according to the Bach and Smith classification discussed above. The
omitted category is the prestige committees, as they are most representative of floor preferences. The table shows that relative to this baseline
category, as congressional–executive conflict increases, policy committees show no significant effects; these committees were restrained at
about the same rate as prestige committees. Constituency committees,
on the other hand, dampened the effect of congressional–executive con-

---

[11]Note that we use the standard deviation of preferences within the majority party
rather than the House as a whole to control for the initial dispersion of member ideal
points. Since our analysis centers on median ideal points rather than means, the
relevant distribution of medians will be drawn from majority-party members. To put
it another way, we can think of committee medians as the outcome of a game played
by the two major parties at the beginning of each Congress. In this game, the
committee median will be under majority-party control; in equilibrium, minority
parties can only change medians in a direction *opposite* to their own preferences. If
we were to use means instead, then the minority-party appointments would matter
as well, and the chamberwide standard deviation would be used.

Table 7.3. *Ordinary Least Squares Estimates of Committee Outliers and Interbranch Conflict*

Dependent Variable: Committee-Floor Outlier

Indep. Var.	By Committee				By Congress		
	Model 1	Model 2	Model 3	Model 4	Model 1	Model 2	Model 3
President-Floor Outlier	0.0002 (0.91)		0.0004 (1.77)**	0.0004 (1.58)*	0.0004 (1.23)		0.0007 (2.55)**
Gridlock		0.001 (2.25)**				0.002 (2.31)**	
Party Polarization			0.38 (3.14)**	0.37 (3.24)**			0.57 (3.80)**
President-Floor Outlier*Policy				0.00004 (0.15)			
President-Floor Outlier*Constituent				-0.0009 (-3.47)**			
President-Floor Outlier*Other				0.001 (4.16)**			
Constant	0.084 (10.14)**	0.048 (2.48)**	-0.006 (-0.21)	-0.003 (-0.10)	0.099 (7.65)**	0.050 (1.80)*	-0.034 (-0.94)
$F^k_{n\ k}$	0.82	5.08**	5.34**	17.30**	1.51	5.34**	8.47**
Num. Obs.	478	478	478	478	23	23	23

Note: t-statistics in parentheses; one-tailed test *<.10; **<.05.

flict; they were not checked to the same extent as the prestige and policy committees. The "other" committee category, which includes House Administration and Standards of Official Conduct, whose primary function is to oversee and investigate abuses within the executive branch, are reined in more than the prestige committees in response to changes in congressional–executive conflict.

Another way to test the prediction that committees are less dispersed under unified government is to examine the variance in committee medians, Congress by Congress. The right-hand side of Table 7.3 therefore reestimates the models above, with the dependent variable now being the standard deviation of committee medians for each Congress. The results obtained are almost identical: Once we control for the dispersion of ideal points, the interbranch conflict measures are positively correlated with committee outliers.

Table 7.4 presents another view of these same data. Our theory predicts not only that committee medians will be less dispersed under unified government but also that those committees closest to the executive will be curbed the most. This asymmetric narrowing of the range of committee medians is shown graphically in Figure 4.5; as the preferences of executive agencies approach those of the median floor voter, the range of acceptable committees shrinks. The explanation again goes back to the logic of iron triangles, which are most likely to form between committees and executive agencies that share similar policy goals. Since the majority party for most of the period studied was the Democrats, this suggests that liberal outlying committees should be checked more than their conservative counterparts.

Table 7.4, then, examines the most liberal outlying committee (the committee with the minimum Nominate score difference) and the most conservative outlying committee (with the maximum difference), as well as the range separating these two, by Congress. As shown, changes in congressional–executive conflict, represented by the president–floor outlier variable, did affect liberal committees significantly, while the impact on conservative committees, though in the expected direction, was significant only in Model 4.[12] And, as illustrated in Models 5 and 6, the range between the most liberal and most conservative committees narrowed significantly as congressional–executive conflict decreased. Furthermore, the standardized coefficients on the president–floor outlier variable in these regressions range from 0.252 to 0.499, indicating that a one standard deviation change in congressional–executive conflict gives

---

[12]This finding is consistent with the observation that constituency committees are pulled in less than others during the period studied, as these committees tend to be conservative outliers (as indicated in Table 7.2).

Table 7.4. *Ordinary Least Squares Estimates of Committee Outliers and Interbranch Conflict*

Dep. Var.	Minimum Diff.		Maximum Diff.		Range	
Indep. Var.	Model 1	Model 2	Model 3	Model 4	Model 5	Model 6
President-Floor Outlier	-0.002	-0.002	0.002	0.002	0.003	0.004
	(-1.77)**	(-2.26)**	(1.20)	(1.73)**	(1.83)**	(2.63)**
Party Polarization		-0.98		1.37		2.34
		(-1.76)**		(1.86)**		(2.44)**
Constant	-0.18	0.046	0.15	-0.17	0.34	-0.21
	(-4.68)**	(0.34)**	(2.90)**	(-0.94)	(4.65)**	(-0.91)
F_n^k	3.12*	3.27*	1.44	2.54	3.36*	5.05**

Note: t-statistics in parentheses; one-tailed test *<.10; **<.05. N = 23

181

rise to anywhere from a quarter to a half of a standard deviation change in the degree to which a given committee is a preference outlier.

These findings all lend support to our hypothesis that committee composition reacts to changes in the larger political environment. Legislative organization may well reflect members' desire to solve their own sets of collective dilemmas, but it also reflects the fact that final policy outcomes are shaped by forces external to Congress. Legislative policy making is but the first step in a long process that ends with executive branch implementation, and our evidence suggests that the preferences of these ultimate actors exert an influence on the way in which legislators initially organize themselves to conduct business.

COMMITTEES, PARTIES, AND DELEGATION

What Do Committee Outliers Predict?

Another strand of the committee composition literature uses committee–floor differences to predict other political variables of interest. Here the focus of the research has been almost exclusively on procedural measures, in particular closed or open rules assigned to bills emerging from a particular committee. The importance of these procedures is highlighted in Bach and Smith (1988, 12): "The Rules Committee stands at the crossroads of the legislative process in the House. Nearly all major legislation passes through Suite H313, its hearing room in the Capitol, so most members make their way there at one time or another to ask the committee to grant them favored treatment or somehow protect their interests in its special rules."[13]

Not only are special rules an important source of parliamentary advantage for committees, they also provide a convenient testing ground for competing theories of legislative organization, as the distributive, informational, and party-based approaches advance different predictions about which committees should receive these restrictive rules. Toward this end, Krehbiel (1991) analyzes all special rules in the 99th Congress, using various proxies for a bill's distributive content and committee specialization as predictive variables for the distributive and informational views, respectively. His results provide support for a majoritarian model of special rules, as the informational variables were correlated with a greater probability of receiving a closed rule, while the distributive variables were associated with more-open rules.

Recently, several studies have reanalyzed restrictive rules data from a

[13]The key role that the Rules Committee plays in the legislative process has long been recognized. See, for example, Alexander (1916), Hasbrouck (1927), Robinson (1963), and Sinclair (1983).

party-based perspective. Sinclair (1995) examines special rules associated with the passage of major legislation in the 100th and 101st Congresses, including as independent variables Krehbiel's measures of distributive and informational content, as well as three party-related indicators: party leadership involvement, party–floor coalition, and omnibus or multiply referred bills. Although Sinclair provides some of the first systematic evidence in support of party control over rules, her findings are somewhat limited by possible endogeneity problems in the measurement of her party variables.

Dion and Huber (1996) present and test an alternative model of the rule assignment process that takes into account the policy preferences of the Rules Committee itself. Their theoretical model predicts that closed rules should be more common when the preferences of the reporting committee lie in between those of the Rules Committee and the floor. The authors test their model against the percentage of closed rules assigned to all committees between the 94th and 98th Congresses and find support for their thesis. Although not explicitly a party-based model, Dion and Huber's approach predicts that expected outcomes will be biased in some cases toward the Rules Committee's preferences, which are usually representative of majority-party leadership.[14]

So far, then, the literature on committee outliers has been limited to predicting the incidences of restrictive rules. While clearly an important aspect of the legislative process, this focus on parliamentary procedures is rather narrow. We shall address issues surrounding restrictive rules and delegation later in the chapter, but our purpose in this section is to broaden the debate by relating the preferences of the committee that reported a given bill directly to final policy outcomes, in particular, to the amount of discretionary authority delegated to the executive branch.

Methods for Measuring Committee Outliers

The model outlined in Chapter 4 predicts that Congress will rely more heavily on the executive branch for policy details as committees become less representative of the median floor voter. Thus, outlying committees should be linked to greater executive discretion. These effects are attenuated, though, at higher levels of congressional–executive policy conflict, so the impact of committee outliers on discretion should fall during times of divided as opposed to unified government.

Testing these hypotheses requires, first, a measure of committee out-

[14]The predictions and empirical tests contained in this paper are further elaborated in an exchange between the authors and Krehbiel (1997).

liers. From the previous section, two immediate alternatives are the committee–floor difference and the committee–party difference. A third possibility derives from the conditional party government literature, which asserts that when the majority party is united (has homogeneous preferences), members will be more willing to delegate resources to party leaders. These leaders, in turn, employ a system of selective incentives to sustain party-based bargains and enact the party's policy agenda. Rohde (1991, 31) states: "Unlike in parliamentary systems, party would not be the dominant influence across all issues, and the leadership would not make policy decisions which would receive automatic support from the rank and file. Rather, there would be party responsibility *only* *if* there were widespread policy agreement among House Democrats." As the majority party becomes less cohesive, then, party leadership will be weak, bargains will be harder to sustain, and policy-making power will devolve to the median floor voter.[15]

If we take the conditional party government theory as a maintained hypothesis, we arrive at two separate predictions for measuring committee outliers. First, cohesive majority parties should be associated with fewer committee outliers, as party leaders will have the authority to align members' preferences through the selective provision of rewards and sanctions. Thus, committee and floor members' preferences will be more closely attuned than their roll-call voting records would otherwise indicate.

Second, one can construct a novel measure of committee outliers that combines both the median voter and partisan approaches. If parties are strongest when the majority coalition is most united on policy issues, then when parties act as a coherent unit the relevant measure of outliers is the committee–party difference; and when parties are disunited, the correct measure will be the committee–floor difference, in line with median voter theories. Thus, we might observe a sliding scale, moving from partisan to majoritarian outcomes as intraparty preferences become more or less homogeneous.

The empirical predictions following from this sliding-scale hypothesis can be represented algebraically as follows. Let d represent the amount of discretion delegated to the executive, let CommOutlier represent the degree to which a committee's policy preferences diverge from those of the median voter, and let MajCoh be the majority party cohesion. Then we can write:

---

[15]For a complete exposition of the conditional party government hypothesis, see also Cooper and Brady (1981) and Brady and Epstein (1997). Banks and Calvert (1992) provide a formal model linking homogeneous intraparty preferences, delegation to party leaders, and more-efficient policy making.

$d = \alpha + \beta(\text{CommOutlier});$
$\text{CommOutlier} = (1 - \lambda)^*\text{FloorOutlier} + \lambda^*\text{PartyOutlier};$
$\lambda = \text{MajCoh}.$

This implies that:

$\text{CommOutlier} = (1 - \text{MajCoh})^*\text{FloorOutlier}$
$\qquad\qquad + (\text{MajCoh}^*\text{PartyOutlier});$
$d = \alpha + \beta_1{}^*\text{FloorOutlier} - \beta_2{}^*(\text{MajCoh}^*\text{FloorOutlier})$
$\qquad + \beta_3{}^*(\text{MajCoh}^*\text{PartyOutlier}).$ (Eq. 7.1)

In other words, we can implement the sliding-scale measure of committee outliers by including a combination of interactive terms in our analysis, the prediction being that the signs on committee–floor outlier and MajCoh*committee–party outlier will be positive, and the sign on MajCoh*committee–floor outlier will be negative.

Committee Outliers and Delegation

The data for this stage of the analysis are the same as in the previous section, with three amendments. First, they are aggregated by bill rather than spanning the entire set of postwar committees, so an observation is a public law–committee pair, the prediction being that bills emerging from outlying committees should delegate more authority to the executive branch. Second, to implement the propositions concerning majority-party unity outlined in equation 7.1, we measure **majority-party cohesion** as the inverse of the party polarization variable above; that is, the inverse of the standard deviation of majority-party Nominate scores, Congress by Congress. Third, the dependent variable in the analysis is the amount of discretion delegated to the executive, law by law, as defined in Chapter 5.

Table 7.5 displays the results of our analysis. The first model includes both the floor and party outlier terms. As shown, the party outlier variable is significant while the floor outlier variable is not, giving some support to the partisan thesis. The next column adds the majority-party cohesion variable to the analysis. Again, the coefficient on party outliers is significant and in the predicted direction, while the floor outlier variable is still insignificant. And as hypothesized, the majority-party cohesion variable is a significant predictor of delegation: The more disunited the majority party, the more discretion is delegated to the executive branch.

The next two models incorporate two measures of the interactive effect between committee outliers and congressional–executive conflict; the first interacts committee–floor outlier with Divided, the second inter-

185

Table 7.5. *Ordinary Least-Squares Estimates of Legislative Organization and Discretion*

Indep. Var.	Dependent Variable: Average Discretion					
	Model 1	Model 2	Model 3	Model 4	Model 5	Model 6
Committee-Floor Outlier	-0.042	-0.063	0.023	-0.097	1.18	1.17
	(-0.32)	(-0.49)	(0.17)	(-0.74)	(2.23)**	(2.21)**
Committee-Party Outlier	0.33	0.30	0.33	0.45		
	(2.18)**	(1.99)**	(2.20)**	(2.59)**		
Majority Cohesion		-0.022	-0.021	-0.021		
		(-1.75)**	(-1.73)**	(-1.74)**		
Committee-Floor Outlier*Divided			-0.28		-0.25	
			(-1.96)**		(-1.80)**	
Committee-Party Outlier*Divided				-0.30		-0.29
				(-1.76)**		(-1.71)**
Committee-Floor Outlier*Cohesion					-0.27	-0.29
					(-2.19)**	(-2.37)**
Committee-Party Outlier*Cohesion					0.075	0.11
					(2.08)**	(2.51)**
Constant	0.14	0.24	0.24	0.24	0.14	0.15
	(10.78)**	(4.09)**	(4.09)**	(4.14)**	(10.73)**	(10.82)**
$F_n^k \; k$	2.92*	3.02**	3.29**	3.02**	3.29**	3.18**
Num. Obs.	251	251	251	251	250	250

Note: t-statistics in parentheses, robust linear regression; one-tailed test *<.10; **<.05. Observations with Cooks distances above 0.04 eliminated from sample.

186

acts committee–party outlier with Divided. In either case, the predicted sign from our model is negative: The impact of committee outliers on discretion should be attenuated as interbranch conflict over policy increases. As the table shows, both variables yield significant coefficients in the predicted direction. Even after accounting for these effects, the party outlier variable remains significant while the floor outlier variable is not. Furthermore, comparing coefficients in standardized regressions showed that the substantive impact of party outliers, majority-party cohesion, and the interactive terms on executive discretion were nearly equal.

These results, taken at face value, might tend to support a party-based view of legislative organization: Differences between majority-party committee contingents and majority-party caucuses predict executive discretion, while overall committee–floor differences do not. On the other hand, as noted above, it may be that both median voters and parties influence delegation, but at different times. If the sliding-scale measure of committee outliers correctly captures committee–floor conflict, then parties will matter when internal cohesion is high, and the pendulum will swing back toward floor majorities when the majority-party caucus is disunited.

Models 5 and 6 of Table 7.5 explore this possibility, incorporating the interactive terms derived in equation 7.1 above. The prediction is that the signs on the committee–floor outlier and committee–party outlier*cohesion variables should be positive, and the sign on committee–floor outlier*cohesion should be negative. As the table shows, all coefficients in these regressions are significant and in the predicted direction, including committee–floor outlier. In other words, when measured correctly, both median voter and partisan influences are significant in predicting executive branch discretion. And the overall results strongly support our theory of delegation under separate powers: The less representative committees are of floor preferences, the more likely Congress is to cede discretionary authority to executive branch actors.

LEGISLATIVE PROCEDURES AND EXECUTIVE DISCRETION

We now extend our analysis to the impact of parliamentary procedures, including restrictive rules and multiple referrals, on delegated authority. Previous studies of congressional policy making suggest that restrictive rules are a key element of a well-functioning legislative system, whether it be to protect distributive logrolls, promote committee specialization, or shield party agendas from unfriendly amendments.[16] If so, our theory would predict that the more restrictive rules are employed the less likely Congress is to delegate authority to the executive. Similarly, multiple referrals are a means by which members can break up monopolistic committee jurisdictions and combine the expertise of many committees on complex policy matters.[17] The use of multiple referrals, then, should also be linked to less authority being delegated to the executive.

Restrictive Rules

We first investigate the use of restrictive rules. For each of the 257 laws in our sample, we coded for whether the rule associated with its passage restricted amendments and debate. We adopt Krehbiel's (1991, 168) definition of restrictive rules: "The key determinants of a restrictive rule are whether it either stipulates that only amendments specified in the rule itself are in order, or provides for consideration of the legislation in the House as opposed to [the] Committee of the Whole." In our sample, 233 laws were assigned a special rule, of which 149 were nonrestrictive and 85 were restrictive. An additional fifteen bills passed under suspension of the rules; these were eliminated from our analysis because they did not pass through both a standing committee and the Rules Committee. For the remaining eight bills, we were unable to obtain special rules.[18]

What explains the incidence of these restrictive rules across time and issues areas? Table 7.6 associates restrictive rules with the committee that reported the bill and the average amount of discretion delegated to the executive. As would be expected, the prestige committees – Appropriations, Budget, and Ways and Means – commonly received restrictive rules. In fact, 93.6 percent of the bills reported from these committees received restrictive rules, as opposed to a rate of about 20 percent for committees in all other categories. Equally notable is the fact that the average amount of discretion is, in general, inversely related to the percentage of restrictive rules; laws reported by committees that receive a high proportion of restrictive rules tend to rely relatively little on executive decision making.

---

[16]Gilligan and Krehbiel (1987), for instance, predict that closed rules will be used more often when committees and floor members share similar policy preferences, as an inducement for committees to gather specialized information.

[17]Austen-Smith (1993) offers a model of multiple referrals, concluding that they will dominate single referrals when committees are less of a policy outlier with respect to the floor.

[18]These were Public Laws 82–165, 84–880, 87–41, 87–415, 90–351, 92–5, 96–39, and 99–177.

Table 7.6. *Restrictive Rules and Discretion, by Committee*

Committee	Number of Laws	Percent of Restrictive Rules	Average Discretion
Agriculture	21	19%	23.81%
Appropriations	2	100%	12.00%
Armed services	3	0%	50.33%
Banking, Finance and Urban Affairs	22	9.1%	19.74%
Budget	3	100%	5.00%
District of Columbia	1	0%	18.00%
Education and Labor	25	12%	16.85%
Energy and Commerce	42	31%	26.53%
Foreign Affairs	10	20%	24.33%
Government Operations	5	0%	20.20%
House Administration	1	100%	7.00%
Internal Security	1	0%	13.00%
Judiciary	18	17%	12.40%
Merchant Marine And Fisheries	1	0%	24.00%
Natural Resources	8	0%	14.90%
Post Office And Civil Service	2	0%	8.33%
Public Works And Transportation	16	31%	21.67%
Rules	1	0.00%	4.00%
Science, Space, And Technology	1	0.00%	50.00%
Ways and Means	41	95%	8.45%

Note: Small Business, Standards of Official Conduct, and Veterans' Affairs reported no laws in our sample.

Another interesting observation is that restrictive rules are more common during times of divided government. Table 7.7 breaks down the percentage of restrictive rules by divided and unified government and shows that Congress was over 50 percent more likely to give committees restrictive rules when a president of the opposite party controlled the White House. This may in part reflect the desire of legislators, faced with a contrary president, to act more cohesively: Members have incentives to streamline the legislative process when faced with the prospect of delegating authority to executive branch actors who do not share their policy preferences.

These findings may also be due in some part to a time trend in the use of restrictive rules. Figure 7.1, showing the percentages of important legislation enacted under a restrictive rule in each Congress, suggests that this claim is not wholly unfounded. Prior to the 94th Congress, only in one session, the 84th, did Congress grant restrictive rules to over 50 percent of all important legislation. After the 94th Congress, the statement is just the opposite; only the 96th Congress enacted less than 50 percent of important legislation under nonrestrictive rules.

189

Table 7.7. *Restrictive Rules by Divided Government*

		Restrictive Rule		
		No	Yes	Total
Unified	Percent	72.55%	27.45%	
	N	74	28	102
Divided	Percent	56.49%	43.51%	
	N	74	57	131
Total	Percent	63.52%	36.48%	100%
	N	148	85	233

Regression analysis of these patterns yields Table 7.8, which reports probit estimates of the likelihood of observing restrictive rules.[19] Model 1 includes divided government and party polarization as independent variables, showing that restrictive rules are more common when congressional–executive conflict is high, and as the majority party becomes more cohesive. Model 2 adds House polarization to the analysis, demonstrating that as overall House preferences diverge, restrictive rules are more likely. Model 3, on the other hand, includes a time trend, which is both significant and swamps the effect of divided government. Therefore, the direct impact of divided government on restrictive rules should be interpreted cautiously.

Taken together, the two polarization variables suggest that partisan forces may be at work in the construction of major legislation. When the majority party is united behind a policy program, restrictive rules help bind the coalition together by preventing unfriendly amendments that might unravel the agreement. When majority caucus members disagree over policy direction, on the other hand, they are less likely to commit to a restrictive rule. And greater polarization in the House as a whole, partly reflected in greater conflict between the parties, will make it even more important to protect the majority-party agenda from minority-party interference.

Finally, we come to our central hypothesis, that restrictive rules should be associated with less discretionary authority being delegated to the executive. As shown in Table 7.9, the average discretion for laws with nonrestrictive rules was 21.9 percent, and the average discretion

[19]In the regression analysis, the Civil Rights Restoration Act of 1987 (PL 100–259) was omitted because it was never considered by a House committee. This controversial measure was passed in the Senate and, to avoid any further delay, bypassed normal House committee procedures and was taken directly from the Senate to the Rules Committee, where it received a restrictive rule.

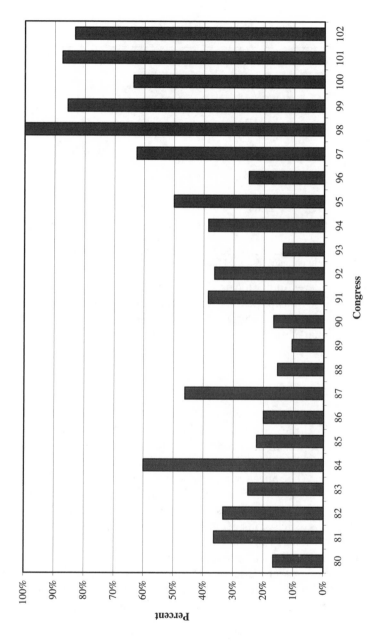

Figure 7.1. Percentage of Restrictive Rules by Congress, 1947–1992

Table 7.8. *Probit Estimates of Restrictive Rules and Congressional–Executive Conflict*

Dependent Variable: Restrictive Rule=1

	Model 1	Model 2	Model 3
Divided	0.43	0.36	0.11
	(2.43)**	(2.01)**	(0.57)
Party	-9.98	-8.53	-7.23
Polarization	(-3.34)**	(-2.81)**	(-2.31)**
House		5.99	6.64
Polarization		(2.54)**	(2.59)**
Congress			0.053
			(3.04)**
Constant	1.64	-0.55	-5.72
	(2.41)**	(-0.50)	(-2.74)**
χ_k^2	17.4**	24.3**	33.8**

Note: z-scores in parentheses; one-tailed test *<.10; **<.05. N=232

for laws considered under a closed rule was 11.1 percent. This difference is statistically significant at the 0.0001 level; so once again, we find that the more reliable the legislative process, the less authority delegated to executive branch actors.

Multiple Referrals

A similar scenario emerges when we examine the use of multiple referrals. Since 1977 (the 95th Congress), the Speaker has had the power to refer bills to more than one committee, representing an end to the sharp delineation of committee jurisdictions that dominated most of the postwar Congresses. The Speaker possesses several procedural options when multiply referring a bill. The bill can be considered in its entirety simultaneously by several committees at once; it can be divided into a series of smaller bills, each considered by a different committee, and then combined into a single bill on the House floor; or the entire bill can be sequentially referred to a series of committees, often with time limits imposed at the Speaker's discretion.[20] In all cases, individual committees lose their monopoly rights over certain areas of legislation in return for access to others. Policy making is consequently less influenced by individ-

[20]See Collie and Cooper (1989) for a review of the use and political significance of multiple referral. See Bawn (1996) for an analysis of the strategies behind multiple referrals and an interesting application to the Energy Mobilization Board of 1979.

Table 7.9. *Restrictive Rules, Multiple Referral, and Discretion*

		Restrictive Rule		
		No	Yes	Total
Single Referral	Avg. Discretion	21.89%	11.24%	**18.21%**
	N	144	76	**220**
Multiple Referral	Avg. Discretion	21.50%	9.44%	**13.15%**
	N	4	9	**13**
Total	**Avg. Discretion**	**21.87%**	**11.05%**	**17.93%**
	N	**148**	**85**	**233**

ual committees as power shifts to both party mechanisms and floor voters.

Insofar as multiple referral helps to curb the excesses of the committee system and allows the expertise of many individual actors to shape legislation, it should increase the efficacy of the legislative process. According to our theory, then, multiple referral should also be associated with less delegation to the executive branch. Unfortunately, as was the case with vetoes in the previous chapter, relatively few bills in our sample were multiply referred. Of the seventy-five public laws passed since the 95th Congress, only twelve were considered by more than one committee.[21] Such a small sample makes robust conclusions difficult.

Nonetheless, such differences as exist are shown in Table 7.9. The average level of executive discretion in laws that were singly referred was 18.2 percent, as opposed to 13.2 percent for all multiple referrals. If we restrict our attention to laws passed from the 95th Congress on, average discretion in single referrals was 14.5 percent as compared to 9.8 percent for multiply referred bills, and this gap is significant at the 10 percent level in a one-tailed test. Though far from conclusive, these results are at least in the predicted direction and offer additional support for the hypothesis that parliamentary devices that make the legislative process more efficient consequently make delegation to the executive less attractive.

[21] In addition, one bill in our sample prior to the 95th Congress, the Federal Election Campaign Act of 1971, was de facto multiply referred. Two committees, the House Administration and Interstate and Foreign Commerce Committees, shared jurisdiction and reported versions that were later merged on the House floor.

SUMMARY

This chapter placed the discussion of legislative organization within the broader institutional context of our separation of powers system. Since policy making does not begin and end within Congress, we argue, the manner in which legislators organize themselves will reflect the preferences of other actors within the governmental system, including the executive branch. Working from this premise, we derive a series of hypotheses relating committee outliers and discretion to interbranch policy conflict.

The results presented above support our hypotheses in all cases. Committee medians move contrary to changes in executive preferences; we observe fewer committee outliers during times of unified government; the presence of committee outliers and a less cohesive majority party are linked to the delegation of greater discretionary authority to executive branch actors; and procedural devices that improve the efficacy of the legislative process also lead legislators to delegate less than otherwise.

Our findings highlight the important and complex linkages between congressional committees and executive branch agencies, the two work engines of policy production. Committees and agencies may at times implicitly collude with each other, as in the classic iron triangle story. Rational floor voters will anticipate this, though, and our results indicate that legislative organization reflects to some degree their desire to limit interbranch collusion. Committees and agencies can also check each other's power: Committees restrain agencies through the oversight process and by serving as an alternative source of expertise in policy production, and agencies provide legislative majorities with a substitute for policy making through committees. Whereas committees have sometimes been portrayed as monopolists in their policy jurisdictions, then, our approach makes it clear that they face credible competition from executive bureaus, and vice versa.

We also address the literatures on legislative organization and the committee system. Theories that explain strong committees as a rational response to legislators' reelection needs must necessarily be incomplete, we argue, as legislators from all political systems share the same basic goals, yet few have instituted a division of labor as complete as that found in the United States. This decentralization of authority must therefore derive from the institutions of governance exterior to Congress, which include first-past-the-post elections, bicameralism, and separate powers.

Taking this perspective on the problem immediately casts new light on some long-standing debates. First, rather than argue over which specific needs committees serve, the question becomes, why fulfill these needs by vesting power in committees rather than elsewhere? Combining the results in the previous two chapters, it seems that Congress continuously recalibrates the division of power between committees and agencies according to the degree to which either of these two actors share legislators' policy preferences. Concerning the measurement of committee outliers, rather than ask whether committees are representative of the floor, the majority party, both, or neither, our approach leads us to ask which factors outside of Congress will influence the degree to which committees are preference outliers. We found support for the proposition that executive branch preferences exert a systematic effect on committee composition, producing contrary outliers. Finally, we developed a statistical technique for modeling situations in which both partisan and median voter influences affect outcomes. Our analysis indicates that committee outliers did influence executive branch discretion, with outliers measured on a sliding scale between the majority-party caucus and the House as a whole.

In passing, we also noted that different categories of committees gave rise to different patterns of committee outliers: Informationally intense issue areas generated representative committees; broad policy committees were given a partisan tilt; and constituency committees were slanted in favor of the narrow groups they served. This division of committees corresponds to the collective action problems highlighted by each theory: the difficulties in incorporating the specialized knowledge possessed by committee members, the breakdown of attempts to formulate and implement the majority party's agenda, and the inability to create and maintain distributive programs, respectively. It may be, then, that each of the distributive, informational, and partisan theories predicts outcomes accurately in its own relevant domain. These areas, of course, need not be mutually exclusive or operate in neatly separable spheres. Still, our approach emphasizes that different policies will have different politics, the subject to which we now turn.

8

Delegation and Issue Areas

Each type of policy generates and is therefore surrounded by its own distinctive set of political relationships. These relationships in turn help to determine substantive, concrete outcomes when policy decisions emerge.

Randall Ripley and Grace Franklin,
Congress, the Bureaucracy, and Public Policy[1]

INTRODUCTION

The notion that different issues are characterized by different politics shaped much of the earlier work on policy making, where it was common to classify issues by the political environment within which they were conceived. For example, Lowi (1964) and Wilson (1974) focus on the degree of concentration of costs and benefits, in order to group different policies by their distributive nature. Fiorina (1982) argues that issues benefiting a few key special interests at the expense of everyone else will be unpopular and are therefore good candidates for legislators to delegate to regulatory agencies. Ripley and Franklin (1984) similarly arrange policies into six different areas, each with its own distinct pattern of interest-group mobilization and congressional–executive relations.

Many analyses of congressional lawmaking follow a similar scheme of distinguishing issue areas by their political patterns. Fenno (1973), in his classic work on the committee system, analyzed six House committees and argued that differences in external constraints, subcommittee power, partisanship, and specialization all influenced the relative overall success of these committees in enacting legislation. Cox and McCubbins (1993) also organize committees according to the political environment

[1]Ripley and Franklin (1984, 22).

196

within which they conduct business, focusing on the homogeneity or heterogeneity of their clientele group and whether the externalities of the policies they generate are targeted, mixed, or uniform. They argue that committees will be representative only in those areas where it is important to party members to keep control of the committee decision process.

This chapter expands on these previous analyses by examining the distinguishing characteristics of those policy areas that are highly delegated to the executive branch. The major prediction arising from our model of strategic delegation in this respect is that, all else being equal, policy areas shrouded in uncertainty will tend to be delegated at higher rates.

The key to testing these predictions is to derive some method of categorizing issues by their distributive and/or informational components. As no single system captures all the facets of our approach, we shall depend on several classifying schemes. First, we divide policy by existing issue-area categories provided in Mayhew (1991) and Poole and Rosenthal (1997) to see if a natural pattern emerges from the data. We then present our measure of informational intensity – committee hearings – and determine if those committees that hold more hearings, including oversight hearings, delegate more to the executive. Finally, we investigate issues surrounding distributive politics and delegation through a series of case studies on agriculture, trade policy, and the line-item veto.

ISSUES, DELEGATION, AND PUBLIC LAWS

Our first approach to delegation and issue areas is simply to classify each of our public laws into categories and then compare average levels of discretion across these categories. This exercise will allow us to examine if those issues with the least potential political benefits relative to informational costs are in fact delegated at higher rates. Here, political benefits are generated by the opportunity to tailor policy for a highly mobilized group, while costs are generated when politicians are associated with policy failure, especially when many constituents are greatly harmed. Our theory predicts that legislators will delegate authority when the political costs of making policy themselves outweigh the corresponding benefits.

Delegation by Issue Area

A number of issue classifications already exist in the literature on policy making, one of which comes from Mayhew himself in *Divided We Govern*, the source from which our data set is drawn. Mayhew classifies those enactments in his sample passed between 1947 and 1986 into a series of forty-three categories. Enactments could be assigned to one or many categories, so classifications are nonexclusive.[2] On average, laws were assigned to 1.36 categories, the maximum for any one law being five. All that remains is to obtain the average discretion for the bills in each of Mayhew's categories, using the discretion measure developed in Chapter 5. The results are shown in Table 8.1 and are arranged in increasing order of delegation, including the number of laws classified in each category.

As indicated, the low end of the delegation spectrum is dominated by tax and social security issues. Also prominent are minimum wage and unemployment insurance laws and laws pertaining to legislative–executive relations. Two anomalies at this end of the table are worth further examination. The first is Soviet Relations, which would seem ripe for delegation along with other foreign policy issues. In fact, the only enactment from this category included in our data set is the Foreign Assistance Act of 1948 (PL 80-472) passed under divided government, which spelled out in detail the amount of foreign aid to be dispersed among several countries. Not included in our data set were three treaties that fell into the Soviet Relations category, all of which necessarily had high executive branch input since they were negotiated by the president and ratified by the Senate.

The other anomalous category is poverty, which seems to fit the description of broad social programs that are usually delegated. Of the eleven enactments classified in this category, though, seven were in fact social security bills or public debt extensions that included social security provisions. These laws had an average discretion index of 3.96 percent. By contrast, the four true antipoverty laws had an average discretion index of 21.75 percent, a score that would place them near the top of the list, alongside public housing.

Those laws that delegate the most authority pertain to foreign relations and space and technology. Also at the high end of delegation ratios are consumer and product safety laws and legislation concerning the environment and public health. Two surprising areas that we see highly delegated are trade and agriculture, usually described as quintessential distributive issues. In both these areas, however, Congress seems to have delegated a considerable amount of discretionary authority to executive agencies. We shall return to these issue in greater detail below.

For another view of the data, we analyze the issue categories that Poole and Rosenthal (1997) assign to roll-call votes, in their study of

[2]This breakdown was the starting point for Mayhew's "Sweep Two" laws, as described in Chapter 5.

Table 8.1. *Mayhew Categorization of Laws and Average Discretion*

Mayhew Category	Number of Laws	Average Discretion
Copyright	1	3.27%
Social Security	7	4.10%
Taxes	22	4.40%
Soviet Relations	1	5.71%
Minimum Wage	6	5.90%
Campaign Finance	2	6.68%
Pensions (Private)	1	7.14%
Unemployment Insurance	2	7.28%
Legislative-Executive Relation	2	9.21%
Civil Service	1	9.63%
Poverty	11	10.43%
Immigration	3	11.73%
Criminal Code	1	12.66%
Labor-Management Relations	2	12.76%
Energy	9	13.62%
Water Projects	2	14.58%
Employment	13	15.39%
Federalism	11	15.92%
Post Office	1	16.12%
Wage & Price Controls	2	17.14%
Deregulation	16	17.50%
Transportation	13	17.84%
Civil Rights	9	18.07%
Employment Opportunity	4	19.66%
Public Lands	5	20.26%
Housing	8	21.03%
DOD Reorganization	1	21.83%
Cities	13	22.69%
Nuclear Energy	3	22.95%
Food Stamps	4	23.42%
Agriculture	13	23.85%
Arts & Humanities	1	24.35%
Occupational Safety	2	24.45%
Education	9	24.76%
Environment	16	26.13%
Consumer Protection	6	29.90%
Health	7	30.15%
Foreign Trade	7	30.25%
Foreign Aid	7	34.93%
Space	5	45.09%

Congress. The authors match every roll-call vote taken in Congress from 1789 through 1988 to one of ninety-nine issue categories. Chapter 6 described the collection of all roll calls associated with the laws in our data set, so starting from this point we were able to identify every issue category associated with at least one roll call for any given bill. Of the ninety-nine categories, fifty-four appeared in our data set.[3] We then averaged the discretion given to the executive branch across bills in the same category.

The results of this tabulation are shown in Table 8.2. The patterns from this table broadly match those from the previous analysis. Again, taxes, minimum wage, and social security are entrenched at the low end of the discretion continuum. More traditional pork barrel programs inhabit the middle region, with agriculture and trade again a bit higher than one might expect. And the high end is dominated by social programs and defense issues, including space exploration and nuclear weapons.

Delegation by Committee

A third method of dividing public laws into different issue categories is to classify them according to the House committee or committees that reported them to the floor. This method of categorization is valid so long as committee jurisdictions remain relatively stable throughout the sample period. Luckily, the years that we analyze are bracketed by the two major reforms in postwar committee jurisdictions, those in 1946 and 1995; the two intervening reforms in 1974 and 1980 did little more than ratify the gradual drift in jurisdictions that had accumulated over the previous years.[4] We therefore analyze the average amount of executive discretion, by reporting committee.

Figure 8.1 graphs each bill by reporting committee and level of discretion for all committees associated with more than one important piece of legislation. One notable omission from this figure is the Appropriations Committee; this is because Mayhew's list of important enactments excludes appropriations bills by construction. Another important committee not on the chart is Rules, which was the original reporting committee for only one bill in our sample.

To help visualize the patterns in the data, each graph also contains a smoothing spline that connects the points according to a best-fit cubic

---

[3] In our sample, seventy-three laws were enacted without a roll call or had no Poole-Rosenthal code assigned to them and therefore are not included in this part of the analysis.

[4] See King (1997, chap. 3) for a discussion of changing committee jurisdictions.

function. The graph shows some interesting trends across committees and over time. Some committees reported important legislation at a fairly constant rate over the period, including Agriculture, Banking, and Ways and Means. And of course, the Budget and Internal Security Committees are relevant only for those years in which they existed. But other committees have clear temporal patterns apparent in the graph. Most of the activity from Foreign Affairs occurred in the 1950s and early 1960s, during the heyday of Cold War legislation. Education, Judiciary, and Public Works were especially active during the Great Society era, but have been less so in the 1970s and 1980s. And Energy and Commerce was active throughout the period, but especially in the post-oil-shock 1970s.

The figure also shows differences in levels of discretion across committees, with discretion levels within each committee remaining fairly stable over time. Thus, Agriculture and Banking bills delegate high levels of discretion, while Ways and Means is uniformly low. Notice also that the pattern of discretion in bills originating from Energy and Commerce seems to decline over time, as indicated by its downward sloping spline function. In fact, this is the one committee whose jurisdiction was most affected by the 1974 and 1980 reforms, so the shift may reflect the committee's desire to move toward more-autonomous issue areas.

Variations in discretion across issue areas are most easily seen in Figure 8.2, which includes all committees in our sample. For each committee, the lighter bar shows the average discretion for all laws referred to that committee, while the darker bar shows the same statistic adjusted for multiple referrals. Thus, if a bill was referred to four committees, the discretion in that law would be weighted one-fourth as much as that in bills referred solely to that committee when calculating averages.

The patterns emerging from this analysis accord well with the results from the two previous classifications. Once again, foreign policy and social issues dominate the high-discretion laws, while budgetary and tax issues exhibit the lowest discretion. Again, Agriculture is perhaps surprisingly high on the discretion scale. Banking, Finance, and Urban Affairs seems rather high as well, until one discovers that most activity in this committee was generated through the latter jurisdiction, urban affairs bills passed mainly in the 1960s and 1970s.

Patterns and Analysis

The three different methods for classifying issues thus lead us to the same conclusion: Legislators closely guard policy-making authority in those areas that afford them an opportunity to target benefits to particular constituents. Tax policy, of course, is the ultimate example of

Table 8.2. *Poole-Rosenthal Vote Categories and Average Discretion*

Poole & Rosenthal Category	Number of Laws	Average Discretion
Tax rates	22	2.46%
Minimum Wage	4	4.23%
Social Security	13	4.53%
Debt Ceilings	2	5.56%
Campaign Contributions/Lobbying	2	6.68%
Women's Equality	2	7.27%
Veterans Benefits	1	9.63%
Civil Service and Patronage	1	9.63%
Alien and Sedition Laws	1	10.04%
Children (aid, infant mortality, etc.)	2	10.43%
Welfare	5	11.30%
Immigration & Naturalization	3	11.73%
South Africa/Rhodesia	1	11.96%
Union Regulation	9	11.98%
Vietnam War	1	12.50%
Banking and Finance	3	12.88%
Civil Rights/Affirmative Action	14	14.25%
Gasoline Rationing	3	14.51%
Handicapped	2	14.92%
Public Works	9	15.03%
un-American Activities	5	15.59%
Energy	4	15.85%
Telecommunications	2	15.85%
Narcotics	2	15.88%
Unemployment/Jobs	12	16.22%
Interstate Commerce	3	16.31%
Coal Mining Regulation	2	17.38%
Public Lands	1	17.46%
Shipping/Maritime	1	18.25%
Judiciary	1	18.37%
Nuclear Power	3	18.56%
Minorities (non-black)	2	18.78%
Airline Industry	2	18.82%
Firearms	1	19.64%
Price Controls	10	19.82%
Parks and Conservation	3	21.81%
Budget resolution	2	21.82%
Consumer Protection	4	21.88%
OSHA	1	22.12%
Agriculture	12	22.16%

Table 8.2. (*cont.*)

Poole & Rosenthal Category	Number of Laws	Average Discretion
Housing/Housing Programs	7	23.21%
Pollution and Environmental Protection	19	23.69%
Voting Rights	1	24.18%
Education	9	24.21%
School Prayer	1	25.32%
Abortion	1	25.32%
Public Health	6	25.69%
Food Stamps/Food Programs	7	28.56%
Public Safety	1	30.00%
Tariffs	5	31.93%
Space Exploration/NASA	1	39.29%
Nuclear Weapons	1	41.27%
Science and Technology	3	55.14%
Selective Service (The Draft)	1	100.00%

this. Tax relief can be granted to specific, narrow constituencies, or even to individual constituents.[5] For legislators eager to solicit favor and campaign contributions, this is a relatively small price to pay for the duty of setting overall tax rates, which must sometimes be raised.

Social Security policy similarly benefits a large and politically well-organized group. This large cache of votes has lured lawmakers into enacting a series of Social Security increases over the years, with benefits spiraling ever upward. And minimum-wage laws are politically valuable not only for the chance they offer to benefit low-wage workers (who vote at lower rates than their elderly counterparts), but also for the opportunity to *exempt* certain businesses from these requirements. The Fair Labor Standards Amendment of 1974 (PL 93–259), for instance, raised the minimum wage but retained overtime exemptions for employees of movie theaters, small logging operations, small telegraph agencies, and for employees engaged in the processing of shade-grown tobacco.

When the targeting of benefits is difficult and the risks of ill-informed policy great, especially in defense and foreign policy issues, legislators are willing if not eager to cede discretionary authority to executive agencies. The benefits generated from these policy areas are widely dispersed, which makes it hard for legislators to point to specific provisions that aid their constituents. In fact, our data support the "two presiden-

[5] One of the items canceled in the maiden voyage of the line-item veto would have benefited a single Texas billionaire, Harold C. Simmons.

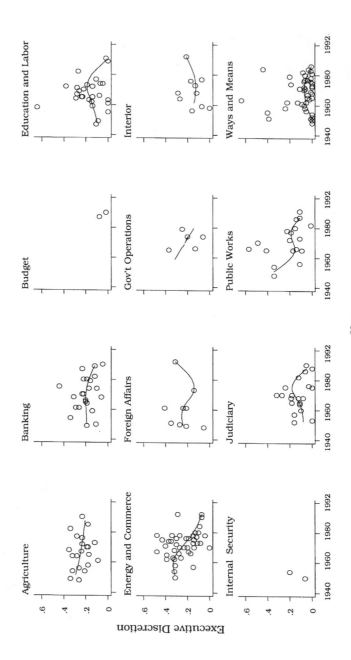

Figure 8.1. Average Discretion in Laws Reported, by Committee, 1946–1992

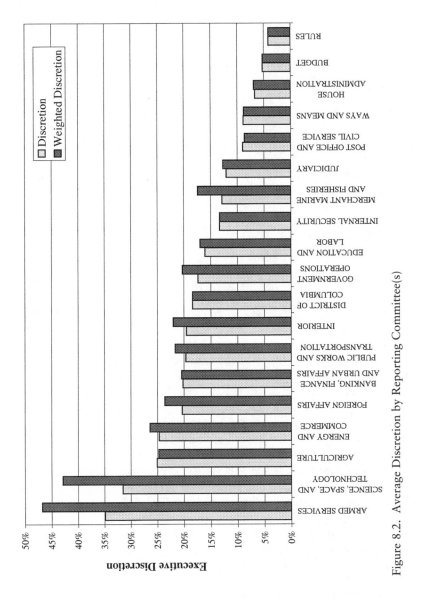

Figure 8.2. Average Discretion by Reporting Committee(s)

205

cies" hypothesis (due to Wildavsky 1975) that presidents have greater latitude to act in foreign as opposed to domestic policy. The foreign policy laws in our data set contained an average of 22.1 percent executive discretion, whereas domestic policy averaged 16.2 percent, a difference significant at the 1 percent level.

Congress also delegates in areas where well-formulated policy causes very little notice but badly made policy can have disastrous effects. Consider the approval of new drugs: Politicians will find it hard to claim credit for new drugs that work, so they concentrate on avoiding the blame for drugs with negative side effects. Finally, these are issue areas that benefit from technical expertise, so legislators are happy to draw on the knowledge of executive branch experts rather than deplete their own scarce resources of time and energy. Overall, we claim that these issue-area breakdowns fit well our theory of strategic delegation by legislators of those areas least favorable to their reelection chances.

ISSUE AREAS AND INFORMATION

Measuring Information

We now proceed to a more direct test of our theoretical prediction that the more informationally intense a committee's issue area, the more discretionary authority is delegated to the executive in bills emerging from that committee, all else being equal. The major hurdle to overcome in running tests of this sort is finding a reasonable proxy for issue complexity that can be applied throughout the time period studied. The two measures most commonly used for this purpose – for instance, in Krehbiel (1991) and Sinclair (1995) – are the number of laws cited in a given bill and committee seniority. The former, however, is unavailable for bills prior to the early 1980s; and the latter is best seen as a measure of committee-specific expertise, as used in the previous chapter, rather than a measure of the intrinsic complexity of an issue area.

We have therefore developed our own measures of issue-area complexity based on committee hearings data available in the Congressional Information Service's *Congressional Masterfile*.[6] This source lists all congressional hearings, by committee, with a subject description of the hearing, witnesses, and dates held.[7] Our hypothesis is that committees dealing with more complex issue areas will be the ones that hold the greatest number of hearings. In fact, many authors have described the

---

[6]Copyright © Congressional Information Service, Inc., 1997. Used by permission.

[7]Committee hearings are published at the discretion of the chairman, with all hearings not vital to national security published thirty years after the original hearing.

key role of hearings in gathering both technical and political information relating to the measure at hand. As Polsby (1976, 136) puts it:

All [these hearings] are necessary – to make a record, to demonstrate good faith to leaders and members of the House and Senate, to provide a background of demonstrated need for the bill, to show how experts anticipate that the bill's provisions will operate, to allay fears, and to gather support from the wavering. Not only does it tell congressmen what the technical arguments for and against a bill are, but, even more important, it tells them *who*, which interests and which groups, are for and against bills and how strongly they feel about them.

The same can be said of oversight hearings in particular, which Aberbach (1990) identified as a key element of committees' "intelligence systems": Committees that hold more oversight hearings in general invest greater resources in monitoring the details of policy implementation. This yields three ways to measure the informational component of legislation: by the average number of hearings (**average hearings**), by the average number of oversight hearings (**average oversight hearings**), and by the **average percent of oversight hearings**, of the committee or committees that reported the legislation.

These data were obtained by tabulating the number of published hearings per committee held between the 80th and 102d Congresses, eliminating those hearings from special, joint, or select committees. Isolating oversight hearings was made difficult by changes in the procedure for coding the hearings adopted by the Congressional Information Service. To account for these differences, oversight hearings from the 80th through 91st Congresses were identified by the appearance of the word "review" in the content description of the committee hearing. Oversight hearings from the 92d through 102d Congresses were identified by the appearance of the word "oversight" (all lowercase) in the content description of committee hearings.[8] The percentage of oversight hearings was calculated as the ratio between these two.

As a check on these measures, we also employ another proxy for informational intensity: the **scope** of a committee's issue domain, as defined by Smith and Deering's (1990) fragmentation ranking of a committee's jurisdiction. Since fragmentation measures a committee's sphere of jurisdiction, it also serves as an indicator of informational intensity in the same vein as Krehbiel's (1991, 169) scope measure, which he defines as the number of laws cited in a given bill. The fragmentation variable is constructed as a combination of the number of departments and agencies under each committee's jurisdiction and the number of areas of

---

[8]Appendix G describes the methodology used to extract these data.

legislative jurisdiction in the chamber rules.[9] Since those committees with more-fragmented jurisdictions would be expected to hold more hearings and especially more oversight hearings, this serves as a useful check on our other measures. Indeed, the scope measure correlates with number of hearings at 0.63 and with oversight hearings at 0.59. Also, this measure ranks the committees in roughly the same order as the hearings-based measures.[10]

For control variables, we also incorporate into our analysis Smith and Deering's measures of **salience** and **conflict**. The former is measured by the number of minutes of evening news broadcasts given to a committee's jurisdiction, while the latter indicates the presence of multiple competing interests surrounding issues under a committee's purview. The level of conflict was ascertained by interviewing committee members and staff; the essence of this measure is captured in one member's description of "pressure": "I don't just mean pressure to do something, I mean pressure to choose between two very polarized sides of an issue – that is pressure."[11] Each of these categorical variables is measured as high, medium, or low.

Table 8.3 lists the committees in decreasing order of fragmentation, with Appropriations having the broadest jurisdictional scope and Post Office the narrowest. Also shown in the table is each committee's level of conflict and salience. The most conflictual committees are the broad-based policy committees: Energy and Commerce and Education and Labor. Also included in this category are the Budget and Ways and Means committees, where members directly clash over the allocation of resources. Note that committees addressing highly salient issues also tend to be associated with high conflict.

Congressional Hearings Data

We first proceed to examine the committee hearing data in a little more detail, before turning to the statistical analysis of discretion. Summary data by committee for average number of hearings and percentage of oversight hearings per Congress are shown in Figure 8.3. As illustrated in the figure, Appropriations, Energy and Commerce, and Armed Services rank at the top in terms of number of hearings per Congress. These committees are indeed associated with complex issue areas that require considerable committee-based expertise. Further down on the list are

---

[9]See Smith and Deering (1990, 80).

[10]Tests on both Spearman and Kendall rank correlation coefficients show that the hypotheses that the measures are independent can be rejected at $p < 0.0001$.

[11]Quoted in Smith and Deering (1990, 83).

Table 8.3. *Committee Classification of Scope, Salience, and Level of Conflict*

Committee Name	Scope of Jurisdiction Rank	Salience	Conflict
Appropriations	20	Medium	Medium
Energy and Commerce	19	High	High
Natural Resources	18	Medium	Medium
Education and Labor	17	High	High
Public Works and Transportation	16	Medium	Medium
Foreign Affairs (current)	15	High	Medium
Judiciary	14	High	High
Agriculture	13	Low	Low
Science, Space, and Technology	12	Low	Low
Government Operations	11	Low	Low
Merchant Marine and Fisheries	10	Low	Low
Banking, Finance and Urban Affairs	9	Medium	Medium
Armed Services	8	Medium	Medium
Ways and Means	7	Medium	High
House Administration	6	N/A	N/A
Small Business	5	N/A	N/A
District of Columbia	4	Low	Low
Veterans' Affairs	3	N/A	N/A
Rules	2	N/A	N/A
Standards of Official Conduct	1	N/A	N/A
Post Office and Civil Service	0	Low	Low
Budget	N/A	High	High

Note: Internal Security Committee was abolished.
Source: Smith and Deering (1990).

more traditionally distributive-based committees, such as Agriculture, Post Office, Merchant Marines, and Veterans' Affairs. Thus the categorization, while not perfect (note the relatively low position of Ways and Means), does capture a good deal of our intended informational intensity.

Oversight as a percentage of total hearings, indicated by the darkened bars in the chart, seems to reflect other aspects of committee activity. This category is headed by Veterans' Affairs and Government Operations, the former of which troubleshoots sticky government bureaucracies for its well-organized clientele, and the latter of which is an oversight committee almost by definition, dedicated as it is to eliminating the ever-present unholy trinity of waste, fraud, and abuse. It seems, then, that

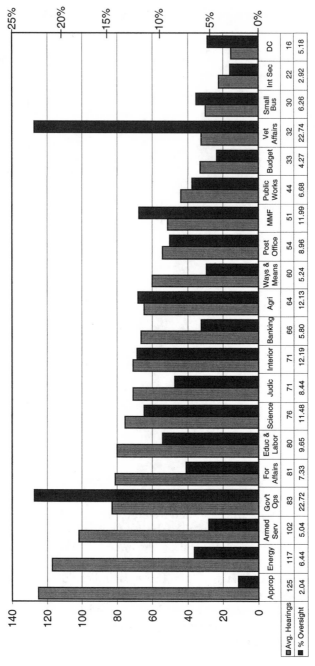

	Approp	Energy	Armed Serv	Gov't Ops	For Affairs	Educ & Labor	Science	Judic	Interior	Banking	Agri	Ways & Means	Post Office	MMF	Public Works	Budget	Vet Affairs	Small Bus	Int Sec	DC
Avg. Hearings	125	117	102	83	81	80	76	71	71	66	64	60	54	51	44	33	32	30	22	16
% Oversight	2.04	6.44	5.04	22.72	7.33	9.65	11.48	8.44	12.19	5.80	12.13	5.24	8.96	11.99	6.68	4.27	22.74	6.26	2.92	5.18

Figure 8.3. Average Number of Hearings and Percentage of Oversight Hearings, by Committee, 1947–1992

oversight hearings capture a different dimension of committee expertise, one dealing more with policy implementation than with policy formation.

Committee Hearings, Oversight, and Delegation

We are now ready to examine whether or not any of our proxies for complexity and information explain a significant proportion of the discretionary authority delegated to the executive. The dependent variable in the analysis is the level of executive discretion per law, as defined in Chapter 5. We use the four measures of informational intensity described above as independent variables: average total hearings per Congress, average oversight hearings per Congress, average percentage of oversight hearings per Congress, and the scope of a committee's policy domain. The hypothesis is that each of these four measures should be positively related to the amount of executive discretion. Summary statistics of all variables are provided in Table 8.4.

As environmental controls, we include, along with the committee's issue-area salience and conflict, the degree to which a committee is an outlier with respect to the floor, as described in the previous chapter. This allows us to control for committee-specific characteristics that might also influence the degree of delegated authority. Finally, we introduce the issue-area divisions provided by Clausen (1973) and Peltzman (1985) in their classic works on roll-call voting. These are descriptors of roll-call votes, where each measure (amendment, rule, final passage, conference report, etc.) is assigned to one of several possible issue categories.[12] We associated each public law in our data set with its modal vote category, similar to the exercise we performed on the Poole and Rosenthal issue codes discussed earlier in the chapter.[13]

---

[12]Clausen defines six possible issue categories: Government Management, Social Welfare, Agriculture, Civil Liberties, Foreign and Defense Policy, and Miscellaneous Policy. Peltzman divides issues more finely into thirteen categories: Budget General Interest, Budget Special Interest, Regulation General Interest, Regulation Special Interest, Domestic Social Policy, Defense Policy Budget, Foreign Policy Budget, Defense Policy Resolutions, Foreign Policy Resolutions, Government Organization, Internal Organization, Indian Affairs, and District of Columbia.

[13]We sometimes confronted the difficulty of roll-call measures associated with the same law being on seemingly unrelated topics. For example, the Tax Reform Act of 1976 (PL 94-455) contained a provision clarifying the authority of Congress to override presidential decisions on remedies by the International Trade Commission when U.S. businesses were injured by foreign imports. To convert these vote classifications into appropriate law classifications, we used modal vote categories, so that the tax reform law, for example, was coded as "Budget Special Interest," because it mainly provided targeted tax breaks for selected industries, rather than "Budget General Interest."

Table 8.4. *Summary Statistics*

Variable	Description	Mean	Std. Dev.	Min	Max
Discretion	The amount of authority that executive agencies have to move policy, as defined in Chapter 5.	0.17	0.15	0.00	1.00
Average Hearings	Average number of hearings held by each reporting committee per Congress.	75.15	24.10	2.66	125.25
Average Oversight Hearings	Average number of oversight hearings held by each reporting committee per Congress.	5.30	2.39	0.08	12.50
Average Percent Oversight Hearings	Average number of oversight hearings as a percent of total hearings held by each reporting committee per Congress.	7.04%	2.45%	1.96%	15.03%
Scope of Jurisdiction	A ranking of each committee based on a composite measure combining the number of departments and agencies under each committee's jurisdiction and the number of areas of legislative jurisdiction in the chamber rules, as defined in Smith and Deering (1990).	13.26	4.79	0.00	20.00
Salience	A categorical variable that takes on three values (High, Medium, and Low), depending on the number of times a committee is mentioned in television network news broadcasts, as defined in Smith and Deering (1990, 84).	2.28	0.71	1.00	3.00
Conflict	A categorical variable that takes on three values (High, Medium, and Low), based on comments of committee members and staff, as defined in Smith and Deering (1990, 84).	2.42	0.73	1.00	3.00
Committee-Floor Outlier	Absolute Value of Committee-Floor Difference, as defined in Chapter 7.	0.08	0.07	0.00	0.31

Number of Observations is 296. The data includes multiple referrals.

A first look at the results is provided in Figure 8.4, which graphs the average number of hearings per Congress and the average level of executive discretion, by committee. As shown, the trend is indeed generally positive. Armed Services has relatively high discretion given the number of hearings held, and Appropriations has relatively low discretion. Otherwise, though, this simple predictor does a fairly good job estimating the amount of discretion in laws reported by the committee.

The full set of regression results is shown in Table 8.5. The findings provide significant support for our hypothesis that informationally intense policies are delegated at higher rates. Of our four key variables, three – number of hearings, number of oversight hearings, and issue scope – are consistently and positively related to discretion. Their standardized regression coefficients are 0.32, 0.11, and 0.19, respectively, so they each have a tangible substantive impact on discretion as well as a statistically significant one. The fourth variable, the percentage of oversight hearings, is consistently in the predicted direction, but it is not significant.

Our findings regarding oversight hearings merit a bit of further commentary. On one hand, these results simply indicate that those policy areas with greater amounts of executive discretion are also associated with more committee oversight hearings. This, of course, may seem unsurprising and even tautological. But some previous accounts had indicated that legislators delegate only in order to distance themselves from adverse policy consequences, and therefore that members have little or no incentive to oversee delegated authority. If this account were true, then we would observe no relation or even a negative relation between delegation and oversight. This, however, is not the case: Legislators may cede authority to bureaucratic actors, but they also monitor the use of that authority to keep executive agents in line.

The salience and conflict measures are generally significant, with positive and negative coefficients, respectively. These findings should be circumscribed somewhat by the fact that the variables are coded only as trichotomous values of high, medium, or low. But insofar as the results are consistently in the same direction across model specifications, they indicate that legislators are more willing to cede the executive discretionary authority in policy areas with high national visibility, and less willing in those areas where many competing groups vie for influence.

The results concerning salience may seem surprising, given legislators' desire for media exposure in order to claim credit on key policy areas. However, media attention can be both positive and negative, so perhaps legislators prefer to retain control in areas where they can quietly provide benefits to key constituents. The latter finding on conflict is a bit more intriguing, as some previous observers, Fiorina (1982) and Mc-

213

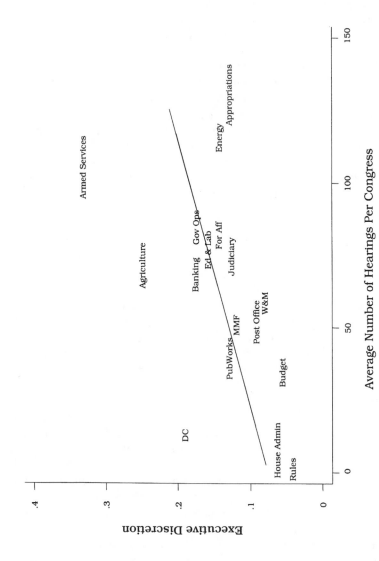

Figure 8.4. Discretion and Number of Hearings, by Committee

Table 8.5. *Information and Discretion*

Dependent Variable: Discretion

Variables	Avg. Hearings		Avg. Oversight Hearings		Avg. Percent Oversight Hearings		Scope of Jurisdiction	
Model	1	2	3	4	5	6	7	8
Avg. Hearings	0.001 (4.37)**	0.002 (4.47)**						
Avg. Oversight Hearings			0.007 (2.55)**	0.007 (2.38)**				
Avg. Percent Oversight Hearings					0.12 (0.43)	0.049 (0.16)		
Scope of Jurisdiction							0.005 (2.68)**	0.006 (2.88)**
Salience	0.045 (2.63)**	0.039 (2.25)**	0.063 (3.94)**	0.061 (3.82)**	0.078 (5.19)**	0.075 (4.96)**	0.039 (1.84)**	0.031 (1.39)*
Conflict	-0.085 (-5.96)**	-0.080 (-5.54)**	-0.084 (-5.58)**	-0.082 (-5.44)**	-0.095 (-6.09)**	-0.093 (-5.96)**	-0.072 (-4.23)**	-0.065 (-3.73)**
Committee-Floor Outlier		0.13 (1.43)*		0.073 (0.81)		0.097 (1.03)		0.13 (1.45)*
Constant	0.14 (5.57)**	0.13 (4.81)**	0.16 (6.25)**	0.16 (5.98)**	0.18 (5.03)**	0.18 (5.02)**	0.16 (6.04)**	0.14 (5.19)**
F_n^k $_k$	22.28**	16.99**	18.09**	13.58**	15.76**	11.84**	17.81**	13.71**

Note: t-statistics in parentheses, calculated from robust standard errors; one-tailed test *< 0.10; **< 0.05. N = 293

Cubbins (1985) being most notable, have hypothesized that greater conflict gives legislators greater incentives for delegation. The positive side to conflict in a policy area, however, is that it allows legislators to reap greater contributions from groups mobilized on either side of an issue. This inducement may be at the heart of legislators' desire to retain control over these policies themselves.[14]

Finally, the issue categories defined by Clausen and Peltzman, as shown in Tables 8.6 and 8.7, convey some interesting information. The omitted category for the Clausen codes is Social Welfare, while the omitted category for Peltzman is General Interest Regulation; in both cases, these are the median categories when ranked by average amounts of executive discretion. Relative to these issue areas, the only Clausen category that differed consistently was Civil Liberties, an area dominated by civil rights bills and crime control acts, with less discretion on average given to executive agencies than on the other issues. The only significant Peltzman categories were Budget General Interest (mainly tax policy) and Domestic Social Policy (mostly Social Security and minimum wage laws), which had less discretion, and Foreign Policy Resolutions, with more executive discretion.

Note that if our perspective on information and delegation is correct, it may be in order to rethink some of the previous literature on committee expertise. According to our view, there is indeed a role for informationally aware committees, but not as large a role as some previous works might suggest. If complex issue areas are to be delegated to the executive, then it will not be worth legislators' while to invest too heavily in expertise of their own, as most of their duties will consist of overseeing delegated authority. They must know enough to write the initial legislation in an effective manner, of course, and they must be able to communicate with executive branch agents concerning policy details. But past a certain point, it makes little sense for legislators (or their staff) to continue investing in issue-specific expertise, as they will be merely duplicating the efforts of bureaucratic policymakers.

DELEGATION AND DISTRIBUTIVE POLITICS

The previous section analyzed our prediction that informationally intense issues are highly delegated to the executive. It may seem natural to assume that distributive issues work in the opposite way – that legislators will delegate little authority in these areas so as best to protect favored constituents. It might also be tempting to classify issues as either

---

[14]This possibility is explored theoretically in Epstein and O'Halloran (1998).

Table 8.6. *Information and Discretion, Clausen Issue Codes*

Dependent Variable: Discretion

Variables	Avg. Hearings	Avg. Oversight Hearings	Avg. Percent Oversight Hearings	Scope of Jurisdiction
Avg. Hearings	0.001 (3.40)**			
Avg. Oversight Hearings		0.01 (1.82)**		
Avg. Percent Oversight Hearings			0.04 (0.14)	
Scope of Jurisdiction				0.004 (1.74)**
Salience	0.06 (3.56)**	0.08 (4.64)**	0.09 (5.92)**	0.06 (2.39)**
Conflict	-0.09 (-5.68)**	-0.08 (-5.15)**	-0.09 (-5.63)**	-0.08 (-4.05)**
Clausen Issue Categories				
Government Management	-0.03 (-1.87)**	-0.02 (-1.23)	-0.02 (-1.49)*	-0.03 (-1.74)**
Agriculture	0.04 (1.09)	0.05 (1.47)*	0.05 (1.56)*	0.04 (1.00)
Civil Liberties	-0.06 (-2.65)**	-0.05 (-2.58)**	-0.06 (-2.76)**	-0.06 (-2.64)**
Foreign & Defense Policy	-0.02 (-0.74)	0.003 (-0.10)	-0.02 (-0.62)	-0.01 (-0.29)
Constant	0.13 (4.16)**	0.15 (4.33)**	0.17 (3.86)**	0.16 (4.87)**
F_{n-k}^{k}	11.41**	9.88**	9.28**	9.67**

Note: t-statistics in parentheses, calculated from robust standard errors; one-tailed test *<0.10; **<0.05. N = 261. Sample includes only those laws associated with a recorded vote.

informational or distributive, so that they can be arrayed along a one-dimensional continuum. If this were the case, then our tests above showing that informationally intense issue areas are delegated at a high rate would simultaneously show that distributive issues are delegated at a low rate.

This optimistic interpretation of our results is, we believe, misplaced. First, we think that issues have both informational and distributive components, so that they fall within a two-dimensional rather than one-dimensional space. The distributive component of policy is not just a lack of informational complexity, that is, but rather the presence of particularized benefits that flow to constituents. In this view, some issues

217

Table 8.7. *Information and Discretion, Peltzman Issue Codes*

Variables	Dependent Variable: Discretion			
	Avg. Hearings	Avg. Oversight Hearings	Avg. Percent Oversight Hearings	Scope of Jurisdiction
Avg. Hearings	0.001 (3.59)**			
Avg. Oversight		0.01 (2.69)**		
Avg. Percent Oversight			0.32 (1.00)	
Scope of Jurisdiction				0.005 (2.30)**
Salience	0.02 (0.78)	0.03 (1.64)*	(0.04) (2.35)**	0.004 (0.16)
Conflict	-0.05 (-2.72)**	-0.04 (-2.57)**	(-0.05) (-2.68)**	-0.03 (-1.49)*
Peltzman Issue Categories				
Budget General Interest	-0.09 (-3.23)**	-0.07 (-2.60)**	-0.08 (-3.14)**	-0.08 (-2.92)**
Budget Special Interest	0.005 (0.27)	0.01 (0.60)	0.004 (0.20)	0.01 (0.47)
Regulation Special Interest	-0.02 (-0.96)	-0.01 (-0.62)	-0.02 (-0.76)	-0.02 (-0.70)
Domestic Social Policy	-0.05 (-2.16)**	-0.04 (-2.00)**	-0.05 (-2.43)**	-0.04 (-1.80)**
Government Organization	-0.05 (-1.73)**	-0.05 (-1.63)*	-0.05 (-1.44)*	-0.03 (-1.06)
District of Columbia	0.04 (0.41)	0.04 (0.36)	0.007 (0.07)	0.03 (0.28)
Defense Policy Budget	0.05 (0.46)	0.07 (0.68)	0.05 (0.51)	N/A
Foreign Policy Budget	0.004 (0.10)	0.03 (0.67)	0.007 (0.16)	0.02 (0.55)
Defense Policy Resolutions	0.01 (0.24)	0.05 (1.06)	0.04 (0.84)	0.06 (1.23)
Foreign Policy Resolutions	0.10 (1.70)**	0.12 (2.03)**	0.10 (1.68)**	0.12 (1.92)**
Constant	0.15 (4.62)**	0.15 (4.62)**	0.16 (3.68)**	0.16 (4.51)**
F_{n-k}^{k}	6.70**	6.20**	5.52**	6.29**

Note: t-statistics in parentheses, calculated from robust standard errors; one-tailed test *<0.10; **<0.05. N = 261.

may have high distributive and informational components – tax policy, for instance – while others are low on both scales – House Administration issues spring to mind.

Second, the politics of distribution is notorious for generating unexpected incentives in the policy game. Legislators can find themselves trapped in collective dilemmas or in chaotic issue-formation problems, such that individually rational behavior aggregates to a collectively irrational result – logrolls may grow out of control, for instance, to everyone's detriment. While it is true that legislators might want to maintain control over policy in these areas, then, they may also have countervailing incentives to delegate in order to escape their collective-choice problems.

This section explores themes of delegation and distribution with reference to three particular policy examples: agriculture, trade, and the line-item veto. Rather than present systematic data analysis, we try here to highlight some important themes in the application of our theory to distributive issues. The basic point of our exercise, though, remains the same: Legislators delegate to the executive more as the costs of internal policy formation rise. When these costs are generated by collective dilemmas in distributive issues, legislators should be willing to delegate just as they were when informational problems encouraged delegation to experts within federal agencies. And, conversely, they will be less willing to delegate the higher the agency costs of doing so.

Agriculture

We begin with the case of agriculture, which has been described as the prototypical example of a small interest group getting its way in the legislative process. Lowi (1979, 68) writes:

Agriculture is that field of American government where the distinction between public and private has come closest to being completely eliminated. This has been accomplished not by public expropriation of private domain . . . but by private expropriation of public authority.

Similarly, Mayhew (1974, 31) states that

Agriculture is an obvious example [of clientelism]. Clientelism, like particularism, gives form to the federal bureaucracy. Congressmen protect clientele systems – alliances of agencies, Hill committees, and clienteles – against the incursions of presidents and cabinet secretaries.

These two classic treatises of interests, committees, and the federal bureaucracy, among others, form the basis of the received wisdom: Agriculture is seen to represent a perfect harmony of interests among the Agriculture Committee, farm lobbies, and the Agriculture Department, forming an iron triangle or an effective subgovernment. According to this view, then, agricultural policy is tailored toward a well-protected farm block constituency in an endless flow of particularized benefits.

Other observers (such as Ferejohn 1986 and Hansen 1991), however, have already noted that this characterization is not quite complete. First, the agriculture lobby fractured after World War II among competing lobby groups (American Farm Bureau Federation vs. the Grange vs. the Farmers' Union) and across commodities (wheat vs. corn vs. dairy vs. soybean), thus destroying the movement's formerly united front.[15] Second, many postwar farm bills were partisan, so their passage was hindered by stiff political resistance. Neither did farm bills receive much protection from floor amendments. Of the twenty-one bills in our sample singly referred to the Agriculture Committee, only four received restrictive rules.[16] For both these reasons, agricultural policy in reality is considerably more nuanced then a straight iron-triangle thesis would have us believe.

To this story of internally divided interests and partisanship we now add a third dimension: delegation to the executive. The broad summaries of issue areas presented earlier in the chapter consistently pointed to agriculture as an area with a relatively high level of executive discretion. The twenty-one agriculture bills in our sample received an average discretion index of 24.4 percent, with a minimum of 9.9 percent, a maximum of 35.7 percent, and a standard deviation of 7.3 percent. In other words, discretion attached to agricultural legislation was consistently high across time and administrations.

Why do we find such significant levels of discretion in what is essentially a distributive program? The logic, derived from our model, is as follows. As discussed in Ferejohn (1986), legislators have a collective-action problem to solve: how to construct a viable bill without falling prey to cycling majorities. The solution eventually settled upon by farm state legislators was to sustain a logroll with urban interests, maintaining urban support for agricultural subsidies in exchange for agricultural support of the food stamp program. The institutionalization of this logroll helped prevent farm policy deals from being picked apart by hostile forces, usually Republicans opposed to pro-farm legislation.

But this intralegislative logroll was not enough, since thin congressional majorities meant that presidential approval would also be neces-

---

[15]See Hansen (1991, chap. 5) for details on the growing rift within the farm lobby.

[16]For instance, fourteen floor amendments were offered to the Agriculture and Consumer Protection Act of 1973 (PL 93-86) on the House floor, of which seven passed.

sary to enact farm legislation, a fact not emphasized by previous commentators. What are the president's preferences regarding farm policy? Presidents are less inclined toward pork barrel projects to begin with, since they have a national constituency and therefore represent those hurt by wasteful spending as well as those helped. But presidents do need votes from farm states, to some degree, for reelection. In general, then, presidents are less enthusiastic about agriculture bills than farm state representatives but may still be willing to support some relief for farmers, especially those hard hit by falling commodity prices.

A considerable amount of disagreement therefore persists between the branches on the subject of agricultural policy. Mayhew (1974, 170–1) notes that "almost every president starting with Coolidge (Johnson and the early Roosevelt are exceptions) has opposed congressional farm programs." Nixon even tried to abolish the Agriculture Department altogether and divide its functions among the proposed departments of Community Development, Economic Affairs, Human Resources, and Natural Resources.[17] And the history of enacting farm legislation consistently reflects this interbranch conflict. Many agriculture bills were negotiated under the threat of a presidential veto, and two farm bills in our sample were passed only after the Eisenhower administration's veto of previous attempts.[18] Likewise, significant interbranch tension preceded the passage of the 1961, 1973, 1977, 1982, 1985, and 1990 agriculture acts.

Enacting farm legislation, then, means including a somewhat reluctant president in a policy logroll, as well as representatives from urban districts. Some presidents can be partially bought off with the same currency as urban representatives, namely, desired social programs such as food stamps. But others, especially Republicans less inclined to favor these social programs, must be bought off with greater discretionary control over the allocation of these farm subsidies.[19] Consequently, for a distributive program like agricultural supports to survive the political shoals of the legislative process, the executive must be given some degree of latitude to set policy.

The untold story of agricultural policy, then, is that it relies heavily on executive discretion for implementation, this authority being supplied as a bribe for presidential support of agricultural programs. For instance,

---

[17]See Seidman and Gilmour (1986, 186).

[18]These were the Agriculture Acts of 1956 and 1958, PL 84-540 and PL 85-835, respectively.

[19]As shown in Chapter 4, presidents always prefer more discretion to less in our model. So a bargaining game carried out in a policy/discretion space will raise equilibrium discretion the more opposed the president is to the policy content of the legislation.

Charles Brannan, Secretary of Agriculture in the Truman administration, introduced in 1949 a plan to eliminate commodity price supports and replace them with direct payments to farmers for the differences between market prices and a predetermined target-price level. Legislators strongly resisted this approach, fearing that it would make agricultural supports more vulnerable to the charge that they were merely a form of welfare for farmers. Eventually, the administration abandoned the Brannan Plan in return for the congressional concession of flexible price supports that, at the administration's discretion, could range between 75 and 90 percent of parity for most basic commodities. As reported in *Congressional Quarterly*:

The Agricultural Act of 1949 [gave] the Secretary of Agriculture more flexibility in setting price support levels. Passage of the legislation in effect reflected a middle position in the debate that Congress would revisit time and time again between those who favored government management of farm prices and those who advocated a free market for agricultural products. (1990 *CQ Almanac*, 323)

Similarly, farm programs were again under attack in 1985, this time from the Reagan administration, which opposed government interference in the marketplace on principle. There followed a bruising legislative fight that divided Republicans loyal to Reagan from those fearing reprisal from farmers at the voting booth. The pro-agriculture lobby was aided both by its traditional alliance with some inner-city Democratic representatives eager to maintain federal support for food stamp programs, and by a depression currently affecting agricultural prices nationwide. The farm bloc eventually beat back administration attempts to slash crop subsidies, but in return they offered the executive broad new discretionary powers to set price support rates for major crops.

The key to understanding farm policy, then, is that crop subsidies benefit a few districts a good deal but impose costs on all others. The support of other legislators *and* the president must therefore be maintained to pass policy. Hence, delegation is the currency used to purchase executive support for an essentially distributive program.

Trade

International trade, on the other hand, can benefit all districts a little. Each legislator would prefer to obtain protectionist benefits for her own constituents at the expense of all other districts, but such a proposal would never garner sufficient support to pass on its own. Therefore, the natural tendency is for legislators to combine their requests together into an omnibus tariff package, where each member gains a little and the costs are divided across all districts.

Once this logroll starts, though, it is hard to limit it to only a few members without the bargain unraveling completely. The process of building trade legislation item by item can thus lead to a collective dilemma of over-logrolling, similar to the much discussed tragedy of the commons. The end result is that all legislators are made worse off than before. The classic trade example is the 1930 Smoot-Hawley Tariff Act, in which Congress revised tariffs on 3,221 items, leading to the highest tariff rates of the twentieth century. Although every member of Congress was able to protect some interest in her district or state, the overall result was to deepen the Great Depression.

In essence, then, trade policy offers legislators too much of a good thing; it imposes a burden of distribution. This situation resembles that of civil service jobs in the late nineteenth century, when the patronage system got so out of hand that the number of people alienated for not receiving a political appointment outnumbered those grateful people who did; Congress had an embarrassment of riches.

The solution in both cases was for Congress to delegate decision-making authority to the executive. In the case of the civil service, professional standards and a meritocracy system were instituted, making it hard to remove and appoint federal bureaucrats and thereby extricating many of the hiring and firing decisions from legislators' hands. The problem of inefficient trade policy was also solved by delegation: Following the disaster of Smoot-Hawley, the 1934 Reciprocal Trade Agreements Act delegated authority to the president to unilaterally cut tariff levels by up to 50 percent in bilateral negotiations with other countries. This represented a break from the previous system in which Congress set tariffs item by item to one in which the president was able to negotiate broad tariff agreements and change rates by executive decree.[20]

Throughout the postwar period, this negotiating authority has been renewed periodically and has been central to worldwide tariff reductions accumulated under the auspices of the General Agreement on Tariffs and Trade (GATT). When the success of these negotiations highlighted the growing importance of nontariff barriers (NTBs), such as quotas and health and safety standards, Congress gave the executive fast-track authority, which consists of expedited, closed-rule procedures for legislative consideration of negotiated trade agreements. Fast-track authority has subsequently been used to negotiate three regional free-trade agreements – U.S.–Israel, U.S.–Canada, and NAFTA – and two GATT agreements – the Tokyo Rounds, and most recently the Uruguay Rounds, which led to the establishment of the World Trade Organization.

---

[20]See Lohmann and O'Halloran (1994) for an explicit model of delegation in trade policy to avoid inefficient distributive logrolls.

So while agriculture saw delegation as a bribe to the executive, trade policy has been delegated as a means to escape from legislative excesses.[21] As in agricultural issues, the president has a national constituency and is therefore less prone to particularistic demands. But there is still a political logic to delegation in trade policy: As demonstrated in Chapter 6, the degree of discretion is not fixed and unchanging; rather it is malleable and has constantly been adjusted to reflect the political realities of the time, and renewals of trade negotiating authority have been circumscribed by political conflict between the branches.

In order to obtain authority over trade policy, then, presidents must periodically barter with legislators who have strategically made this authority renewable at regular intervals. Negotiation over fast-track authority therefore inherits some of the distributive aspects of congressional trade policy making. To illustrate this dynamic, we offer an extended discussion of the 1991 fast-track renewal.[22]

The 1988 Omnibus Trade and Competitiveness Act renewed fast-track authority for three years, with the possibility of an additional two years if the president requested authority by March 1991 and if neither house passed a resolution disapproving the extension. Congress had until June 1 to block the fast-track extension; after that, fast-track procedures would continue automatically for two more years. The original intent of Congress in providing the short time frame was to ensure that the Uruguay Round GATT negotiations were making significant progress and to give U.S. negotiators bargaining leverage.[23]

This procedural measure had the unanticipated effect of allowing Congress the opportunity to set further guidelines for the president in negotiating the North American Free Trade Agreement, and the Democratically controlled Congress took the opportunity of the renewal of fast track to ensure that many of the most controversial issues – the environment, labor concerns, and workers' rights – were written directly into the authorizing legislation.

The sequence of events was as follows. On March 4, 1991, President Bush requested the extension of fast-track procedures.[24] This set up an unlikely scenario in which organized labor, environmental groups, and human rights activists formed a loose coalition in opposition to extend-

---

[21]Another important factor distinguishing these two policy areas is the reversion point if interbranch bargaining breaks down: In agricultural policy, it is no price supports to farmers, which is more favorable to the president; in trade policy, the reversion point is no executive negotiating authority, which is more favorable to Congress.

[22]For details on fast track and its evolution, see O'Halloran (1994, chap. 6).

[23]*Congressional Quarterly Almanac 1988*, 209.

[24]Message from the President of the United States: *The Extension of Fast Track Procedures*, 102d Cong., 1st sess., H. Doc. 51.

ing fast-track authority. The AFL-CIO strongly opposed the talks and made defeating fast track a top priority. Environmental groups warned that a U.S.–Mexico free-trade agreement would exacerbate pollution along the border and create pressure to weaken U.S. environmental laws as businesses relocated to take advantage of lax Mexican enforcement of its pollution controls. Human rights advocates worried that poor working conditions in Mexico would result in lower health and safety standards for American workers.

The administration lobbied hard for the fast-track extension, seeing the procedure as crucial to the success of the negotiations. But this required that the president make concessions to key congressional leaders. By early May, USTR Carla Hills had met individually with about 150 members of Congress, including two-thirds of the Senate, while Bush met with key Democrats Bentsen, Rostenkowski, and House Majority Leader Gephardt to discuss the extension of fast track. To counter the attacks made by labor and environmentalist groups and quench congressional opposition, on May 1, 1991, the administration put forth an "action plan," containing three main points:

1. Transition and safeguard provisions to phase in tariff reductions, including an escape clause and "snapback" provisions;[25]
2. An enhanced trade adjustment assistance program to provide services to workers displaced by imports resulting from the trade pact; and
3. A vow not to negotiate lower environmental standards than were currently in law in the areas of pesticides, energy conservation, toxic waste, and health and safety.

With the action plan, the administration succeeded in driving a wedge between organized labor and the mainstream environmental organizations, thereby diffusing much of the congressional opposition. Appeased by the president's promises to prevent further environmental degradation and to include them in the negotiation process, environmental leaders withdrew their opposition to the extension of fast track. Still not satisfied with the president's assurances, labor continued to fight against the extension. The defection of the environmentalists, though, proved to be a mortal blow to labor's cause, as Democratic members of Congress now had sufficient cover to vote for the extension. The disapproval resolution consequently failed, 192 to 231 in the House and 36 to 59 in the Senate. This episode is typical of bargaining under fast track: The president traded off the gains and losses from meeting certain interest group demands in order to win congressional support. Congress, on the

---

[25]If domestic producers were injured by imports, the tariff rate would "snap back" to the rate prior to the agreement.

other hand, by extracting public promises from Bush on contentious provisions, strengthened its bargaining position vis-à-vis the administration.

A nearly identical scenario played itself out in late 1997, as the Clinton administration sought to renew fast-track authority to include Chile in the North American Free Trade Agreement. The administration had been without fast-track authority since 1994, and an effort to renew it in 1995 failed because Republicans, who had gained control of Congress, and minority Democrats battled over whether labor and environmental issues should be included in international trade agreements. Republicans opposed muddling the trade debate with these additional issues, while some Democrats refused to support legislation that did not address safeguards for the environment and labor. Administration officials, meanwhile, worked hard on compromise legislation that would win support from both parties.

The efforts to renew fast track culminated in late 1997, when Clinton mounted a major political and public relations offensive. Fast-track reauthorization bills were drafted in both the House Ways and Means and the Senate Finance Committees, with language allowing for the discussion of labor and environmental issues, but only if they were "trade-related." As House floor action grew near, it became clear that the Republicans could muster only 150 Aye votes from their side of the aisle. In response, as he had done with NAFTA and GATT, Clinton shifted into bargaining mode, cutting deals for the additional seventy or so Democratic votes necessary to pass the measure. One administration official privately admitted "the bazaar is open," while a congressional spokesman stated more directly that "It's been like 'Let's Make a Deal' up here the last couple of days." Increased trade adjustment assistance to the tune of $750 million was put on the table, as were programs of $250 million each for assistance to communities hurt by plant closings and to businesses indirectly affected by trade, including suppliers and subcontractors.

But on this occasion, even a frenzy of deal making and an unusual televised appeal for support were not enough to save the legislation. Clinton offered special deals for peanuts, tomatoes, citrus fruit, air pollution along the Mexican border, child-labor laws, wheat trade with Canada, and even Mississippi homeowners who rent out their homes during large furniture sales – all to no avail. With organized labor pushing hard against the bill and no obvious rallying point for the pro-trade forces, many Democrats and some Republicans felt that they could not risk a vote for fast track. Still two dozen or so members short of a majority, the administration, in consultation with Republican leaders, pulled the bill on November 10 rather than risk an embarrassing defeat on the House floor, and as of this writing, fast-track authority is no closer to being passed than it was before.

Line Item Veto

The most puzzling of our examples of distributive delegation is the (now defunct) line-item veto law, passed by a Republican-controlled Congress while a Democrat occupied the White House. Although forty-three state governors possess line-item veto authority of some form, every president from Ulysses S. Grant onward had requested similar authority, and all had been left empty-handed. Why then was this impasse finally broken in 1996, under divided government? This section reviews the history of enacting the line-item veto law and outlines a series of factors contributing to its passage.

Although a presidential line-item veto had been discussed for over a century, the first version to pass a chamber of Congress came in 1992, when the House passed an "expedited rescissions" bill. To digress briefly, the 1974 Budget and Impoundment Act allowed the president to suggest that certain appropriations be rescinded. However, Congress was in no way obliged to act on these proposals. The expedited-rescissions approach would force legislators to vote on presidential proposals within a certain number of days under a closed rule, similar to fast-track procedures in trade policy. Thus a simple majority in both houses could approve presidential requests; conversely, a simple majority in either chamber could reject them.

Republicans eagerly supported the 1992 act, but further action was blocked in the Senate by Robert Byrd (D-W.Va.), an ardent supporter of congressional prerogatives in appropriations. The same scenario repeated itself in 1993 and in 1994: The House passed expedited rescissions bills (along partisan lines; Republicans cooled to the idea once Clinton entered office), but the measures once again died in the Senate.

The biggest push toward the enactment of a line-item veto law came when the proposal was included in the Republicans' platform, the "Contract with America," prior to the 1994 midterm elections. Once the Republicans surprised observers by regaining control of Congress, the House at least was obliged to pass some form of a line-item veto law. They did so on February 6, 1995, enacting an "enhanced rescissions" bill, stronger than the previous expedited-rescissions approach but less aggressive than the proposal actually included in the Contract with America, which would have extended to any tax cuts or spending increases in any bill passed by Congress.

Under enhanced rescissions, the president could veto a block of items within five days of signing appropriations legislation. If Congress disagreed with any of the rescissions, the law allowed for expedited congressional procedures to consider and pass a disagreement bill, which would then be subject to bicameral presentment and the possibility of a presidential veto. In effect, this procedure gave the president the unilateral authority to cancel tax breaks or new spending, with a two-thirds majority in both chambers necessary to override him. The new authority applied to (*a*) enhanced entitlements; (*b*) tax breaks going to a hundred or fewer individuals; and (*c*) staying requirements going to ten or fewer firms. The savings from any of these rescissions were to go into a "lock box," which had to be used for deficit reduction.[26]

The Senate, however, remained deadlocked between the expedited and enhanced rescissions options. In fact, the two Senate committees considering the bill, the Budget Committee and the Governmental Affairs Committee, eventually reported both versions to the floor favorably. The deadlock was broken only when Majority Leader Robert Dole (R-KS) proposed a third alternative, which would fragment appropriations legislation into many individual bills, each of which could be signed or vetoed; for example, a separate bill on each agricultural subsidy and each transportation project. Senator Byrd, still a foe of any line-item veto authority, ridiculed this approach in a floor speech, saying that the 1995 appropriations bills would have to be broken up into almost ten thousand "billettes, or actlettes, or public lawlettes." Nonetheless, this was the version passed by the Senate on March 23, 1995.

There ensued a long period of negotiations and maneuvering among House and Senate Republicans. Speaker Gingrich (R-Ga.), for instance, delayed appointing conferees until after the August recess in order to restrict the opportunity of House floor members to instruct them. Work on reaching a compromise was already getting bogged down when the budget battle between congressional Republicans and Clinton erupted, shutting the federal government down and putting a damper on any further moves to strengthen the president's hand in budget negotiations.

Given the degree of conflict and animosity generated by the budget fight, it is rather surprising that any line-item veto bill was passed at all. The fact that it was finally adopted is probably the result of no one overriding factor, but rather a confluence of a number of different forces. First, legislators did face a collective-action problem in the passing of appropriations legislation with numerous special-interest tax breaks and spending provisions. Like targeted tariff reductions, each item helped an individual member, but the package as a whole was detrimental to Congress's reputation, as the federal deficit loomed ever larger. With

---

[26]For an overview of the line-item veto, see the 1995 *Congressional Quarterly Weekly Report*, 687, 779, 864, and 3134.

consistently negative public evaluations of Congress and legislators, the line-item veto held the promise of burnishing their image. And because Republicans over the years had been strong rhetorical supporters of the line-item veto, they would seem inconsistent if they failed to enact one now that they controlled both chambers of Congress.

Second, Senator Dole put his weight behind finishing the bill, jump-starting negotiations in March of 1996. Dole was running for president at the time and wanted a major legislative victory under his belt. Since both chambers had approved versions of the bill already, it seemed that a compromise should be possible. Without Dole's pressing the issue forward, though, the bill would likely have laid dormant yet again.

Third, the final compromise bill was tailored to garner sufficient Republican support for passage (with Clinton in the White House, most Democrats were now an easy sell). For one thing, the authority would not come into effect until 1997, by which time, it seemed likely to some members, Dole might be the first to use it. And after the Senate's approach of breaking legislation into thousands of bills was deemed unworkable, attention reverted to the House-enhanced rescissions version, which was agreed by observers to be the plan least likely to withstand constitutional scrutiny by the Supreme Court – after all, it gave the president the unprecedented unilateral power to cancel not only spending provisions, but tax breaks as well. A number of Republican legislators were therefore convinced that by seeming to give the president the greatest possible amount of authority, they were in fact giving him none at all; in this way, the Republicans could have their legislative cake and eat it too.

As it turned out, of course, they were correct. On June 25, 1998, the Supreme Court ruled the Line Item Veto Act to be an unconstitutional violation of the presentment clause.[27] Up until that point, the president had used the veto eighty-two times on eleven laws, to cancel a total of $1.9 billion in anticipated spending over five years.[28] However, the court struck down the law on the grounds that Congress had, in essence, given the president the authority to create a new law outside of the requirements of bicameral presentment from Article I, Section 7 of the Constitution. Regardless of one's assessment of the Court's reasoning,[29]

[27] *Clinton v. City of New York*, Case No. 97-1374.
[28] This included Clinton's veto of thirty-eight military construction projects, worth $287 million, which was later overturned by the procedure provided in the law: Congress passed a disagreement bill, Clinton vetoed this bill, and his veto was then overridden by two-thirds of each house of Congress, thereby restoring the projects to the budget. The total does not include savings through closing tax loopholes; the Medicare payments at issue in the line-item veto case alone were worth $2.6 billion to New York City over five years.
[29] The authors disagree on this point.

it is clear that the national experiment with line-item veto authority has come to a temporary end, and the unhappiness that many members expressed with canceled projects in their districts while the law was in operation indicates that it is unlikely to be revived in the near future.

SUMMARY

This chapter began with a general declaration that different issues will generate different politics and the specific hypothesis that issues can have both informational and distributive components, each with its own set of political imperatives. Our formal model of the policy-making process offers the predictions that (1) the higher the informational content of an issue area, the more authority Congress will delegate to the executive; and (2) legislators will be loath to delegate in those policy areas with a high ratio of political benefits to costs, and eager to delegate when the opposite is true.

The first two substantive sections of the chapter tested these two propositions. To determine if delegation followed general patterns of legislators' political advantage, we examined a series of issue-area break-downs for the laws in our sample. According to all measures, legislators jealously guard their authority in taxing and spending areas while they delegate in foreign policy and broad social issues. We argue that this configuration matches our prediction that issues with large political downsides are good candidates for delegation.

We then set about measuring the informational content of laws to test our predictions regarding information and delegation. We constructed a number of such measures, based on congressional-hearings data and on the scope of a committee's jurisdiction. Our regression analysis supported our theoretical hypothesis in every case: On average, complex issue areas are delegated at higher rates. Thus, committee-based expertise may be employed more to oversee authority delegated to the executive rather than to fashion the initial legislation.

Finally, we entered the murky waters of distributive politics and delegation. On the one hand, it may seem obvious that legislators will want to retain control over distributive, pork barrel programs to ensure that the right benefits get to the right constituents. On the other hand, distributive politics is notorious for generating a series of collective dilemmas, such as cycling in policy formation and excessive logrolling. These pathologies of policy making contribute to the inefficiency of the legislative process and therefore may encourage some level of delegation. We closely examined three policy areas traditionally thought of as distributive – agriculture, trade, and appropriations – and showed that in all cases legislators delegated rather more authority than one might think from previous descriptions of these issue areas. The relationship between distribution and delegation is therefore not straightforward: Legislators have conflicting incentives to secure district-specific benefits on the one hand and to mitigate costly logrolls on the other.

9

Conclusion

Separation of powers . . . operates on a horizontal axis to secure a proper balance of legislative, executive, and judicial authority. Separation of powers operates on a vertical axis as well, between each branch and the citizens in whose interest powers must be exercised.
Supreme Court Justice Anthony Kennedy, *Clinton v. New York*, 4.

SUMMARY OF RESULTS

In this book, we have presented what we consider a null theory of policy making under separate powers. When legislators have the option of delegating authority to the executive, the division of policy-making authority will follow the natural fault lines of political advantage: Legislators will rationally choose to delegate in exactly those areas where the political advantages of doing so outweigh the costs. The balance of power across the branches will therefore depend on the efficacy of both delegation and legislative action, from one issue area to the next.

To capture this logic of national policy making, we constructed a formal model of policy formation in which committees and agencies both possess some degree of technical expertise. The median voter in Congress could choose to delegate to the executive or make the details of policy herself, and if any authority was delegated, the discretion accompanying this authority could be circumscribed by restrictive administrative procedures. From the model, we derived a series of propositions predicting that executive discretion should rise when legislative committees are outliers, fall under divided government, and rise when the issue area at hand is characterized by informational intensity or uncertainty.

One of the goals of this project is to link theories of policy making with systematic empirical analysis. Toward this end, we derived a series of testable hypotheses from our theoretical propositions. The subsequent

232

chapters were dedicated to detailing a new data set on executive discretion in 257 pieces of important postwar legislation, which was then used to test these hypotheses. Our general methodology was to approach our estimation and measurement problems from several vantage points to see if they yielded confirmatory results. In all cases, our theoretical predictions were borne out in the data, lending substantial support to our transaction cost politics approach to policy formation.

THE GRAND REGRESSION: INTEGRATING THEORIES OF AMERICAN POLITICAL INSTITUTIONS

As a summary of our previous empirical analysis, and as a robustness check on it, we provide a final test of our theory by combining all three effects – divided government, committee outliers, and issue-area characteristics – into a single statistical equation. The comparative-statics predictions in our model are, theoretically, independent from one another, so each effect should explain a significant amount of the total variation when combined into a multiple regression. Conversely, if the coefficient on one dimension of our analysis became insignificant when estimated with the others, we would be led to conclude that its effects are subsumed by the action of the other variables.

Therefore, Table 9.1 presents a "grand regression," including committee, divided government, and issue-area effects. In the analysis, two measures of congressional–executive conflict are employed: divided government and the seat share measure discussed in Chapter 6. Committee effects are captured in the same combination of interactive terms as were employed in Chapter 7, reflecting the fact that the locus of control may swing from the floor median to the majority-party caucus median as the majority party becomes more cohesive. And the three alternative measures of issue-area complexity from Chapter 8 were used: average committee hearings, average oversight hearings, and the scope of jurisdiction.

The results shown in the table suggest that in all cases our major variables were significant in predicting the level of discretionary authority delegated to the executive. More congressional–executive conflict leads to less discretionary authority; the combination of committee measures collectively indicates that outlying committees induce the floor to delegate more authority to the executive; and as issue areas become more informationally intense, more authority is delegated. These findings reinforce our earlier conclusions drawn independently in each chapter: Delegation does respond to changes in legislative organization, interbranch conflict, and issue-area characteristics.

The empirical analysis in this book has also allowed us to take a number of claims from the literature on interbranch relations and test

Table 9.1. *Grand Regression*

Independent Var.	Model 1	Model 2	Model 3	Model 4	Model 5	Model 6
Dependent Variable: Executive Discretion						
Interbranch Conflict						
Divided	-0.04	-0.04	-0.04			
	(-2.95)**	(-3.16)**	(-3.03)**			
Seat Share				-0.17	-0.18	-0.18
				(-2.43)**	(-2.54)**	(-2.51)**
Legislative Organization						
Committee-Floor Outlier	1.32	0.98	1.03	1.30	1.00	1.05
	(2.85)**	(2.03)**	(2.19)**	(2.76)**	(2.07)**	(2.24)**
Committee-Floor Outlier*Cohesion	-0.32	-0.25	-0.25	-0.32	-0.25	-0.25
	(-3.02)**	(-2.24)**	(-2.30)**	(-2.91)**	(-2.22)**	(-2.30)**
Committee-Party Outlier*Cohesion	0.09	0.07	0.08	0.09	0.07	0.08
	(3.08)**	(2.16)**	(2.59)**	(3.03)**	(2.24)**	(2.69)**
Issue-Area Characteristics						
Avg. Hearings	0.001			0.001		
	(5.02)**			(5.05)**		
Avg. Oversight Hearings		0.01			0.01	
		(3.96)**			(3.89)**	
Scope of Jurisdiction			0.01			0.01
			(4.88)**			(4.86)**
Constant	0.06	0.11	0.07	0.03	0.08	0.04
	(2.33)**	(5.63)**	(3.20)**	(1.30)	(4.63)**	(2.06)**
F_{n-k}^{k}	11.90**	8.92**	10.98**	11.29**	8.66**	10.91**

Note: t-statistics in parentheses, calculated from robust standard errors; one-tailed test *< 0.10; **< 0.05. N=292. The data includes multiple referrals. High leverage outliers with Cook's distances greater than 0.014 omitted from the sample.

them against hard, systematic data. For the most part, the extant hypotheses performed well: The more Congress delegates, the more it constrains; legislators do enfranchise outside interest groups to oversee the executive, even more so in recent years and when interbranch conflict has been high; and legislators do strategically design the institutions of delegation, so that actors further removed from the president's direct control gain authority under divided government. But other informal hypotheses have not fared as well. Overall, total executive discretion has fluctuated over time but declined on average in the postwar era, and legislators do not wash their hands of policy once delegated to the executive; rather, they oversee more intensely those issues on which they delegate the greatest amount of discretion.

Our analysis also, as a by-product, casts light on some important themes in American politics. Regarding legislative organization, many of our results broadly support a median-voter approach to policy making: Outlying committees are associated with more delegation to executive agencies, and the impact of divided government on delegation is attenuated when committees are less representative of floor preferences. On the other hand, distributive and partisan theories also predicted well some patterns of committee assignments and delegation: Contentious, bipolar issue areas generated a partisan tilt in committee assignments, while distributive issues gave rise to committees representative of narrower interests. Further, committee outliers with respect to the majority-party caucus predict delegation to the executive under conditions of high intraparty unity. It seems, therefore, that each of these three major approaches to understanding committees and legislative organization may predict outcomes well in its own sphere of operation.

Regarding legislative-executive relations, we find that divided partisan control of government does significantly affect policy making. Previous analyses had established that the same number of significant laws are passed under unified and divided government. But we show that the content of these laws changes predictably with partisan conflict between the branches: Congress gives less discretionary authority to executive agencies controlled by the opposite party, reducing agencies' latitude and flexibility when making regulatory policy. And in at least one specific area – trade policy – these changes in executive discretion had an appreciable impact on policy outcomes.

It is also our contention that theories of legislative organization and congressional–executive relations, hitherto developed in relative isolation from one another, should be seen as intertwined, as opposite faces of a single decision on where policy should be made. The organization and activities of the executive branch, for instance, are in part shaped by the fact that the greatest delegation occurs in those areas that legislators would rather not decide themselves. Under this view, executive branch agencies will naturally become embroiled in contentious, difficult policy domains, ones in which the potential political benefits from success are outweighed by the penalties for failure. Small wonder, then, that bureaucratic miscues are far more prominent and publicized than well-executed agency policy making. And it should be little surprise that executive branch organization is so often seen as chaotic; the executive is, after all, a branch of leftovers.

On the other side of the coin, legislative organization is influenced by its position in a larger separation of powers system. Institutional structures within Congress are often seen as the result of a purely internal decision-making process, with no reference being made to actors outside of the legislative domain. According to this view, for instance, congressional committees have monopoly power over detailed policy making; the alternative to committee deliberation and expertise is uninformed policy made by the chamber floor. But legislators' choices are not so restricted, as power not reserved to committees can instead be delegated to the executive, to experts within executive branch agencies with considerable technical knowledge of their own. When committees are seen as less reliable agents for the floor, rational legislative actors can choose to shift more policy-making authority to the executive, checking both wayward committees and bureaucrats alike by shifting the locus of decision-making authority from one to the other.

Furthermore, we have shown that committee medians move predictably in response to changes in interbranch conflict, as contrary outliers. Legislative organization, in our view, should be brought out of the legislature and seen as part of our larger constitutional system of policy making, where it exists in the shadow of delegation to the executive. More broadly, the executive branch would not have its present organization and contours if it were not for the fact that it mostly exercises authority delegated by Congress, nor would Congress have the structure and procedures it does were it not separated from the branch that executes its laws.

SEPARATION OF POWERS IN THE UNITED STATES

How, then, do our results relate to the debate over the impact of delegation on our system of separate powers? That is, can the virtues of separate powers intended by the Founders be maintained alongside significant delegation to executive actors? On one side of this issue, some commentators have claimed that congressional delegation of authority to the executive undermines the very foundations of our representative government, citing *Federalist 47* as affirmation: "The accumulation of all powers, legislative, executive and judiciary, in the same hands . . . may justly be pronounced the very definition of tyranny." One way that power can come to reside within a single branch is through the practice of Congress delegating the details of policy making to executive agencies. As Justice Kennedy put it in his concurring opinion for the Line Item Veto case, "Liberty demands limits on the ability of any one branch to influence basic political decisions. . . . Abdication of responsibility is not part of the constitutional design." Therefore, the argument goes, to ensure liberty it is necessary to limit such delegations of authority.

Nor do the debates surrounding the adoption of the Constitution offer much guidance in resolving this dispute, as the Founders assumed that the legislature would jealously guard its policy-making prerogatives. They were therefore much more concerned about the possibility of congressional aggrandizement of authority than the possibility that legislators would willingly relinquish policy-making power. For the first century of governance under the Constitution, events flowed more or less according to the original scheme. But with the turn of the twentieth century, social, demographic, and political changes led the federal government to take a more active role in the regulation of society, and since the time of the New Deal legislators have assimilated the electoral advantages of delegating broad social policy to the executive. Ever since, new areas of federal policy making – product safety, public housing, environmental protection, and civil rights, for instance – have all been accompanied by a generous role for the executive.

Attacks on delegation, in short, operate under three assumptions: first, that legislators delegate many important policy decisions to executive agencies; second, that once authority has been delegated, legislators show little interest in overseeing its exercise; and third, that restricting Congress's ability to delegate will improve the quality of public policy. Hence, delegation is equivalent to the surrender of Congress's legislative duties under Article I of the Constitution, the result of which is policy detrimental to the public good.

To this argument, our work provides three responses. First, our data show that Congress does not delegate wholesale to the executive. Even on important policy issues – some of which, like the budget and tax policy, require considerable time and expertise – Congress takes a major role in specifying the details of policy. Second, when Congress does delegate, it also constrains executive discretion with restrictive administrative procedures. Legislators carefully adjust and readjust discretion over time and across issue areas so as to balance the marginal costs and benefits of legislative action against those of delegation. Congress is not free from particularistic legislation, but neither does it devote its energies solely to narrow, individually tailored policy while delegating larger issues indiscriminately to the executive.

Third, delegation is not only a convenient means to allocate work across the branches; it is also a necessary counterbalance to the concentration of power in the hands of committees. In an era where public policy becomes ever more complex, the only way for Congress to make all important policy decisions internally would be to concentrate significant amounts of authority in the hands of powerful committee and subcommittee leaders, once again surrendering policy to a narrow subset of its members. From the standpoint of floor voters, this is little better than complete abdication to executive branch agencies. As it now works, the system of delegation allows legislators to play committees off against agencies, dividing the labor across the branches so that no one set of actors dominates. Given this perspective, limits on delegation would not only be unnecessary, they would threaten the very individual liberties they purport to protect.

What, then, should the attitude of the courts be toward delegation, say through a resuscitation of the nondelegation doctrine? In our view, delegation is a self-regulating system not in need of closer attention from the judiciary. Legislators will, over time, adjust the boundaries of the administrative state so that the executive branch considers those issue areas that Congress handles less effectively itself, keeping the system in a rough equilibrium. Forcing Congress to do more legislating would only push back into the halls of the legislature those issues on which the committee system, with its lack of expertise and tendency toward uncontrollable logrolls, produces policy most inefficiently – hardly a step in the right direction.

Or consider the position, implied in the majority opinion from the Line Item Veto case discussed in Chapter 8, that, when delegating, Congress should provide agencies with a road map or algorithm for translating technical findings into policy, rather than relying more substantially on agencies' policy judgment. In the Supreme Court's opinion, Justice Stevens distinguished the Line Item Veto case from *Field v. Clark*, an early trade-related delegation case, by claiming that in the latter, "Congress itself made the decision to suspend or repeal the particular provisions at issue upon the occurrence of particular events subsequent to enactment, and it left only the determination of whether such events occurred up to the President" (27). The president did not *legislate*, that is, because Congress had made the fundamental policy decisions itself, and, subsequent to any given finding of facts, the president was *obligated* to take a certain set of actions.[1] The assumption is that, as legislators are elected and bureaucrats are not, policy decisions made in Congress gain legitimacy that agency rulings lack.

But consider a fairly complex policy area – say airline safety – in which legislators are confident that the regulator's policy goals are nearly identical to their own. Then, delegating with broad discretion will result in outcomes close to those preferred by legislators and, by transitivity, to those preferred by their constituents as well. Where is the illegitimacy here? And why would Congress delegate broadly to those who do not

---

[1] *Field v. Clark*, 143 US 649 (1892). This, in essence, is a restatement of Stewart's (1975) transmission belt hypothesis from Chapter 2.

share their policy goals?[2] In contrast, forcing Congress to provide a detailed policy algorithm may result in the regulator's having to implement policy that neither she nor the legislators in the enacting coalition would have preferred. True, a good algorithm will deliver good policy, but relatively uninformed legislators may not even possess sufficient expertise to be sure that their road map will lead to the desired destination, rather than a dead end. Must we sacrifice unanimously agreed-upon policy goals in the name of strict procedural orthodoxy?

We believe not, and conclude with the observation that the overall impact of separate powers on both the substance and pace of policy making is ambiguous. The original idea was that separate powers combined with checks and balances would inhibit or impede the process of producing new government action, making policy movement incremental. By setting ambition against ambition, and by having representatives selected from a large, diverse republic by different modes of election, policy making would perforce be a continuous process of compromise and accommodation.

But this logic does not take delegation into account, which generates a political dynamic of its own. Legislators can now avoid some hard decisions they would otherwise have to face, thus making possible the enactment of certain laws that would otherwise be politically infeasible or technically unattainable. And when bargaining with the executive, legislators can barter discretionary authority for presidential support, as in agricultural policy. So the possibility of delegation produces countervailing forces that make policy movement more rather than less likely. In the final analysis, separate powers may not decrease the volume of policy making, just change its location – this is the paradox of separate powers.

---

[2]Some may protest here that the shared policy goal between legislators and bureaucrats might be the protection of special interests rather than the public good. But then, this is a dissatisfaction with politics in general not delegation in particular; legislators have provided benefits to favored constituents from day one of the republic, and there is no evidence that the problem has intensified in the present Era of Delegation.

An Afterword on Comparative Institutions

After we had circulated initial drafts of this work, several colleagues inquired how our transaction cost politics framework could be adapted to a comparative setting. Comparative specialists, after all, love to remind us that American politics is the last bastion of area studies. This afterword therefore offers a few speculative remarks about the application of our findings to other governmental systems, both presidential and parliamentary.

The logic of our approach begins with the observation that the U.S. system of separate powers allows two general methods of policy making, through legislative committees or through executive agencies. Since legislators can control which of these two methods is chosen by writing explicit or vague legislation, the location of policy making will maximize legislators' basic political goal of reelection. So the means of policy production is explicable in terms of rational politicians' behavior.

PRESIDENTIAL SYSTEMS

Our theory should be directly applicable to other separation of powers systems (or presidential systems, as they are now called). Here, too, legislative and executive policy making are both possible, with legislators having the option of delegating power or making explicit policy themselves. If our transaction cost politics approach holds elsewhere, we should see legislatures delegating those issues that have the least electoral advantages for them and retaining control over issues whose disposition is most crucial to their reelection concerns.

Of course, lessons from the United States will not apply to other presidential systems unamended. For one thing, the U.S. government is the longest-running, most stable of all presidential systems.[1] This is

[1] This fact has generated a debate over the general performance of other presidential

240

partly due to the fact that the United States had the advantage of beginning with a relatively weak executive, so that the first century and a half of our republic saw policy making dominated by the legislature. Many other presidential systems derived directly from autocracies, so that legislative policy making was never firmly established. Indeed, many presidential constitutions were written by individuals who expected to be chief executive in the near future, and consequently they tended toward stronger executive powers from the very start. In these circumstances, the question may be, not whether legislatures decide to delegate their policy-making powers strategically, but whether the legislature is competent to make policy on its own. In other words, there may exist no viable alternative to executive policy making.[2]

In addition to these considerations, structural features of other presidential systems alter the roles of policy proposition and disposition. In the United States, the policy-making powers of the president are limited to his ability to veto legislation, which can be overridden by a two-thirds congressional vote. In other presidential systems, executives have the power of a line-item veto; constitutionally reserved decree powers;[3] budgetary powers, such as the exclusive preparation of a budget or the requirement that the legislature can reduce but not increase spending on any one item; exclusive power to introduce legislation in certain policy areas, sometimes coupled with privileged parliamentary procedures for considering this legislation; and the power to directly propose referenda.[4] In addition to these legislative powers, some presidents can unilaterally appoint and dismiss ministers, dismiss their cabinets, and even dissolve the assembly.

Given these differences in the legislative powers of the executive, the roles of proposer and administrator may in some cases be reversed with respect to the model we outlined in Chapter 4. Where presidents can propose legislation, they may choose to push politically difficult problems onto the legislature to maximize their own political advantage. And constitutionally specified decree powers are in effect delegations of authority hard-wired into the system. On the other hand, many executive decree powers are delegated by assemblies to the executive, as in the

systems, with Sartori (1997, 86) claiming that, "By and large, presidentialism has performed poorly. With the sole exception of the United States, all other presidential systems have been fragile – they have regularly succumbed to coups and breakdowns." Shugart and Carey (1992) defend presidentialism, noting that the probability of breakdown per system-year is not very different from that in parliamentary systems.

[2]This is often the case, for instance, in U.S. state governments lacking a professionalized legislature. See Fiorina (1994) for a discussion.

[3]For a comparative view of decree powers, see Carey and Shugart (1998).

[4]These powers are summarized in Shugart and Carey (1992, chap. 8).

241

Russian Duma.[5] In these cases, our theory should still hold; legislators should delegate more authority the more fractured and incoherent their internal decision-making processes are, delegate less when they have large policy differences with the executive, and delegate more on technically difficult and politically contentious issues.

PARLIAMENTARY SYSTEMS

On its face, our theory would seem to have little to offer the study of parliamentary forms of government. In the pure "Westminster model" (Lijphart 1984), a majority party in parliament elects a cabinet, essentially delegating to that body all policy-making responsibilities. The cabinet then formulates and implements policy until the next set of elections, with any formal ratification by elected legislators being perfunctory. Other than the initial maneuvering to form a government and instilling it with the power to make policy, members of parliament serve a less active role in the details of policy formation than their U.S. counterparts.

In these circumstances, it is true that no bill-by-bill strategic calculations need be performed on how much authority to cede executive actors. But, as is becoming more generally recognized in the comparative institutions literature, the Westminster model is at the far end of a spectrum that includes a variety of forms of parliamentary governments; in general, there are multiple points at which substantive policy decisions can be made. First, if a coalition government is to be formed, then the coalitional contract will often be explicit about certain policy decisions to be undertaken. Second, there is the normal ministerial policy-making stage that takes place at the cabinet level, possibly constrained by policy bargains made in phase one.[6] Third, members of parliament, sometimes acting through legislative committees, may have input into the content of public policy. And fourth, civil service bureaucrats will make important decisions when implementing policy directives.

At each of these stages, institutional variables will determine the nature and scope of policy input. Coalition governments will form only if there is no majority party and if a minority government is not feasible. Therefore, plurality winner electoral systems, which tend to produce a majority party, will often eliminate the need for intracoalitional bargaining, while proportional-representation systems encourage multiparty coalitions. Ministerial policy making may be constrained by the degree of

[5]See Chase (1999) for an exposition.
[6]The essays in Laver and Shepsle (1994) explore issues of cabinet policy making across modern European democracies.

control that the parliament has over the government in general and individual ministers in particular, as when the assembly can pass a censure vote on a particular minister. The strength of parliamentary committees varies greatly from one country to another; in some instances, they are nonexistent, whereas other countries have well-developed and influential committee systems, including Japan, Germany, Sweden, and Italy.[7] And finally, political control over bureaucrats varies according to the civil service laws of different countries. In some instances, control is well defined and strict, while in others, like France, ministries have a reputation for independent policy making.[8]

The general point, then, is that within parliamentary systems a range of institutions exists, some exhibiting a complete fusion of legislative and executive powers and others possessing independent centers of decision making within the legislature. Note that our theory would predict that, as policy conflict increases between parliaments and the government, assemblies will have incentives to cultivate their own policy-making prerogatives.[9] This is an example of our paradox of separate powers in reverse; in the United States, the presence of separate powers gives legislators incentives to delegate and thereby blur the distinctions between legislation and implementation, while in parliamentary systems the domination of policy making by the cabinet gives backbenchers incentives to create their own independent sources of expertise and policy influence.

To the extent that a given parliamentary system exhibits multiple points where policy details can be amended, the division of labor should follow our general theory of transaction cost politics. Fractured legislatures with little policy-making expertise should be willing to let cabinets and technocrats handle the intricate details of complex policy. Legislatures with policy goals distinct from the cabinet or ruling coalition (as in

---

[7]In the Italian case, there are even some instances in which committees can write and pass legislation on their own. We have argued elsewhere that the Japanese committee system under LDP domination derived from members' need to garner the personal vote under a single nontransferable vote. See Epstein, Brady, Kawato, and O'Halloran (1997).

[8]See Huber (1996) on the policy-making process in France. The Japanese bureaucracy has traditionally been regarded as an independent policy-making force as well (Johnson 1982), but see Ramseyer and Rosenbluth (1993) for an argument that political control is greater than previously supposed. See also Horn (1995), who argues that independent bureaucracies help governments commit to a set of future policies, thereby alleviating the time consistency problem legislators face when enacting policy.

[9]In fact, Peters (1997, 68) argues that just such a transformation is now taking place. For instance, British legislators established a system of select committees to serve as a counterweight to Prime Minister Thatcher's attempts to dominate all cabinet policy making.

the case of minority governments) may find it in their interest to establish competing centers of legislative power and oversight.[10] And technical issues may be safely delegated to professional civil servants with minimal political interference, since policy expertise is at a premium.

COMPARATIVE POLICY-MAKING STRUCTURES

These predictions await testing against systematic data, both across countries and within countries over time. But they do illustrate the power of our general approach to policy making, which consists of three steps. First, identify the various centers of decision making in a given governmental system; this includes all areas in which the details of policy are specified. Second, from the institutions governing policy choice, determine which actors have the power to choose one of these alternatives on a case-by-case basis. Third, identify the political interests of these actors, as generated by the electoral and constitutional structures in place. This three-step process should yield predictions on the circumstances under which policy will be made in one way or another.

Again, this division of labor may or may not coincide with technical efficiency. Sometimes rational political actors will find it to their advantage to ensure that policy incorporates the greatest technical expertise available, they may delegate to escape their own internal collective action problems, or they may insulate policy making from political control to ensure the durability of political bargains. But this need not be the case; unequal political pressures, political information, and political power – via the ballot box or otherwise – create the possibility that policy will reflect more parochial concerns rather than doing the greatest good for the greatest number.

Our approach also emphasizes that, in any political system, the advantages or disadvantages of a particular mode of policy making must always be judged relative to the next best feasible alternative. That is, it makes little sense to evaluate policy outcomes in a vacuum or against a theoretically more desirable outcome that cannot be supported by any set of self-sustaining political institutions. Politics is the art of the possible, and institutions that implement the best possible outcome are therefore the most conducive to the greater public good.

[10]See Strom (1990) for a discussion of parliamentary policy committees under minority governments.

Proofs from Formal Model in Chapter 4

Appendix A. *Proofs from Formal Model in Chapter 4*

Here stands Theory, a scroll in her hand, full of deep and mysterious combinations of figures, the least failure in which may alter the result entirely, and which you must take on trust; for who is expected to go through and check them?

Sir Malachi Malagrowther [Sir Walter Scott], 1826[1]

GAME FORMS

We assume four players: the median Floor voter in Congress (F), a congressional Committee (C), the President (P), and an Agency (A), all of whom have single-peaked preferences that can be summarized by ideal points x_i, i = F, C, P, A in a unidimensional policy space $X = \mathfrak{R}^1$; for convenience, we set $x_F = 0$ and $x_P \geq 0$. All players have quadratic preferences over outcomes: $U_i(x) = -(x - x_i)^2$ for i = F, C, P, A. Outcomes x in turn depend on both the policy passed and an exogenous parameter ω, according to the formula $x = p + \omega$. Legislators treat ω as unknown when deciding where policy will be made; all other parameters are common knowledge. The *ex ante* prior probability distribution over ω is $f(\omega)$, where $f(\omega)$ is uniform in the interval [-R,R].

The first move of the game is made by nature, which randomly selects the value of ω from the distribution $f(\omega)$. Then the Committee observes only the sign of ω, so it receives the signal ω^- if $\omega < 0$ and ω^+ if $\omega \geq 0$. The Committee then reports a bill $b(\omega; X_P)$ to the Floor, where $b \in \{\omega^-, \omega^+, \varnothing\}$, standing for a report that ω is negative, positive, and no report, respectively. The Floor voter then chooses the value of a variable $\mathcal{D} \in \{0,1\}$, where $\mathcal{D} = 0$ [1] indicates that the Floor chooses to play the Congressional Policy-Making [Agency Delegation] game.

In the Congressional Policy-Making game, the Floor player observes

---

[1]The quote from Scott was borrowed from Nicholson (1893).

the committee bill, updates her beliefs over ω to g(ω), and then passes policy $p^F(b) \in \mathfrak{R}^1$, giving a final policy outcome of $x = p^F + \omega$. In the Agency Delegation game, the Floor sets two parameters, $\hat{p}$ $(b,x_P) \in \mathfrak{R}^1$ and $d(b,x_P) \in \mathfrak{R}^1_+$. The President then sets the ideal point of the Agency, $X_A(\hat{p}, d) \in \mathfrak{R}^1$, after which the Agency observes the exact value of ω and sets policy $p^A(\hat{p}, d, \omega)$ such that $|p^A| \le d$, giving a final outcome of $x = \hat{p} + p^A + \omega$. After final policy is set, all players receive their utility payoffs and the game ends.

SUBGAME EQUILIBRIA

A strategy for the Floor is a vector $(\mathcal{D}, p^F, \hat{p}, d)$, consisting of a choice of where to make policy, how to respond to all committee bills, and the status quo and discretion given to the agency. The Committee chooses a bill b(ω; X_P) depending on its information about the random variable and the President's ideal point. The President chooses an agency ideal point $x_A(\hat{p}, d)$, and the Agency chooses a policy $p^A(\hat{p}, d, \omega)$. We solve for the set of Bayesian Nash equilibria.

> *Proposition 1:* Assume that F believes that $\omega \sim [-R, R]$. The equilibrium to the Agency Delegation game consists of the status quo $\hat{p}$, agency discretion d, and agency ideal point $x_A(\hat{p}, d)$ given by:
>
> $$\hat{p} = 0;$$
> $$d = R - x_P \text{ if } x_P \le R, d = 0 \text{ otherwise;}$$
> $$x_A = x_P, \forall \hat{p}, d.$$

Proof

It is immediately apparent that the Agency will choose final outcomes according to the rule:

$$x = \begin{cases} \omega + \hat{p} + d & \text{if} - R \le \omega \le x_A - \hat{p} - d; \\ x_A & \text{if } x_A - \hat{p} - d \le \omega \le x_A - \hat{p} + d; \\ \omega + \hat{p} - d & \text{if } x_A - \hat{p} + d \le \omega \le R. \end{cases}$$

This equation implies that the Agency will choose the outcomes closest to its ideal point, given discretion level d. Therefore, P will maximize utility by setting $x_A = x_P$. In choosing $\hat{p}$ and d, Congress maximizes its expected utility given the agency's decision rule, which is equivalent to solving:[2]

---

[2]Note that the following integral has three terms, while the equilibrium behavior it describes in Figure 4.4 has only two regions. The reason is that the third term will have length 0 at the optimal values for $\hat{p}$ and d.

$$\max_{\acute{p},d} EU_F = -\int_{-R}^{x_P-\acute{p}-d} (\omega + \acute{p} + d)^2 \frac{1}{2R}d\omega - \int_{x_P-\acute{p}-d}^{x_P-\acute{p}+d} x_P^2 \frac{1}{2R}d\omega$$

$$-\int_{x_P-\acute{p}+d}^{R} (\omega + \acute{p} - d)^2 \frac{1}{2R}d\omega$$

$$= \frac{R[(d - R)^3 - 3x_p^2 d + 3(d - R)\acute{p}^2]}{3}.$$

To find the optimal status quo, we solve:

$$\frac{\partial EU_F}{\partial \acute{p}} = 0 \Rightarrow \acute{p} = 0.$$

We now solve for the optimal agency discretion:

$$\frac{\partial EU_F}{\partial d} = 0$$

$$(x_p + R - d)(x_P - R + d) = 0.$$

This equation has two solutions: $d = R - x_P$ and $d = R + x_P$. Given our assumption that $x_A > 0$, $d^* = R - x_P$ is the appropriate choice. Since $d \geq 0$, when $x_P > R$ the optimal amount of discretion is $d = 0$. Notice that $\frac{\partial d^*}{\partial x_p} < 0$, so as the President's ideal point diverges from that of Congress, the agency will be given less discretion to set policy. **QED**

Notice that the President always prefers more discretion to less:

$$EU_P = \frac{R(d - R)[(d - R)^2 + 3(x_P - 2\acute{p})^2]}{3};$$

$$\frac{\partial EU_P}{\partial d} = R[(d - R)^2 + (x_P - 2\acute{p})^2] > 0.$$

On the other hand, the committee will want the agency to have more discretion if it is on the same side of the floor as the Agency:

$$EU_C = \frac{R[-3x_P^2 d + 6x_P x_C d - 3x_C^2 R + (d - R)((d - R)^2 + 12\acute{p}(\acute{p} - x_C))]}{3};$$

$$\frac{\partial EU_C}{\partial d} = R[-x_P^2 + 2x_P x_C + (d - R)^2].$$

Substituting in the equilibrium condition that $d = R - x_P$, this becomes $2x_P x_C R$, which is positive if $x_C > 0$, given the assumptions that x_P and R are both non-negative. Thus, committees that share an agency's policy views, compared to the Floor, prefer Agencies to have more latitude when setting policy than they actually do in equilibrium.

We now solve for the Floor's equilibrium choice of institutions, setting $\mathcal{D}$ equal to 0 or 1. Assume that $\mathcal{D} = 0$ unless the Floor strictly prefers to delegate, and note that in equilibrium, the bill from the committee will either be separating, in which case Floor beliefs will be $g(b(\omega^-)) = \omega^-$ and $g(b(\omega^+)) = \omega^+$, or it will be pooling, in which case $g(b(\omega)) = [-R, R]$ for all ω; it is impossible for the Committee to reveal information for one value of ω without revealing the complementary set of information for the other value of ω. For convenience, denote the Committee's strategy as $b(\omega = \omega^-, \omega = \omega^+)$, so that the separating equilibrium is characterized as $b^* = (\omega^-, \omega^+)$ and in the pooling equilibrium $b^* \in \{\omega^-, \omega^+, \varnothing\}$.

Proposition 2

> $\mathcal{D} = 0$ if $x_P > R$, or if $b^* = (\omega^-, \omega^+)$ and $R/2 \leq x_p \leq R$;
> $\mathcal{D} = 1$ otherwise.

Proof

Given the assumption above, the Floor will choose to play the Agency Delegation game only if $EUF_{\mathcal{D}=1} - EUF_{\mathcal{D}=0} > 0$. From Proposition 1, the Agency will receive discretion $d > 0$ only if x_P falls inside of the range of possible values of ω, after the Floor has set the status quo. In a separating equilibrium, the Floor will adjust the status quo $\hat{p} = E(\omega)$, so that the relevant range for ω is $[-R/2, R/2]$. Similarly, even if the equilibrium is pooling, the Agency will receive no discretion if $x_P > R$. **QED**

We now calculate the circumstances under which the message from the Committee will be separating, and when it will be pooling.

Proposition 3

Define condition α to hold if:

$$\begin{cases} x_P > R \text{ and } |x_C| \leq \dfrac{R}{2}, \text{ or} \\[2mm] \dfrac{R}{2} < x_P \leq R \text{ and } x_C \in \left[-\dfrac{R}{2}, \min\left(x_C^{Sep_2}, \dfrac{R}{2} \right) \right], \text{ or} \\[2mm] x_P \leq \dfrac{R}{2} \text{ and } x_C \in [x_C^-, x_C^{Sep_1}]; \end{cases}$$

where $x_C^{Sep_2} = \dfrac{8x_P^3 - 12Rx_P^2 + R^3}{24x_P^2 - 24x_pR}$, $\quad x_C^{Sep_1} = \dfrac{x_P}{3}$,

and $x_C^- = \dfrac{4x_P^3 + 3R^2x_P + R^3}{3(4x_P^2 - 4Rx_P - R^2)}$.

Equilibrium proposals $b^*(\omega)$, policies $p^{F*}(b)$, and Floor beliefs $g^*(b)$ are given by:

$b^* = (\omega^-, \omega^+)$ if condition α holds,

$b^* \in \{\omega^-, \omega^+, \varnothing\}$ otherwise;

$$p^*(b) = \begin{bmatrix} \dfrac{R}{2} & if & \alpha \text{ holds and } b = \omega^-, \\ -\dfrac{R}{2} & if & \alpha \text{ holds and } b = \omega^+, \\ 0 & otherwise; \end{bmatrix}$$

$$g^*(b) = \begin{bmatrix} \{\omega \mid \omega \in [-R, 0]\} & if & \alpha \text{ holds and } b = \omega^-, \\ \{\omega \mid \omega \in [0, R]\} & if & \alpha \text{ holds and } b = \omega^+, \\ \{\omega \mid \omega \in [-R, R]\} & otherwise. \end{bmatrix}$$

Proof

We need only check under which conditions a separating equilibrium exists, for a babbling equilibrium will exist for all values of ω. For a separating equilibrium to be supported, the Committee must prefer not to lie, and it must prefer separation to pooling. Assume first that $x_P > R/2$; so if the Committee separates, the Agency will receive no discretion, and for convenience assume $x_C \geq 0$. In a separating equilibrium, the Floor will respond to a message of $\omega = \omega^-$ with $p = R/2$ and respond to $\omega = \omega^+$ with $p = -R/2$. Then the Committee will be tempted to misinform the Floor player only when $\omega = \omega^+$. The Committee will lie if:

$$-\int_{-\frac{R}{2}}^{\frac{R}{2}} (\omega - x_C)^2 \cdot \frac{1}{R} d\omega > -\int_{\frac{R}{2}}^{\frac{3R}{2}} (\omega - x_C)^2 \cdot \frac{1}{R} d\omega;$$

$$x_C > \frac{R}{2}.$$

Thus, a separating equilibrium exists for all $x_C \leq R/2$. Similarly, if $x_C \leq 0$, then the Committee will separate whenever $x_C \geq -R/2$.

We must also check whether the Committee prefers pooling to separation, for if the Committee pools, then the Agency will receive greater delegated authority than otherwise. In a pooling equilibrium, the Floor sets $\hat{p} = 0$ and the Agency will get discretion $(R - x_P)$, and in a separating equilibrium the Agency will get no discretion and the Floor will adjust the status quo according to the signal it receives from the Committee. The Committee will therefore prefer pooling to separation iff:

$$-\int_{-R}^{2x_{P-R}} [x_C - (\omega + R - x_P)]^2 \frac{1}{2R} \, d\omega - \int_{2x_{P-R}}^{R} (x_C - x_P)^2 \frac{1}{2R} d\omega >$$

$$-\int_{-R}^{0} (x_C - \omega - \frac{R}{2})^2 \frac{1}{2R} \, d\omega - \int_{0}^{R} (x_C - \omega + \frac{R}{2})^2 \frac{1}{2R} \, d\omega$$

$$\frac{R[8x_P^3 + 24x_P x_C R + R^3 - 12x_P^2(2x_C + R)]}{12} > 0$$

$$x_C > \frac{8x_P^3 - 12Rx_P^2 + R^3}{24x_P^2 - 24x_P R} \equiv x_C^{Sep_2}.$$

This quantity is positive for all $0 < x_P < R$, and it equals $R/6$ when $x_P = R/2$.

Now assume that $x_P \leq R/2$, so that discretion d will be positive for all possible signals. Then, in a separating equilibrium, the Floor will set the status quo $\hat{p} = 0$ and grant the Agency discretion $d = R/2 - x_P$. If the Committee misleads the Floor, then the Agency will use all its discretion to move policy toward its ideal point. So when $x_c > 0$, the Committee will prefer to mislead the Floor if:

$$\int_{\frac{R}{2}}^{\frac{3R}{2}} U_C\left(\omega - \frac{R}{2} + x_P\right) \frac{1}{R} \, d\omega > \int_{-\frac{R}{2}}^{2x_P - \frac{R}{2}} U_C\left(\omega + \frac{R}{2} - x_P\right) \cdot \frac{1}{R} \, d\omega +$$

$$\int_{2x_P - \frac{R}{2}}^{\frac{R}{2}} U_C(x_P) \cdot \frac{1}{R} \, d\omega;$$

$$x_C > \frac{4x_P^3 + 3R^2 x_P + R^3}{3(4x_P^2 + R^2)} \equiv x_C^+.$$

Similarly, when $x_C \leq 0$, then the Committee will mislead when:

252

$$\int\limits_{-\frac{3R}{2}}^{-\frac{R}{2}} U_C\left(\omega + \frac{R}{2} - x_P\right)\frac{1}{R}\,d\omega > \int\limits_{-\frac{R}{2}}^{2x_P-\frac{R}{2}} U_C\left(\omega + \frac{R}{2} - x_P\right)\cdot\frac{1}{R}\,d\omega +$$

$$\int\limits_{2x_P-\frac{R}{2}}^{\frac{R}{2}} U_C(x_P)\cdot\frac{1}{R}\,d\omega;$$

$$x_C < \frac{4x_P^3 + 3R^2 x_P + R^3}{3(4x_P^2 - 4Rx_P - R^2)} \equiv x_C^-.$$

The Committee will prefer to pool if:

$$-\int\limits_{-R}^{2x_P-R} (\omega + R - x_P)^2 \frac{1}{2R}\,d\omega - \int\limits_{2x_P-R}^{R} x_P^2 \frac{1}{2R}\,d\omega >$$

$$-\int\limits_{-R}^{2x_P-R} (\omega + R - x_P)^2 \frac{1}{2R}\,d\omega - \int\limits_{2x_P-R}^{0} x_P^2 \frac{1}{2R}\,d\omega$$

$$-\int\limits_{0}^{2x_P} (\omega - x_P)^2 \frac{1}{2r}\,d\omega - \int\limits_{2x_P}^{R} x_P^2 \frac{1}{2R}\,d\omega$$

$$\frac{2x_P^2(x_P - 3x_C)R}{3} > 0$$

$$x_C > \frac{A}{3} \equiv x_C^{Sep_1}.$$

This last quantity is always greater than 0 and equals R/6 when $x_P = R/2$, so at the boundary it matches up with $x_C^{Sep_2}$. Furthermore,

$$x_C^+ - x_C^{Sep_1} = \frac{R^2(2x_P + R)}{3(4x_P^2 + R^2)} > 0,$$

so the conditions for preferring to pool always dominate those for telling the truth in this range.

Finally, note that the Floor player always prefers that the Committee separate rather than pool; F is never better off under a babbling equilibrium. Even in the most difficult case, when $x_A = R/2$, the equilibrium outcomes with an informative committee are distributed $U[-R/2, R/2]$

for all ω, while equilibrium outcomes with a babbling committee are distributed U[−R/2,R/2] for ω < 0, plus a segment with p = R/2 for ω > 0. **QED**

Note that this last point – that the Floor always prefers an informative committee – is equivalent to the statement that for any given value of x_A the Floor's utility is maximized by any value of x_C for which a separating equilibrium can be sustained. Thus, the set of optimal committees is not unique. Also, this set narrows as the preferences of the Floor and the President become closer, as shown in the equilibrium diagram, Figure 4.5. For convenience, these regions are reproduced in Figure A.1, which shows the Floor's utility as a function of x_C and x_A, drawn for R= 1.

On the other hand, the difference in equilibrium discretion between separating and babbling committees is $(R- x_A) - 0 = (R- x_A)$ for $R/2 \leq x_A \leq R$, and it is $(R- x_A) - (R/2- x_A) = R/2$ for $0 \leq x_A \leq R/2$. This difference therefore declines as x_A becomes larger, so the interaction between the preference difference between Congress and the executive, and the impact of committee outliers on discretion, should be negative.

COMPARATIVE STATICS

From Propositions 1 through 3 above, there are three cases to consider, depending on the value of x_P.

(A) $x_P > R$: $\mathcal{D} = 0$ (the Congressional Policy-Making game is always played). Equilibrium is separating if $|x_C| \leq R/2$, pooling otherwise.

(B) $R/2 \leq x_P \leq R$: $\mathcal{D} = 0$ and equilibrium is separating if $x_c \in [-R/2, x_C^{Sep_2}]$; $\mathcal{D} = 1$ and equilibrium is pooling otherwise.

(C) $x_P \leq R/2$: $\mathcal{D} = 1$ (the Agency Delegation game is always played). The equilibrium is separating if $x_C \in [x_C^-, x_C^{Sep_1}]$ and pooling otherwise.

Implicitly define $d(x_C, x_P, R)$ as the equilibrium amount of discretion given the executive agency from Propositions 1 through 3 above. Then the three hypotheses stated in the chapter follow directly:

1. $d(x_C, x_P, R) \geq d(x_C', x_P, R)$ if $|x_C| \geq |x_C'|$;
2. $d(x_C, x_P, R) \geq d(x_C, x_P', R)$ if $|x_P| \leq |x_P'|$;
3. For any R^0, there exists $\lambda(R^0) \geq 1$ such that $\lambda \geq \lambda(R^0) \Rightarrow$ $d(x_C, x_P, \lambda R) \geq d(x_C, x_P, R^0)$.

AGENCY INDEPENDENCE

Consider the following variant on the game described above. If Congress delegates, then it can set, in addition to $\hat{p}$ and d, a variable $\alpha \in [0,1]$.

254

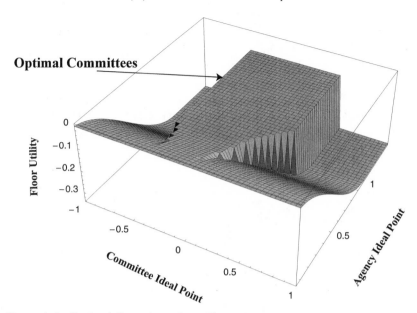

Figure A-1. Optimal Committees from Floor's Perspective

The higher the value of α, the closer is the expected agency ideal point $\bar{x}_A$ to that of Congress: $\bar{x}_A = \alpha x_F + (1 - \alpha)x_P$. However, the actual agency ideal point x_A will be $\bar{x}_A + \delta$ with probability $\frac{1}{2}$ and $\bar{x}_A - \delta$ with probability $\frac{1}{2}$. Finally, $\delta = \delta(\alpha) = \alpha^2$, so that the more control Congress has over the agency, the less predictable will be the outcomes of the regulatory process. Note that this game reduces to the baseline game when $\alpha = 0$.

Then the Floor must solve:

$$
\max_{\hat{p},d,\alpha} EU_F = \frac{1}{2}\left(-\int_{-R}^{x_A^- - \hat{p} - d} (\omega + \hat{p} + d)^2 \frac{1}{2R}\, d\omega - \int_{x_A^- - \hat{p} - d}^{x_A^- - \hat{p} + d} x_P^2 \frac{1}{2R}\, d\omega - \right.
$$

$$
\left. \int_{x_A^- - \hat{p} + d}^{R} (\omega + \hat{p} - d)^2 \frac{1}{2R}\, d\omega \right) + \frac{1}{2}\left(-\int_{-R}^{x_A^- - \hat{p} - d} (\omega + \hat{p} + d)^2 \frac{1}{2R}\, d\omega - \right.
$$

$$
\left. \int_{x_A^- - \hat{p} - d}^{x_A^- - \hat{p} + d} x_P^2 \frac{1}{2R}\, d\omega - \int_{x_A^- - \hat{p} + d}^{R} (\omega + \hat{p} - d)^2 \frac{1}{2R}\, d\omega \right)
$$

$$
= -\frac{R[-d^3 + 3d^2R + R^3 + 3\hat{p}^2R + 3d(-R^2 - \hat{p}^2 + x_P^2(\alpha - 1)^2 + \alpha^4)]}{3},
$$

where $x_A^- = x_P - \alpha^2$ and $x_A^+ = x_P + \alpha^2$.

This leads to the Floor's setting $\hat{p} = 0$ as before, and setting

$$\alpha^3 = \frac{x_P^2[-6x_P^2 + (9 + \sqrt{81 + 6x_P^2})^2]}{6(9 + \sqrt{81 + 6x_P^2})},$$

which is an increasing function of x_P, so that agencies are given more independence during times of divided government. Optimal discretion still falls as a function of x_P, so, overall, more-independent agencies will also be given less discretionary authority.

Sample of Public Laws

Appendix B *Sample of Public Laws*

Year	Cong	PL Num	Final Bill	Title
1947	80	80-101	HR3020	Labor Management Relations Act of 1947
1948	80	80-471	HR4790	Revenue Act of 1948
1948	80	80-472	S2202	Foreign Assistance Act of 1948
1948	80	80-845	S418	Water Pollution Control Act of 1948
1948	80	80-897	HR6248	Hope-Aiken Agricultural Act of 1948
1949	81	81-171	S1070	Housing Act of 1949
1949	81	81-329	HR5895	Mutual Defense Assistance Act of 1949
1949	81	81-393	HR5856	Fair Labor Standards Amendments of 1949
1949	81	81-439	HR5345	Agricultural Act of 1949
1950	81	81-507	S247	National Science Foundation Act of 1950
1950	81	81-535	HR7797	Foreign Economic Assistance Act of 1950
1950	81	81-734	HR6000	Social Security Act Amendments of 1950
1950	81	81-774	HR9176	Defense Production Act of 1950
1950	81	81-814	HR8920	Revenue Act of 1950
1950	81	81-831	HR9490	Internal Security Act of 1950
1950	81	81-909	HR9827	Excess Profits Tax Act of 1950
1951	82	82-165	HR5113	Mutual Security Act of 1951
1951	82	82-183	HR4473	Revenue Act of 1951
1951	82	82-50	HR1612	Reciprocal Trade Agreements Act of 1951
1952	82	82-414	HR5678	Immigration and Nationality Act
1952	82	82-590	HR7800	Social Security Increase of 1952
1953	83	83-31	HR4198	Submerged Lands Act
1954	83	83-358	S2150	Saint Lawrence Seaway
1954	83	83-480	S2475	Agricultural Trade Development and Assistance Act of 1954
1954	83	83-560	HR7839	Housing Act of 1954
1954	83	83-591	HR8300	Internal Revenue Code of 1954
1954	83	83-637	S3706	Communist Control Act of 1954
1954	83	83-690	HR9680	Agricultural Act of 1954
1954	83	83-703	HR9757	Atomic Energy Act of 1954
1954	83	83-761	HR9366	Social Security Amendments of 1954
1955	84	84-381	S2168	Minimum Wage Increase of 1955
1955	84	84-86	HR1	Trade Agreements Extension Act of 1955
1956	84	84-485	S500	Colorado River Storage Project—Authority to Construct, Operate, and Maintain
1956	84	84-540	HR10875	Agricultural Act of 1956
1956	84	84-627	HR10660	Highway Act of 1956
1956	84	84-880	HR7225	Social Security Amendments of 1956
1957	85	85-256	HR7383	Atomic Energy Act of 1954 Amendment
1957	85	85-315	HR6127	Civil Rights Act of 1957
1958	85	85-508	HR7999	Alaska—Admission into Union
1958	85	85-568	HR12575	National Aeronautics and Space Act of 1958

(cont.)

Year	Cong	PL Num	Final Bill	Title
1958	85	85-599	HR12541	Department of Defense Reorganization Act of 1958
1958	85	85-625	S3778	Transportation Act of 1958
1958	85	85-686	HR12591	Trade Agreements Extension Act of 1958
1958	85	85-835	S4071	Agricultural Act of 1958
1958	85	85-840	HR13549	Social Security Amendments of 1958
1958	85	85-864	HR13247	National Defense Education Act of 1958
1959	86	86-257	S1555	Labor-Management Reporting and Disclosure Act of 1959
1959	86	86-3	S50	Hawaii—Admission into Union
1959	86	86-372	S2654	Housing Act of 1959
1960	86	86-449	HR8601	Civil Rights Act of 1960
1960	86	86-778	HR12580	Social Security Amendments of 1960
1961	87	87-128	S1643	Agricultural Act of 1961
1961	87	87-195	S1983	Foreign Assistance Act of 1961
1961	87	87-27	S1	Area Redevelopment Act
1961	87	87-293	HR7500	Peace Corps Act
1961	87	87-297	HR9118	Arms Control and Disarmament Act of 1961
1961	87	87-30	HR3935	Fair Labor Standards Amendment of 1961
1961	87	87-41	HR6518	Inter-American Program—Appropriation
1961	87	87-64	HR6027	Social Security Increase, 1961
1961	87	87-70	S1922	Housing Act of 1961
1962	87	87-415	S1991	Manpower Development and Training Act of 1962
1962	87	87-543	HR10606	Public Welfare Amendments of 1962
1962	87	87-624	HR11040	Communications Satellite Act of 1962
1962	87	87-781	S1552	Drug Amendments of 1962
1962	87	87-794	HR11970	Trade Expansion Act of 1962
1962	87	87-834	HR10650	Revenue Act of 1962
1963	88	88-129	HR12	Health Professionals Educational Assistance Act of 1963
1963	88	88-156	HR7544	Maternal and Child Health and Mental Retardation Planning Amendments of 1963
1963	88	88-164	S1576	Mental Retardation Facilities and Community Health Centers Construction Act of 1963
1963	88	88-204	HR6143	Higher Education Facilities Act of 1963
1963	88	88-206	HR6518	Clean Air Act of 1963
1963	88	88-38	S1409	Equal Pay Act of 1963
1964	88	88-272	HR8363	Revenue Act of 1964
1964	88	88-297	HR6196	Agricultural Act of 1964
1964	88	88-352	HR7152	Civil Rights Act of 1964

(cont.)

Year	Cong	PL Num	Final Bill	Title
1964	88	88-365	S6	Urban Mass Transportation Act of 1964
1964	88	88-452	S2642	Economic Opportunity Act of 1964
1964	88	88-525	HR10222	Food Stamp Act of 1964
1964	88	88-577	S4	Wilderness Act of 1964
1965	89	89-10	HR2362	Elementary and Secondary Education Act, ESEA of 1965
1965	89	89-110	S1564	Voting Rights Act of 1965
1965	89	89-115	HR2984	Health Research Facilities Amendments of 1965
1965	89	89-117	HR7984	Housing and Urban Development Act of 1965
1965	89	89-174	HR6927	Department of Housing and Urban Development (HUD)
1965	89	89-209	S1483	National Foundation on the Arts and the Humanities Act of 1965
1965	89	89-234	S4	Water Quality Act of 1965
1965	89	89-236	HR2580	Immigration and Nationality Act— Amendments
1965	89	89-272	S306	Motor Vehicles—Air Pollution—Solid Waste Disposal Act of 1965
1965	89	89-285	S2084	Highway Beautification Act of 1965
1965	89	89-321	HR9811	Food and Agriculture Act of 1965
1965	89	89-329	HR9567	Higher Education Act of 1965
1965	89	89-4	S3	Appalachian Regional Development Act of 1965
1965	89	89-44	HR8371	Excise Tax Reduction Act of 1965
1965	89	89-97	HR6675	Social Security Amendments of 1965
1966	89	89-563	S3005	National Traffic and Motor Vehicle Safety Act of 1966
1966	89	89-601	HR13712	Fair Labor Standards Amendments of 1966
1966	89	89-670	HR15963	Department of Transportation Act
1966	89	89-675	S3112	Clean Air Act Amendments of 1966
1966	89	89-753	S2947	Clean Waters Restoration Act of 1966
1966	89	89-754	S3708	Demonstration Cities and Metropolitan Development Act of 1966
1966	89	89-755	S985	Fair Packaging and Labeling Act of 1966
1967	90	90-129	S1160	Public Broadcasting Act of 1967
1967	90	90-148	S780	Air Quality Act of 1967
1967	90	90-201	HR12144	Meat Inspection—State Programs
1967	90	90-202	S830	Age Discrimination in Employment Act of 1967
1967	90	90-248	HR12080	Social Security Amendments of 1967
1968	90	90-284	HR2516	Civil Rights Riots—Fair Housing—Civil Obedience

(cont.)

Year	Cong	PL Num	Final Bill	Title
1968	90	90-321	S5	Consumer Credit Protection Act
1968	90	90-321	S5	Consumer Credit Protection Act
1968	90	90-351	HR5037	Omnibus Crime Control and Safe Streets Act
1968	90	90-364	HR15414	Revenue and Expenditure Control Act of 1968
1968	90	90-448	S3497	Housing and Urban Development Act of 1968
1968	90	90-481	S1166	National Gas Pipeline Safety Act of 1968
1968	90	90-492	HR16363	Wholesale Poultry Products Act
1968	90	90-537	S1004	Colorado River Basin Project Act
1968	90	90-543	S827	National Trails System Act
1968	90	90-618	HR17735	Gun Control Act of 1968
1969	91	91-124	HR14001	Selective Service Amendments Act of 1969
1969	91	91-172	HR13270	Tax Reform Act of 1969
1969	91	91-173	S2917	Federal Coal Mine Health and Safety Act of 1969
1969	91	91-190	S1075	National Environmental Policy Act of 1969
1970	91	91-222	HR6543	Public Health Cigarette Smoking Act of 1969
1970	91	91-224	HR4148	Water and Environmental Quality Improvement Act of 1970
1970	91	91-258	HR14465	Airport and Airway Development Act of 1970
1970	91	91-285	HR4249	Voting Rights—Tests
1970	91	91-373	HR14705	Employment Security Amendments of 1970
1970	91	91-375	HR17070	Postal Reorganization Act of 1970
1970	91	91-379	S3302	Defense Production Act—Amendments— Economic Stabilization
1970	91	91-452	S30	Organized Crime Control Act of 1970
1970	91	91-453	S3154	Urban Mass Transportation Assistance Act of 1970
1970	91	91-513	HR18583	Comprehensive Drug Abuse Prevention and Control Act of 1970
1970	91	91-518	HR17849	Rail Passenger Service Act of 1970
1970	91	91-524	HR18546	Agricultural Act of 1970
1970	91	91-596	S2193	Occupational Safety and Health Act (OSHA) of 1970
1970	91	91-604	HR17255	Clean Air Amendments of 1970
1970	91	91-644	HR17825	Omnibus Crime Control Act of 1970
1970	91	91-671	HR18582	Food Stamp Act—Amendments
1971	92	92-178	HR10947	Revenue Act of 1971
1971	92	92-218	S1828	National Cancer Act of 1971

(cont.)

Year	Cong	PL Num	Final Bill	Title
1971	92	92-5	HR4690	Public Debt Limit—Interest Rate—Social Security Wage Base
1971	92	92-54	S31	Emergency Employment Act of 1971
1972	92	92-225	S382	Federal Election Campaign Act of 1971
1972	92	92-261	HR1746	Equal Employment Opportunity Act of 1972
1972	92	92-318	S659	Education Amendments Act of 1972
1972	92	92-336	HR15390	Public Debt Limitation—Extension
1972	92	92-500	S2770	Federal Water Pollution Control Act Amendments of 1972
1972	92	92-512	HR14370	State and Local Fiscal Assistance Act of 1972
1972	92	92-516	HR10729	Federal Environmental Pesticide Control Act of 1972
1972	92	92-573	S3419	Consumer Product Safety Act of 1972
1972	92	92-603	HR1	Social Security Amendments of 1972
1973	93	93-148	HJRE542	War Powers Resolution
1973	93	93-153	S1081	Trans-Alaska Pipeline Authorization Act
1973	93	93-159	S1570	Emergency Petroleum Allocation Act of 1973
1973	93	93-198	S1435	District of Columbia Self-Government and Governmental Reorganization Act
1973	93	93-203	S1559	Comprehensive Employment and Training Act (CETA) of 1973
1973	93	93-222	S14	Health Maintenance Organization Act of 1973
1973	93	93-233	HR11333	Social Security Benefits—Increase
1973	93	93-236	HR9142	Regional Rail Reorganization Act of 1973
1973	93	93-86	S1888	Agriculture and Consumer Protection Act of 1973
1973	93	93-87	S502	Federal Aid Highway Act of 1973
1974	93	93-259	S2747	Fair Labor Standards Amendment of 1974
1974	93	93-344	HR7130	Congressional Budget and Impoundment Control Act of 1974
1974	93	93-383	S3066	Housing and Community Development Act of 1974
1974	93	93-406	HR2	Employment Retirement Income Security Act (ERISA) of 1974
1974	93	93-438	HR11510	Energy Reorganization Act of 1974
1974	93	93-443	S3044	Federal Elections Campaign Act Amendments of 1974
1974	93	93-502	HR12471	Freedom of Information Act of 1974
1974	93	93-503	S386	National Mass Transportation Assistance Act of 1974

(cont.)

Appendix B *(cont.)*

Year	Cong	PL Num	Final Bill	Title
1974	93	93-618	HR10710	Trade Act of 1974
1974	93	93-637	S356	Magnuson-Moss Warranty Act—Federal Trade Commission Improvement Act
1974	93	93-641	S2994	National Health Planning and Resources Development Act of 1974
1975	94	94-12	HR2166	Tax Reduction Act of 1975
1975	94	94-143	HR10481	New York City Seasonal Financing Act of 1975
1975	94	94-145	HR6971	Consumer Goods Pricing Act of 1975
1975	94	94-163	S622	Energy Policy and Conservation Act
1975	94	94-29	S249	Securities Act Amendments of 1975
1975	94	94-73	HR6219	Voting Rights Act of 1965—Extension
1976	94	94-210	S2718	Railroad Revitalization and Regulatory Reform Act of 1976
1976	94	94-455	HR10612	Tax Reform Act of 1976
1976	94	94-469	S3149	Toxic Substances Control Act
1976	94	94-553	S22	Copyrights Act
1976	94	94-566	HR10210	Unemployment Compensation Amendments of 1976
1976	94	94-579	S507	Federal Land Policy and Management Act (FLPMA) of 1976
1976	94	94-580	S2150	Resource Conservation and Recovery Act of 1976
1976	94	94-588	S3091	National Forest Management Act (NFMA) of 1976
1977	95	95-113	S275	Food and Agriculture Act of 1977
1977	95	95-151	HR3744	Fair Labor Standards Amendments of 1977
1977	95	95-216	HR9346	Social Security Amendments of 1977
1977	95	95-217	HR3199	Clean Water Act of 1977
1977	95	95-30	HR3477	Tax Reduction and Simplification Act of 1977
1977	95	95-87	HR2	Surface Mining Control and Reclamation Act
1977	95	95-95	HR6161	Clean Air Act, Amendments of 1977
1978	95	95-454	S2640	Civil Service Reform Act of 1978
1978	95	95-504	S2493	Airline Deregulation Act of 1978
1978	95	95-600	HR13511	Revenue Act of 1978
1978	95	95-617	HR4018	Public Utility Regulatory Policies Act of 1978
1978	95	95-618	HR5263	Energy Tax Act of 1978
1978	95	95-619	HR5037	National Energy Conservation Policy Act
1978	95	95-620	HR5146	Power Plant and Industrial Fuel Use Act of 1978
1978	95	95-621	HR5289	Natural Gas Policy Act of 1978

(cont.)

Year	Cong	PL Num	Final Bill	Title
1979	96	96-185	HR5860	Chrysler Corporation Loan Guarantee Act of 1979
1979	96	96-39	HR4537	Trade Agreements Act of 1979
1979	96	96-88	S210	Department of Education Organization Act
1980	96	96-221	HR4986	Depository Institutions and Monetary Control Act of 1980
1980	96	96-223	HR3919	Crude Oil Windfall Profits Tax Act on Oil
1980	96	96-294	S932	Energy Security Act
1980	96	96-296	S2245	Motor Carrier Act of 1980
1980	96	96-448	S1946	Staggers Rail Act of 1980
1980	96	96-487	HR39	Alaska National Interest Lands Conservation Act
1980	96	96-510	HR7020	Comprehensive Environmental Responses, Compensation, and Liability Act of 1980
1981	97	97-34	HR4242	Economic Recovery Tax Act of 1981
1982	97	97-205	HR3112	Voting Rights Act Amendments of 1982
1982	97	97-248	HR4961	Tax Equity and Fiscal Responsibility Act of 1982
1982	97	97-253	HR6955	Agriculture and Food Act of 1982 (Omnibus Budget Reconciliation Act)
1982	97	97-300	S2036	Job Training Partnership Act
1982	97	97-320	HR6267	Garn-St. Germain Depository Institutions Act of 1982
1982	97	97-424	HR6211	Surface Transportation Assistance Act of 1982
1982	97	97-425	HR3809	Nuclear Waste Policy Act of 1982
1983	98	98-144	HR3706	Public Holiday—Birthday of Martin Luther King, Jr.
1983	98	98-21	HR1900	Social Security Amendments of 1983
1984	98	98-369	HR4170	Deficit Reduction Act of 1984
1984	98	98-473	HJRES648	Continuing Appropriations, 1985—Comprehensive Crime Control Act of 1984
1984	98	98-549	S66	Cable Communications Policy Act of 1984
1984	98	98-573	HR3398	Trade and Tariff Act of 1984
1985	99	99-177	HJRES372	Public Debt Limit—Balanced Budget and Emergency Deficit Control Act of 1985
1985	99	99-198	HR2100	Food Security Act of 1985
1986	99	99-433	HR3622	Goldwater-Nichols Department of Defense Reorganization Act of 1986
1986	99	99-440	HR4868	Comprehensive Anti-Apartheid Act of 1986
1986	99	99-499	HR2005	Superfund Amendments and Reauthorization Act of 1986
1986	99	99-514	HR3838	Tax Reform Act of 1986

(cont.)

Year	Cong	PL Num	Final Bill	Title
1986	99	99-570	HR5484	Anti-Drug Abuse Act of 1986
1986	99	99-603	S1200	Immigration Reform and Control Act (IRCA) of 1986
1986	99	99-662	HR6	Water Resources Development Act of 1986
1987	100	100-17	HR2	Surface Transportation and Uniform Relocation Assistance Act of 1987
1987	100	100-203	HR3545	Omnibus Budget Reconciliation Act of 1987
1987	100	100-242	S825	Housing and Community Development Act of 1987
1987	100	100-4	HR1	Water Quality Act of 1987
1987	100	100-77	HR558	McKinney Homeless Assistance Act of 1987
1988	100	100-259	S557	The Civil Rights Restoration Act of 1987
1988	100	100-360	HR2470	Medicare Catastrophic Coverage Act of 1988
1988	100	100-383	HR442	Wartime Relocation of Civilians
1988	100	100-418	HR4848	Omnibus Trade and Competitiveness Act of 1988
1988	100	100-485	HR1720	Family Support Act of 1988
1988	100	100-690	HR5210	Anti-Drug Abuse Act of 1988
1989	101	101-157	HR2710	Fair Labor Standards Amendments of 1989
1989	101	101-73	HR1278	Financial Institutions Reform, Recovery, and Enforcement Act of 1989
1990	101	101-336	S933	Americans with Disabilities Act of 1990
1990	101	101-508	HR5835	Omnibus Budget Reconciliation Act of 1990
1990	101	101-549	S1630	Clean Air Act—Amendments
1990	101	101-624	S2830	Food, Agriculture, Conservation, and Trade Act of 1990
1990	101	101-625	S566	Cranston-Gonzalez National Affordable Housing Act
1990	101	101-649	S358	Immigration Act of 1990
1991	102	102-166	S1745	Civil Rights Act of 1991
1991	102	102-240	HR2950	Surface Transportation Efficiency Act
1992	102	102-385	S12	Cable Television Consumer Protection and Competition Act of 1992
1992	102	102-486	HR776	Energy Policy Act of 1992
1992	102	102-511	S2532	Freedom for Russia and Emerging Eurasian Democracies and Open Markets Support Act of 1992
1992	102	102-575	HR429	Reclamation Projects Authorization and Adjustment Act of 1992

APPENDIX C

Sample Coding Sheet

Sample Coding Sheet

Discretion

Year: `1979`　Congress: `96`　PLNum: `96-39`　Final Bill: `HR4537`

Title: `Trade Agreements Act of 1979`

Description: `Foreign Trade Act Extension. Approved Tokyo Round nontariff barrier reductions.`

Delegation

Yes | No

# of Major Provisions: `59`　# With Delegation: `24`　# With Exec Deleg: `24`

Agencies Receiving Authority:

Agency Name		Agency Type	Created by this Law?
Agriculture, Department of	Add...	Cabinet	☐
Commerce, Department of	Add...	Cabinet	☐
Customs Court	Add...	Judicial Actors	☐
Customs Service	Add...	Cabinet	☐
Domestic Manufactures	Add...	Private Corporation	☐
International Trade Commission	Add...	Independent Agencies	☐
President	Add...	Executive Office of the Pr	☐
Special Trade Representative	Add...	Independent Agencies	☐
Treasury, Department of	Add...	Cabinet	☐
United States Trade Representative	Add...	Executive Office of the Pr	☐

Constraints On Discretion

Appointment Power Limits: ☐   Comment:

Time Limits: ☑   Comment: (52) President's authority to negotiate trade agreements with foreign countries to reduce or eliminate NTBs is extended for an additional 8 years until Jan 3, 1988.

Spending Limits: ☐   Comment:

Legislative Action Required: ☑   Comment: (4) Any legislation would be considered under fast-track procedures.

Executive Action Required: ☐   Comment:

Legislative Veto: ☐   Comment:

Reporting Requirements: ☑   Comment: (28) President to submit a report to Congress that assessed the effect of the procurement provisions in areas of high unemployment.

Consultation Requirements: ☑   Comment: (4) If any future change in US law was necessary to conform to a code agreement, the president must consult with congressional committees, at least a month before submitting a draft bill.
(33) USTR is directed to resolve complaints from other nations that had signed the code or observed its provisions through consultations and, if consultations failed, submit it to international arbitration.
(46) USTR to request consultation with the foreign country involved in the dispute as part of its investigation.

Public Hearings: ☐   Comment:

Appeals Procedures: ☑   Comment: (33) Other nations that signed the code could file a complaint with the USTR alleging that specific domestic practices violated US obligations under the standards code.
(45) Any interested person could file a petition alleging unfair trade practices with the USTR's office.
(48) Provided increased opportunities for judicial review of some provisional and all final rulings by the Treasury Department and the ITC in antidumping and countervailing duty cases.
(50) Any interested party involved in the proceeding is allowed to take legal action and any party can challenge the amount of countervailing or antidumping duty as well as the failure to assess a duty.
(51) Provided expedited review procedures for antidumping and countervailing duty cases and these cases would be given priority in Customs court.

Rule-Making Requirements: ☑   Comment: (3) The president could accept a particular agreement if only one industrial country had not accepted the agreement and acceptance by that country was not considered essential.
(5) Countervailing duties can offset foreign governments' export subsidies if the Treasury Department determined that an import was either directly or indirectly subsidized and the ITC determined that a domestic industry had been

"materially injured" or threatened with injury.
(6) Defined material injury as "a harm which is not inconsequential, immaterial, or unimportant."
(10) Treasury Department to verify the accuracy of any information submitted to it before making a final determination. If it was not able to verify the information, it must rely on the best information available, which could include information submitted by the domestic industry.
(12) Provided for an antidumping duty if the Treasury Department found that merchandise was being or was likely to be sold in the U.S. at less than fair value and if the ITC determined that a domestic industry was materially injured or threatened with material injury. The duty would be the amount by which the home market price exceeded the U.S. price for the merchandise.
(17) Established 5 methods of determining the value of imports to simplify the process of assessing duties.

Direct Oversight: ☐	Comment:	

Exemptions: ☑	Comment:	(24) Excluded from the waiver provision several U.S. agencies, including the Departments of Transportation and Energy, the Tennessee Valley Authority, and the Army Corps of Engineers. Also excluded state and local governments and small and minority businesses.

Compensations: ☐	Comment:	

Notes:

These are not examples of time limits. Removed from the list:

(14) Custom service has 6 months to determine the amount of dumping and assess the duty.
(45) USTR office has 45 days to determine if an investigation is necessary when an affected person files a petition alleging unfair trade practices.
(57) President must submit a trade reorganization proposal to Congress by July 10, 1979, and then congressional committees have to make their best efforts to take final action on a reorganization bill by Nov. 10, 1979.

Rechecked by Sharyn O' 9/31/96

Date/Typist Entered:	CheckedBy:	DateChecked:
11/20/95 EG/slo	Barak	2/27/96

Coding Rules for Discretion

Appendix D. *Coding Rules for Discretion*

This appendix details the coding rules used to compile the data sets in our study. As a general rule, each of the data sets was coded independently by two different researchers, and then checked over by a third. Upon final entry, each law was then checked a fourth and final time by the authors.

MAJOR PROVISIONS

For the most part, counting the number of major provisions listed in *Congressional Quarterly*'s legislative summaries was straightforward: Each new paragraph counted as a provision. In difficult cases, we followed these rules:

- Bullets and paragraphs count as separate provisions.
- Sub-bullets do not count if they merely elaborate on the previous paragraph.
- Sub-bullets do count if they include new substantive authority.
- Unbulleted paragraphs count as a separate provision if they are substantively distinct from the previous, bulleted paragraph.
- If a paragraph is followed by a colon and a list of elements, and if the elements of the list merely elaborate on the main point of the paragraph, then we count the paragraph and accompanying list as one provision.

DELEGATION

Our definition of delegation is any major provision that gives another governmental body the authority to move policy away from the status quo. To maintain consistency across laws, we developed the following guidelines.

Examples of what delegation *is*:

- The authorization of a new program with some discretionary powers;
- Discretion to make or modify decision-making criteria;
- Extension of discretionary authority that would otherwise expire;
- The creation of a new commission, board, or agency;
- Demonstration projects;
- Grants and loans where the agency determines the size of the award and/or the recipients;
- The right to issue subpoenas;
- The right to bring suit or intervene in an existing suit;
- The right to issue waivers;
- The ability to enter into contracts.

Examples of what delegation is *not*:

- Authorizing appropriations or funds for a program;
- Requiring reports, studies, or publication of information;
- The hiring of staff or personnel;
- Transferring delegated authority from one executive branch actor to another without increasing the scope of that authority;
- Evaluations, recommendations, and assessments that do not directly alter policy;
- Audits, which are considered constraints and not delegation to, for instance, the GAO.

CONSTRAINTS

The next step is to define how we coded the fourteen categories of administrative procedures associated with each law. These categories are all defined as constraints on executive action above and beyond those specified in the 1946 Administrative Procedure Act.

Appointment Power Limits

These are defined as limits on whom the president can appoint to commissions or to be heads of agencies, beyond requiring the advice and consent of the Senate. Typical limits include the requirement that a commission be bipartisan, that it be composed of experts in a certain field, that some of its members be the heads of certain other agencies, or that congressional actors get to name some of the appointees. However, simply limiting the size of a commission, the length of its term, or its members' pay were not coded as appointment power limits.

For example, in the Foreign Assistance Act of 1948, Congress required that the Joint Committee on Foreign Economic Cooperation consist of two majority members and one minority member of the Senate Foreign Relations Committee, one minority and one majority member from the Senate Appropriations Committee, and similarly for the House.

Time Limits

Time limits arise when delegated authority is associated with sunset provisions (i.e., it expires after a certain specified time period), or when the amount of time that an agency regulation can affect a private party is limited. The most common time limit arises when a program automatically expires after a fixed period; other typical cases include a limit on the duration of contracts between the government and private parties or loans that can be extended for only a specified time frame. Funds authorized for a program for a set number of years, however, were *not* coded as a time limit.

Examples include the Excess Profits Tax of 1950, which was scheduled to expire at the end of June 1953; the Foreign Assistance Act of 1948, where the program was to terminate on June 30, 1952, or upon concurrent resolution of Congress; and the Trade Agreements Extension Act of 1958, which extended tariff-cutting authority through June 30, 1962. In each of these cases, the law specified a fixed time frame within which the agency was to act or no further action could be taken, or the act itself would expire unless Congress renewed or extended the authority. We see similar limits in the Atomic Energy Act of 1954, which allowed the Atomic Energy Commission to issue licenses for ten years, and in the National Aeronautics and Space Act of 1958, in which the president could transfer functions to NASA for four years. We also see limits on the number of years funds could be used, as in the National Defense Education Act of 1958, which authorized the commissioner of education from 1959 to 1962 to make loans and grants to state agencies for up to four years.

Spending Limits

Spending limits define a maximum amount that an agency can allocate to any activity or set of activities, either stated explicitly or in a formula. This does *not* include authorizations or appropriations for an act in general; we focus instead on whether or not Congress sought explicitly to limit how (in which ways) the agency could allocate monies, typically by limiting the percentage of a project's cost that the federal government could pay, the requirement of matching grants, or a cap on the amount of benefits payable to any one recipient.

For example, the Clean Water Restoration Act of 1966 eliminated existing dollar ceilings on the amount of federal assistance a single sewage treatment plant could receive, thus permitting the federal government to provide up to a flat 30 percent of the construction costs of an approved treatment project. In the same act, we find incentive grants that provided that the federal government could contribute up to 40 percent of a project's construction costs if the state in which the project was to be built agreed to pay at least 30 percent of costs of all projects within its boundaries receiving such federal grants. The 1967 Social Security Act similarly provided that day-care centers be set up to take care of the preschool children of those mothers who take training and hold a job, and provided for 80 percent federal matching grants for the cost of the work training and day-care programs. Moreover, the act specified that 50 percent of the total authorization would be for formula grants, 40 percent for project grants, and 10 percent for research and training.

Legislative Action Required

Another constraint that limits the ability of executive agencies to alter policy is the requirement that Congress must act prior to the agency's action becoming effective by passing a bill or resolution that approves the policy proposed by the agency. In these cases, the agency's decision does not constitute final policy action, but rather the final action is placed in the hands of Congress. This category of constraint is more stringent than a legislative veto, which allows an agency's decision to take effect *unless* Congress acts to stop it. Here, in order for the agency's decision to take effect at all, Congress must first take some positive action, usually requiring at least a majority in each chamber.

The shining example of the use of legislative action required was the 1974 Trade Reform Act. Before international trade agreements affecting domestic regulations could be enacted, Congress had to vote to implement the legislation through what have come to be known as fast-track procedures. Similarly, extensions of Most Favored Nation status require congressional approval. We see like provisions in the Atomic Energy Act of 1954, which specifies that Congress must authorize the construction of large-scale atomic electric demonstration plants approved by the Atomic Energy Commission.

Executive Action Required

Another means of limiting arbitrary actions by agencies is to require that their rulings or decisions be approved by a separate agency or the president himself. This is less restrictive than requiring congressional action, since executive actors appointed by the same president may tend to have similar policy preferences, but it is also less costly from legislators' point of view. This category contained only provisions that required final agency actions to be approved by another executive branch actor to take effect; requirements that one executive branch actor merely consult with another before taking action were coded in the separate category of consultation requirements.

Examples include the 1954 St. Lawrence Seaway Act, which requires that the decisions of the St. Lawrence Seaway Development Corporation be subject to presidential approval. Similarly, according to the Trade Agreements Extension Act of 1958 the president must approve the Tariff Commission's recommendations regarding tariff alterations for them to become effective. The Airport and Airway Development Act of 1970 requires that airport runway extension locations approved by the Department of Transportation must also be approved by either the Secretary of the Interior or the Secretary of HEW to affirm that these plans conform to applicable air- and water-quality standards. And the Postal Reorganization Act of 1970 specifies that postal service rates be subject to approval by the Board of Governors and the Interstate Commerce Commission.

Legislative Veto

In some sense, of course, Congress can always override the decisions taken by an agency by passing a law that makes null and void the agency's action and by overriding a presidential veto with a two-thirds vote. A legislative veto establishes a special procedure outside the normal bicameral approval and presentment process that allows Congress to overturn specific agency decisions through a unicameral resolution or a two-house concurrent resolution.

Throughout the postwar period, legislative vetoes of one sort or the other were rather common. For example, the Federal Land Policy and Management Act (FLPMA) of 1976 included several such override provisions. The act specified that Congress could veto by concurrent resolution within ninety days any decision to exclude from one or more principal uses (including timber production, grazing, fish, and wildlife development) a tract of 100,000 acres, or to sell a tract of more than 2,500 acres, or to withdraw federal lands from uses such as mining or grazing for twenty-year periods. Moreover, the secretary of agriculture could terminate any of those withdrawals, unless Congress disapproved that termination by concurrent resolution within ninety days.

Reporting Requirements

One of the central ways in which Congress is able to keep tabs on what the bureaucracy is doing is through reporting requirements. Usually after – or even in some cases prior to – the agency's promulgating a rule or making a decision, they are to report to Congress or the oversight committees as to the actions taken, or those that will be taken, and their proposed economic impact. Reporting requirements can be very detailed – often Congress specifies exactly the type of information it wishes to consider – or can just require that the agency report to Congress annually about its general activity.

For example, the Energy Policy and Conservation Act of 1975 stated that the president was to report to Congress by April 15, 1977, on the adequacy of the incentive provided under existing price ceilings for development of Alaskan oil. More typically, we find, as in the Toxic Substances Control Act, that the EPA is required to submit an annual report on the administration of the law to the president and Congress.

Consultation Requirements

Sometimes Congress requires that before an agency promulgates any regulations it must consult with other agencies as well. In many ways, this is similar to the category of Executive Action Required, but here final agency action does not require the approval of another actor – the agency simply has to consult with a specified actor prior to making its final ruling. Other instances of this category arise when agencies must consult with affected private interests or with Congress before promulgating regulations.

The Clean Air Act Amendments of 1977, for example, required that before the EPA could redesignate federal lands, it had to consult with a federal land manager. The Civil Service Reform Act of 1978 required agencies to consult with unions that had exclusive representation rights about government-wide rules or regulations that would make a substantial change in employment conditions. The Depository Institutions and Monetary Control Act of 1980 authorized the Federal Reserve Board to consult with other regulatory bodies to initiate supplemental reserves. And the Nuclear Waste Policy Act of 1982 required that the Energy Department consult closely throughout the site-selection process with states or Indian tribes that might be affected by its decision.

Public Hearings

Section 553 of the 1946 APA sets out the basic elements of "notice and comment" rule making: Advance notice of proposed rules must be published in the *Federal Register*, and interested parties given the opportunity to express their opinions. Thus public hearings will be a normal element of policy making in any case. This category of constraints identifies those acts that specifically call for an agency to hold public hearings at certain times or under certain circumstances over and above the requirements of the APA.

For example, the Hope-Aiken Agricultural Act of 1948 states that the Secretary of Agriculture must hold public hearings before raising support prices above a given maximum level. In the Housing Act of 1949, the Housing and Home Finance Agency was required to hold public hearings before slum clearings. And in the Internal Security Act of 1950, the Subversive Activities Control Board was to hold hearings on whether a group is a communist action or front group. On more regular business, under the Trade Expansion Act of 1962 the Tariff Commission was to hold hearings on proposed tariff changes; in the Clean Air Act of 1963 the HEW Secretary had to hold hearings on alleged air pollution problems before taking action; and the Civil Rights Act of 1964 formalized procedures for public hearings and required that agencies hold hearings before enforcing any nondiscrimination provisions.

Appeals Procedures

All agency decisions are subject to judicial review and can be appealed by a person or group that can show that they are adversely affected by the ruling. Here, we coded for whether the act established explicit procedures by which an agency's decision could be appealed. This includes giving a group standing, expediting the review process, or defining in which court's jurisdiction a case will be heard. Over time, appeals procedures have become an effective way for environmental and civil rights groups to force effective change on a case-by-case basis, and by the 1970s most social policy contained rather detailed appeals procedure provisions.

The Omnibus Crime Control and Safe Streets Act of 1968, for instance, made provisions to curb potential abuses of the system by allowing individuals who file a discrimination suit to follow up in court, by establishing that the subject of wiretapping can ask the court to suppress the contents of recorded conversations, and that the subject can sue any person who makes illegal interceptions. In the Gun Control Act of 1968, the aggrieved party can go to a U.S. district court and appeal the treasury secretary's decision to deny a gun license. The Occupational Safety and Health Act (OSHA) of 1970 provided that the OSHA Appeals Committee had to conduct hearings if an employer contested a violation and issued penalties and orders to enforce the act; that any person affected by an employment commission order could obtain review in the U.S. court of appeals; and that any person could file for a judicial review of a safety and health standard within sixty days of its promulgation. Similarly, one of the major changes in the Clean Air Amendments of 1970 was that affected persons could bring suit in federal court against the EPA for failure to perform specified duties or prosecute violators. Moreover, standing was expanded in the Federal Water Pollution Control Act Amendments of 1972 so as to authorize citizen suits against the U.S. government, federal agencies, or the EPA, and provided for judicial review of the EPA's actions.

Rule-making Requirements

The most common way for Congress to limit the discretionary authority that an agency has in implementing policy is to specify detailed rules and procedures in the form of standards and criteria by which an agency must make a decision. Sometimes the agency is merely directed to regulate in the public interest; for example, in the Hope-Aiken Agricultural Act of 1948 we find general mandates that allow the agriculture secretary to raise price supports if necessary to ensure national security. But more often than not, Congress specifies in intricate detail what the agency can and cannot do, and how an agency can do what it does.

For example, in the Labor Management Relations Act of 1947, Congress went into great detail as to what defined unfair labor practices by unions. The Fair Labor Standards Amendments of 1949, which raised the minimum wage to 75 cents, carefully defined categories of workers covered by minimum-wage regulations. The Agricultural Act of 1949 allowed the secretary to set price supports between 75 and 90 percent of parity and defined the conditions of eligibility for price supports. The St. Lawrence Seaway Act of 1954 stated what projects the St. Lawrence Seaway Development Corporation could undertake, including canals, locks, and dredging. And the California Water Policy Reform Act of 1992 required that the Bureau of Reclamation could temporarily reduce water reserves for wildlife and the environment only if natural conditions, such as droughts, mandated such a change.

Exemptions

Here we coded whether a specific group or class of interests was exempted from the effects of a regulation, either permanently or for a given period of time. Often exemptions were explicitly noted as such in the *Congressional Quarterly* legislative summaries; at other times, the content of the provision made it clear that an exemption was being offered.

The Fair Labor Standards Amendments of 1949, for instance, listed exemptions from coverage under the wages and hours section, including retail sales, dry cleaning, sharecroppers, and newspapers. Industries excluded from hours section only included airline employees and fish canneries. And industries excluded from child-labor laws included agricultural workers and newspaper delivery. The Foreign Economic Assistance Act of 1950 exempted cotton from the provision that the Economic Cooperation Administration could not pay higher prices for commodities procured in the United States than the prevailing world price. The Trade Agreements Extension Act of 1958 exempted articles covered under the national security provision. And the Clean Water Act of 1977 exempted from industrial cost recovery requirements those industries discharging 25 thousand gallons or less per day into municipal treatment plants, as long as the sludge was not toxic.

Compensations

This category includes provisions that the government directly compensate private interests for the adverse impact of federal regulations. Under the Fifth Amendment to the Constitution, of course, any government takings must be accompanied by just compensation, so again this category of constraint accounted for compensations over and above this baseline standard. Provisions that awarded special privileges to an industry in return for any adverse consequences of regulation were also counted as compensations.

Examples include the Trade Agreements Act of 1979, which reduced tariffs on imported cheese products but compensated cheese producers by allowing the president to proclaim import quotas up to an annual level of 111,000 metric tons on 85 percent of cheeses currently imported, and established fast-track complaint procedures to protect domestic producers against subsidies on foreign cheeses. The Cable Communications Policy Act of 1984 specified compensation for firms forced to sell property when franchises were revoked. The Surface Transportation and Uniform Relocation Assistance Act of 1987 provided compensation for homeowners displaced by federally funded transportation projects. And the Omnibus Trade and Competitiveness Act of 1988 authorized a new training program for workers who lost jobs due to increased trade.

Direct Oversight

All bureaucratic agencies are subject to oversight by congressional committees. But in certain cases, we find that Congress takes the time to specify how agencies' actions will be overseen, for example, by a General

Accounting Office (GAO) audit or by holding congressional hearings. These procedures are coded separately from other devices used to oversee agencies, such as reporting requirements or public hearings, because they entail a level of direct involvement by a third party exterior to the agency's daily functioning and routines. While direct oversight activities are intrusive and time-consuming, they are not as uncommon as one might expect.

One example of direct oversight occurred in the Public Broadcasting Act of 1967, which required that the Corporation for Public Broadcasting's accounts be audited by the GAO. Similarly, the Federal Water Pollution Control Act Amendments of 1972 required an oversight study by the GAO of research and demonstration programs; the Health Maintenance Organization Act of 1973 required the GAO to evaluate the operations of at least fifty HMOs funded under the act; the Employment Retirement Income Security Act (ERISA) of 1974 authorized the Internal Revenue Service to audit plans receiving tax consideration; the Energy Policy and Conservation Act of 1975 authorized the GAO to conduct verification audits of the records of any person required to submit energy information to the Federal Energy Administration, the Interior Department, or the Federal Power Commission; the Civil Service Reform Act of 1978 authorized the GAO to conduct audits and reviews of agency compliance with civil service laws and regulations; and finally, the Staggers Rail Act of 1980 required the United States Railway Association to audit the railroads' benefits program annually.

Gridlock Interval and Other Measures of Interbranch Conflict, 1947–1992

Appendix E. Gridlock Interval and Other Measures of Inter-branch Conflict, 1947–1992

Year	House Veto-	House Median	House Veto+	Senate Veto-	Senate Filibuster-	Senate Median	Senate Filibuster+	Senate Veto+	President	Gridlock	Seat Share	Divided
1947	1.9	17.0	39.2	-4.8	-4.8	12.7	33.0	33.0	66.4	44.0	9.6%	1
1948	0.1	8.1	38.3	3.8	3.8	15.0	27.2	27.2	71.2	34.5	9.6%	1
1949	9.2	34.1	58.2	7.6	7.6	18.1	34.6	34.6	72.2	50.7	-17.0%	0
1950	15.4	26.5	54.6	-0.3	-0.3	17.7	35.7	35.7	80.6	54.9	-17.0%	0
1951	10.7	23.7	50.5	2.7	2.7	16.9	37.6	37.6	78.3	47.7	-5.2%	0
1952	4.3	23.1	42.0	5.1	5.1	17.8	30.4	30.4	75.3	36.9	-5.2%	0
1953	13.1	21.8	39.1	4.3	4.3	18.3	33.2	33.2	35.2	30.8	-1.4%	0
1954	8.9	19.4	40.4	7.4	7.4	13.9	35.1	35.1	23.6	16.3	-1.4%	0
1955	12.7	33.1	53.5	6.8	6.8	16.8	36.7	36.7	54.0	46.6	3.6%	1
1956	15.4	30.7	45.0	6.9	6.9	26.3	44.7	44.7	41.0	34.1	3.6%	1
1957	12.0	24.4	49.1	7.9	7.9	28.2	47.4	47.4	47.1	39.2	4.6%	1
1958	14.9	29.0	51.0	9.5	9.5	23.6	38.7	38.7	37.8	28.3	4.6%	1
1959	13.0	36.0	59.0	17.3	17.3	35.7	54.0	54.0	18.0	36.0	30.4%	1
1960	14.7	38.9	64.7	11.3	11.3	40.8	55.4	55.4	24.3	31.1	30.4%	1
1961	10.0	31.7	60.5	18.2	18.2	40.4	55.3	55.3	68.1	42.3	-25.0%	0
1962	10.0	31.7	60.5	18.2	18.2	40.4	55.3	55.3	72.4	42.3	-25.0%	0
1963	9.7	35.7	64.9	16.6	16.6	39.6	61.2	61.2	81.2	48.4	-26.6%	0
1964	9.7	35.7	64.9	16.8	16.8	40.0	60.3	60.3	81.2	48.1	-26.6%	0
1965	18.1	43.5	69.8	11.8	11.8	48.0	63.5	63.5	86.3	58.0	-35.8%	0
1966	15.0	38.6	72.0	10.6	10.6	43.2	63.7	63.7	79.6	61.4	-35.8%	0
1967	16.5	29.5	66.5	22.0	22.0	36.5	59.7	59.7	87.3	44.5	-21.0%	0
1968	13.2	35.1	57.0	16.6	16.6	37.6	59.9	59.9	99.7	43.3	-21.0%	0
1969	13.3	32.5	51.7	13.8	13.8	40.0	63.4	63.4	21.2	42.1	12.8%	1
1970	16.8	29.0	57.4	14.6	14.6	36.7	62.5	62.5	49.1	34.5	12.8%	1
1971	17.2	33.0	59.8	19.3	19.3	34.8	60.1	60.1	9.8	43.0	13.8%	1

Appendix E. (cont.)

Year	House Veto-	House Median	House Veto+	Senate Veto-	Senate Filibuster-	Senate Median	Senate Filibuster+	Senate Veto+	President	Gridlock	Seat Share	Divided
1972	14.5	31.5	57.1	19.4	19.4	35.9	60.7	60.7	38.6	19.2	13.8%	1
1973	18.2	35.8	61.3	18.1	18.1	49.6	63.8	63.8	11.7	45.7	13.2%	1
1974	18.5	32.9	62.9	16.6	16.6	46.0	66.9	66.9	12.3	50.3	13.2%	1
1975	24.0	48.1	73.2	19.0	31.5	50.2	63.7	65.5	29.0	34.7	28.8%	1
1976	21.6	47.6	68.3	25.6	35.9	46.2	56.5	65.1	2.9	34.8	28.8%	1
1977	20.8	48.0	64.3	20.8	31.1	46.6	59.2	67.5	71.4	36.4	-28.8%	0
1978	24.9	44.5	64.0	23.4	29.6	48.4	54.6	60.8	94.7	34.3	-28.8%	0
1979	20.5	43.9	68.4	24.4	29.5	47.4	53.8	59.0	79.8	38.9	-22.4%	0
1980	22.0	44.0	70.0	25.7	32.7	46.6	57.1	64.1	69.6	36.8	-22.4%	0
1981	17.8	33.4	59.4	13.9	18.5	32.5	41.8	51.0	1.1	27.9	2.4%	1
1982	14.6	37.4	70.3	9.8	17.6	36.3	45.6	59.7	8.5	35.8	2.4%	1
1983	17.6	51.5	75.8	13.1	18.0	33.0	48.0	57.3	4.2	38.5	8.0%	1
1984	18.9	49.2	69.3	12.5	25.9	39.3	48.3	55.8	-3.3	36.7	8.0%	1
1985	13.3	44.7	65.6	10.6	21.4	33.0	44.6	55.4	-0.4	34.1	5.0%	1
1986	19.4	44.0	68.7	12.0	25.5	34.4	52.4	59.8	4.7	40.4	5.0%	1
1987	19.9	50.9	74.1	15.1	29.3	48.2	57.6	62.4	-5.9	42.5	13.4%	1
1988	22.6	53.1	73.5	16.1	29.5	47.3	54.5	65.2	-4.9	38.4	13.4%	1
1989	18.6	51.9	70.9	18.9	28.2	37.6	56.2	62.5	-0.1	37.6	14.8%	1
1990	25.3	47.6	69.9	21.1	27.7	43.5	54.9	64.0	-3.1	33.8	14.8%	1
1991	26.4	46.6	71.8	15.7	29.2	47.3	56.3	65.3	-0.5	40.5	17.4%	1
1992	23.5	54.5	75.1	15.9	29.3	51.7	60.6	65.2	-2.7	44.8	17.4%	1

Note: Before 1975 a two-thirds majority was needed to cut off debate in the Senate, so the filibuster pivots are the same as the veto pivots. Afterward, this requirement was reduced to three-fifths of the Senate.
Source: Calculated using real ADA scores provided in Groseclose, Levitt, and Snyder (1997).

288

Coding Rules for Roll-Call Votes

Appendix F. *Coding Rules for Roll-Call Votes*

We identified each of the roll calls associated with the passage of our sample laws and coded if the measure sought to increase or decrease executive discretion. Here we relied on the *Congressional Quarterly*'s vote summaries contained in the *CQ Almanac* and the ICPSR brief descriptions of each roll call. When these briefs were ambiguous, we located the discussion of the roll-call measure in the *CQ* legislative summary. If, after reviewing these secondary sources, it was still unclear if the vote was over delegation, we turned to the primary sources, including committee reports and the debates surrounding consideration of the measure.

A. DEFINING ROLL CALLS OVER DELEGATION

The first step in coding each roll call is to determine whether or not the motion under consideration (amendment, rule, passage, etc.) directly affects delegation. The step-by-step procedure is as follows:

1. For each roll call, read the ICPSR description.
2. Compare this with the associated *Congressional Quarterly* roll-call brief.
3. Determine if the roll call is a vote on delegation or not.
4. If in doubt about step 3, consult the *CQ* legislative summaries of each bill.
5. If the vote is not over delegation, stop and go to the next record. Otherwise, proceed to the steps below.

B. CODING FOR DISCRETION IN ROLL CALLS

Once it has been determined that a measure concerns delegation, the next step is to code if the motion increases or decreases delegated au-

Table F-1. *Relevant Status Quo for Different Types of Roll-Call Votes*

Motion	Status Quo	Sources
Rule	Bill as reported by committee	• *CQ* summary of legislation
Passage	Existing law	• *CQ* background summary • *Congressional Record* • *Committee Reports*
Amendment	Bill	• *CQ* summary of legislation
Motion to Recommit with Instructions	Bill	• *CQ* summary of legislation
Conference Report	Version of the bill passed by the House	• *CQ* summary on Conference Report

thority. The key here is to compare the motion with its *alternative* – that is, how much authority would the executive have if the motion passed as opposed to the status quo if it failed. For each type of motion, then, we identified the relevant alternative:

1. Rules

Most rules specify the terms for consideration of a bill, not its content. So for the most part, unless the rule also contains an amendment (as some rules do for the consideration of conference reports), rules will be coded as no delegation. If a rule does somehow alter the bill, the relevant status quo to determine if the bill increases or decreases discretion is the bill itself.

2. Amendments

Here the relevant comparison is between the proposed amendment and the section of the bill or amendment that it changes.

3. Motions to Recommit with Instructions

Again, the relevant comparison is the section of the bill that would be changed under recommital.

4. Passage

The relevant comparison here is existing law. The *CQ Almanac* background summaries usually provide a description of existing legislation and how the proposed bill would alter it. If after reading the *CQ* summary we were still unclear, we consulted the committee reports and the accompanying text in the *Congressional Record*.

5. Conference Report

Here the relevant status quo is the *House* version of the bill. Did the conference committee decrease (increase) the amount of authority the House was willing to cede the administration? *CQ* summaries usually provide a comparison between the House and the Senate versions. Table F-1 provides a quick overview of the relevant status quo for coding discretion.

APPENDIX G

Committee Hearings Data

Appendix G. *Committee Hearings Data*

Committee hearings data were collected for two purposes: first, to gauge the relative extent to which congressional committees oversee the federal bureaucracy; second, to measure the average "informational intensity" of the issues that fall within the jurisdiction of a congressional committee. This section outlines how these data were collected and compiled.

DATA SOURCE

We relied on a third-party commercial vendor, Congressional Information Service, Inc. (CIS), which publishes summaries of all published committee hearings. CIS also makes these summaries available on-line. We obtained these on-line briefs and created a file containing all the hearings held by each standing committee from the 80th to 103d Congress. We used two of CIS's products: *Congressional Masterfile 1* and *Congressional Masterfile 2*.[1] The former provides an on-line summary of each published hearing from the second session of the 91st Congress through to the present (or, at the time of the study, the 103d Congress). The latter provides a summary of each published hearing and a summary of selected unpublished hearings. The congressional masterfiles come with their own extraction software, which allows the researcher to search by using keywords, subject, date of hearings, or serial set number. As our needs are somewhat specialized, we were forced to rely on our own search engines, which we now detail.

[1] Copyright © Congressional Information Service, Inc., 1997. Used by permission.

DATA EXTRACTION METHOD

To analyze this data, we wrote two UNIX shell script programs.[2] The first program counted the number of times a particular committee held hearings during a Congress. The second program counted the number of hearings per committee in which the term "review" or "oversight" occurred in the content notation section of the summaries (the term "oversight" was tracked from the second session of the 91st Congress up to the 103d Congress; the term "review" was tracked from the 80th Congress through the first session of the 91st Congress). Finally, the data for the different Congresses were aggregated for each Congress by committee, as detailed in Chapter 8.

Several particularities of these data should be noted. First, the files for the pre-1970 Congresses include the unpublished hearings. Unpublished hearings are, mostly, hearings that the chairperson of the committee deemed inappropriate to make public at the time of the hearing. Under the House rules, hearings must be made public thirty years after the date of the hearing. The implementation of this rule remains uneven.

Second, CIS claims that unpublished hearings were included when the masterfile was generated because of: (1) uncertainty at the time of file generation of the meaning of "unpublished" hearings; and (2) the rule of thumb of "Better safe than sorry." Consequently, the forms of the summaries of the two products (and the subsequent structure of the files generated by the two products) are not the same. This is reflected in the somewhat different Awk programs run for the two groups of hearings (i.e., the post-1969 and pre-1970 files).

Third is the issue of unpublished hearings for the 80th through 91st. Congresses. Unpublished hearings were only available prior to 1959. Furthermore, most unpublished hearings had multiple CIS numbers. Nor have all unpublished hearings thirty years old or older been made public. After discussion, we decided to exclude the unpublished hearings to ensure that the file for all Congresses (i.e., 80th through 103d) was consistent in including published hearings only. The Awk programs were modified to do this.

Our fourth concern was the issue of multiple CIS numbers per published hearing for the 80th–91st Congresses. Upon review of the data files and the text files (and discussion with CIS personnel), it became apparent that some published hearings had multiple CIS numbers. This is due to the fact that a hearing that was bound in multiple volumes received multiple CIS numbers – one for each volume of the hearing

[2]These programs, written in Awk, are available from the authors upon request. We would like to thank Greg Wawro for supplying the original programs upon which ours are based.

(e.g., h1231–1-A, h1231–1-B, etc.). Consequently, two approaches were developed to ensure that there was no multiple counting of a hearing: one for assigning all hearings to a committee and the other for assigning hearings with the term "review" in the content notation section to a committee.

Approach 1

When counting the total number of published hearings per Congress, we were able simply to modify the Awk program to exclude all CIS numbers (and their associated records) that ended with a B – Z. In other words, of those records which ended with a capital letter, we only included those ending with a capital A.

Approach 2

Such an approach was not possible for keeping track of hearings that had "review" in the content notation section of the record. Assume, for instance, that hearing h1231–1-B had "review" in the content notation section of the record but h1231–1-A did not. In other words, the content notation section was not the same for all volumes of a hearing. Such an approach would have unnecessarily missed hearings that had "review" in the content notation section of the record. To check for this possibility, all oversight hearing files were concatenated and sorted and then reviewed manually to identify and count identical lines. Once the number of duplicate lines per committee per Congress were counted, these numbers were subtracted from the generated file.

MATCHING LAWS AND COMMITTEE HEARINGS

It may seem most natural to measure informational intensity by hearings data for the reporting committee in the Congress where the measure was passed. For example, if an appropriations bill is passed in the 89th Congress, it may seem reasonable to use the number of hearings from the Appropriations Committee in the 89th Congress alone to measure informational intensity. But there are a number of reasons to aggregate committee data across years rather than relying on any one given year.

First, a set of hearings across more than one Congress may culminate in a single piece of legislation. For example, the 1988 Omnibus Trade Act took three years from its original introduction to finally become a law. And the Post Office Committee considers rates hikes nearly continuously, but actual legislation is produced only every few Congresses. Second, other committees may visit issues sporadically, so that when an important piece of legislation is enacted, the number of hearings in that Congress will be unrepresentative of the committee's usual workload. That is, measuring informational intensity by the number of hearings that occurred in a given committee during the Congress in which a measure was passed would confound general notions of complexity with the specific hearings that would have to be held to pass a major piece of legislation. Finally, given the changes in coding mentioned above, we would not want our inferences to be influenced by the CIS coding period in which a bill was enacted. We therefore use period-wide averages per committee to measure informational content.

References

Aberbach, Joel D. 1990. *Keeping a Watchful Eye: The Politics of Congressional Oversight*. Washington, D.C.: Brookings Institution.

Aldrich, John. 1995. *Why Parties? The Origin and Transformation of Political Parties in America*. Chicago: University of Chicago Press.

Alexander, De Alva Stanwood. 1916. *History and Procedure of the House of Representatives*. Boston: Houghton Mifflin.

Alt, James, and Charles Stewart. 1990. "Parties and the Deficit: Some Historical Evidence." Paper presented at National Bureau of Economic Research Conference on Political Economics, Cambridge, MA.

American Political Science Association, Committee on Political Parties. 1950. *Toward a More Responsible Party System: A Report*. New York: Rinehart.

Aranson, Peter, Ernest Gellhorn, and Glen Robinson. 1982. "A Theory of Legislative Delegation." *Cornell Law Review* 68:55–63.

Arnold, Douglas. 1990. *The Logic of Congressional Action*. New Haven, CT: Yale University Press.

Arrow, Kenneth J. 1951. *Social Choice and Individual Values*. New York: Wiley.

Austen-Smith, David. 1993. "Interested Experts and Policy Advice: Multiple Referrals Under Open Rule." *Games and Economic Behavior* 5:3–43.

Austen-Smith, David, and William H. Riker. 1990. "Asymmetric Information and the Coherence of Legislation." *American Political Science Review* 81: 897–918.

Bach, Stanley, and Steven Smith. 1988. *Managing Uncertainty in the House of Representatives: Adaptation and Innovation in Special Rules*. Washington, DC: Brookings Institution.

Banks, Jeffrey. 1989. "Agency Budgets, Cost Information, and Auditing." *American Journal of Political Science* 33:670–99.

Banks, Jeffrey, and Randall Calvert. 1992. "A Battle-of-the-Sexes Game with Incomplete Information." *Games and Economic Behavior* 4:347–72.

Banks, Jeffrey, and Barry Weingast. 1992. "Political Control of Bureaucracies under Asymmetric Information." *American Journal of Political Science* 36:509–24.

Bawn, Kathleen. 1995. "Political Control versus Expertise: Congressional

Choices About Administrative Procedures." *American Political Science Review* 89:62–73.

———. 1996. "Strategic Response to Institutional Change: Parties, Committees and Multiple Referral." *Public Choice* 88:239–58.

Bendor, Jonathan. 1988. "Review Article: Formal Models of Bureaucracy." *British Journal of Political Science* 18:353–95.

Bendor, Jonathan, Serge Taylor, and Roland Van Gaalen. 1985. "Bureaucratic Expertise versus Legislative Authority: A Model of Deception and Monitoring in Budgeting." *American Political Science Review* 79:1041–60.

———. 1987. "Politicians, Bureaucrats, and Asymmetric Information." *American Journal of Political Science* 31:797–828.

Bensel, Richard. 1980. "Creating the Statutory System: The Implications of a Rule of Law Standard in American Politics." *American Political Science Review* 74:734–44.

Bibby, John. 1968. "Congress's Neglected Function." In *Republican Papers*, ed. Melvin Laird. New York: Praeger.

Black, Duncan. 1958. *The Theory of Committees and Elections.* Cambridge University Press.

Bollen, Kenneth, and Robert Jackman. 1990. "Regression Diagnostics: An Expository Treatment of Outliers and Influential Cases." In *Modern Methods of Data Analysis*, eds. John Fox and J. Scott Long. Newbury Park, CA: Sage Publications.

Brady, David. 1993. "The Causes and Consequences of Divided Government: Toward a New Theory of American Politics." *American Political Science Review* 87:734–44.

Brady, David, and David Epstein. 1997. "Intraparty Preferences, Heterogeneity, and the Origins of the Modern Congress: Progressive Reformers in the House and Senate, 1890–1920." *Journal of Law, Economics, and Organization* 13:26–49.

Brady, David, and Morris Fiorina. 1997. "New Perspectives on Congressional Elections." Manuscript. Stanford University.

Brady, David, and Craig Volden. 1998. *Revolving Gridlock.* Boulder, CO: Westview Press.

Bruff, Harold, and Peter Shane. 1988. *The Law of Presidential Power.* Durham, NC: Carolina Academic Press.

Bryce, James. 1888. *The American Commonwealth.* New York: Macmillan.

Calvert, Randall. 1985. "The Value of Biased Information: A Rational Choice Model of Political Advice." *Journal of Politics* 47:530–55.

Calvert, Randall, Mathew McCubbins, and Barry Weingast. 1989. "A Theory of Political Control and Agency Discretion." *American Journal of Political Science* 33:588–611.

Calvert, Randall, Mark Moran, and Barry Weingast. 1987. "Congressional Influence over Policy Making: The Case of the FTC." In *Congress: Structure and Policy*, ed. Mathew McCubbins and Terry Sullivan. Cambridge: Cambridge University Press.

Cameron, Charles, Albert Cover, and Jeffrey Segal. 1990. "Senate Voting on

Supreme Court Nominees: A Neoinstitutional Model." *American Political Science Review* 84:525–34.

Carey, John, and Matthew Shugart, eds. 1998. *Executive Decree Authority*. New York: Cambridge University Press.

Cass, Ronald, and Colin Diver. 1987. *Administrative Law: Cases and Materials*. Boston: Little Brown & Company.

Chase, Judith. 1999. "Placating the President: Legislative Struggle and Surrender in Russia, 1993–1996." Ph.D. diss., Columbia University.

Clausen, Aage. 1973. *How Congressmen Decide: A Policy Focus*. New York: St. Martin's Press.

Coase, Ronald. 1937. "The Nature of the Firm." *Economica* 4:386–405.

——— 1960. "The Problem of Social Cost." *Journal of Law and Economics* 3:1–44.

——— 1988. *The Firm, the Market, and the Law*. Chicago: University of Chicago Press.

Collie, Melissa, and Joseph Cooper. 1989. "Multiple Referral and the 'New' Committee System in the House of Representatives." In *Congress Reconsidered*, eds. Lawrence Dodd and Bruce Oppenheimer. Washington, DC: Congressional Quarterly Press.

Cook, R. Dennis, and Sanford Weisberg. 1983. "Diagnostics for Heteroskedasticity in Regression." *Biometrika* 70:1–10.

Cooper, Joseph, and David Brady. 1981. "Institutional Context and Leadership Style: The House from Cannon to Rayburn." *American Political Science Review* 75:411–25.

Cox, Gary, and Samuel Kernell, eds. 1991. *The Politics of Divided Government*. Boulder, CO: Westview Press.

Cox, Gary, and Mathew McCubbins. 1993. *Legislative Leviathan: Party Government in the House*. Berkeley: University of California Press.

Crawford, Vincent, and Joel Sobel. 1982. "Strategic Information Transmission." *Econometrica* 50:1431–51.

Cutler, Lloyd. 1988. "Some Reflections about Divided Government." *Presidential Studies Quarterly* 18:485–92.

——— 1989. "Now Is the Time for All Good Men. . . ." *William and Mary Law Review* 30:485–92.

Davidson, Roger, Walter Oleszek, and Thomas Kephart. 1988. "One Bill, Many Committees: Multiple Referrals in the US House of Representatives." *Legislative Studies Quarterly* 13:3–28.

Davis, Kenneth. 1978. *Administrative Law Treatise*. San Diego: Kenneth Davis.

Denzau, Arthur T., and Robert J. Mackay. 1983. "Gatekeeping and Monopoly Power of Committees: An Analysis of Sincere and Sophisticated Behavior." *American Journal of Political Science* 27:740–61.

Diermeier, Daniel, and Roger Myerson. 1996. "Lobbying and Incentives for Legislative Organization." Manuscript. Stanford University Graduate School of Business.

Dion, Douglas, and John D. Huber. 1996. "Procedural Choice and the House Committee on Rules." *Journal of Politics* 58:25–53.

Dion, Douglas, John D. Huber, and Keith Krehbiel. 1997. "Restrictive Rules Reconsidered." *American Journal of Political Science* 41:919–64.

Dixit, Avinash. 1996. *The Making of Economic Policy: A Transaction-Cost Perspective*. Cambridge, MA: MIT Press.

Dodd, Lawrence C., and Richard L. Schott. 1986. *Congress and the Administrative State*. New York: Macmillan.

Epstein, David. 1997. "An Informational Rationale for Committee Gatekeeping Power." *Public Choice* 91:271–99.

1998. "Partisan and Bipartisan Signaling in Congress." *Journal of Law, Economics, and Organization* 14:183–204.

Epstein, David, David Brady, Sadafumi Kawato, and Sharyn O'Halloran. 1997. "A Comparative Approach to Legislative Organization: Careerism and Seniority in the United States and Japan." *American Journal of Political Science* 41:965–88.

Epstein, David, and Sharyn O'Halloran. 1994. "Administrative Procedures, Information, and Agency Discretion." *American Journal of Political Science* 38:697–722.

1995. "A Theory of Strategic Oversight: Congress, Lobbyists, and the Bureaucracy." *Journal of Law, Economics, and Organization* 11:227–55.

1996. "Divided Government and the Design of Administrative Procedures: A Formal Model and Empirical Test." *Journal of Politics* 58:373–97.

1998. "Modeling Madison: A Multiple Principals Model of Interest Group Competition." Manuscript. Columbia University.

1999. "Delegation and the Structure of Policy Making: A Transaction Cost Politics Approach." *Journal of Theoretical Politics* 11:37–56.

Farber, Daniel, and Philip Frickey. 1991. *Law and Public Choice: A Critical Introduction*. Chicago: University of Chicago Press.

Farrell, Joseph, and Nancy Gallini. 1988. "Second-Sourcing as a Commitment: Monopoly Incentives to Attract Competition." *Quarterly Journal of Economics* 103:673–94.

Fenno, Richard. 1973. *Congressmen in Committees*. Boston: Little, Brown.

Ferejohn, John. 1986. "Logrolling in an Institutional Context: A Case Study of Food Stamp Legislation." In *Congress and Policy Change*, eds. Gerald Wright, Leroy Rieselbach, and Lawrence Dodd. New York: Agathon Press.

Fiorina, Morris. 1977. *Congress: The Keystone of the Washington Establishment*. New Haven, CT: Yale University Press.

1982. "Legislative Choice of Regulatory Forms: Legal Process or Administrative Process?" *Public Choice* 39:33–71.

1986. "Legislator Uncertainty, Legislative Control, and the Delegation of Legislative Power." *Journal of Law, Economics, and Organization* 2:33–51.

1992. *Divided Government*. New York: Macmillan.

1994. "Divided Government in the American States: A Byproduct of Legislative Professionalism?" *American Political Science Review* 88:304–16.

Ford, Henry Jones. 1898. *The Rise and Growth of American Government*. New York: Macmillan.

Froman, Lewis. 1967. *The Congressional Process*. Boston: Little, Brown.

References

Gibson, Martha. 1994. "Politics and Divided Government." Paper presented at the American Political Science Association Annual Meeting, New York.

Gilligan, Thomas, and Keith Krehbiel. 1987. "Collective Decision-Making and Standing Committees: An Informal Rationale for Restrictive Amendment Procedures." *Journal of Law, Economics, and Organization* 3:287–335.

——— 1989. "Collective Choice without Procedural Commitment." In *Models of Strategic Choice in Politics*, ed. Peter Ordeshook. Ann Arbor: University of Michigan Press.

Goldberg, Victor. 1976. "Regulation and Administered Contracts." *Bell Journal of Economics* 7:426–52.

Greene, William. 1993. *Econometric Analysis*. 2d ed. New York: Macmillan.

Groseclose, Timothy, Steve Levitt, and James Snyder. 1997. "An Inflation Index for ADA Scores." Manuscript. MIT.

Hamilton, Alexander, John Jay, and James Madison. 1937 *The Federalist. A Commentary on the Constitution of the United States*. New York: Modern Library.

Hammond, Thomas H. 1986. "Agenda Control, Organizational Structure, and Bureaucratic Politics." *American Journal of Political Science* 30:379–420.

Hammond, Thomas H., and Gary J. Miller. 1985. "A Social Choice Perspective on Expertise and Authority in Bureaucracy." *American Journal of Political Science* 29:1–28.

Hansen, John Mark. 1991. *Gaining Access: Congress and the Farm Lobby, 1919–1981*. Chicago: University of Chicago Press.

Harris, Joseph. 1964. *Congressional Control of Administration*. Washington, DC: Brookings Institution.

Hart, Oliver. 1995. *Firms, Contracts, and Financial Structure*. Oxford: Clarendon Press.

Hasbrouck, Paul. 1927. *Party Government in the House of Representatives*. New York: Macmillan.

Hawkins, Keith. 1992. *The Uses of Discretion*. New York: Oxford University Press.

Heclo, Hugh. 1977. *A Government of Strangers: Executive Politics in Washington*. Washington, DC: Brookings Institution.

Hess, Stephen. 1976. *Organizing the Presidency*. Washington, DC: Brookings Institution.

Hogben, Lancelot. 1983. *Mathematics for the Millions*. New York: W. W. Norton.

Holmström, Bengt. 1982. "Moral Hazard in Teams." *Bell Journal of Economics* 13:324–40.

Holmström, Bengt, and Jean Tirole. 1989. "The Theory of the Firm." In *Handbook of Industrial Organization*, eds. Richard Schmalensee and Robert Willig. Amsterdam: North-Holland.

Horn, Murray J. 1995. *The Political Economy of Public Administration*. Cambridge: Cambridge University Press.

Huber, John. 1996. *Rationalizing Parliament*. New York: Cambridge University Press.

References

Huntington, Samuel. 1971. "Congressional Responses to the Twentieth Century." In *Congress and the President: Allies and Adversaries*, ed. Ronald Moe. Pacific Palisades, CA: Goodyear Publishing Co.

Jaffe, Louis. 1965. *Judicial Control of Administrative Action*. Boston: Little, Brown.

Jensen, Michael, and William Meckling. 1976. "Theory of the Firm: Managerial Behavior, Agency Costs and Ownership Structure." *Journal of Financial Economics* 3:305–60.

Johnson, Chalmers. 1982. *MITI and the Japanese Miracle*. Stanford, CA: Stanford University Press.

Jones, Charles O. 1979. "American Politics and the Organization of Energy Decision-Making." *Annual Review of Energy* 4:99–121.

Joskow, Paul. 1985. "Vertical Integration and Long-Term Contracts: The Case of Coal Burning Electric Generating Plants." *Journal of Law, Economics, and Organization* 1:33–80.

Kafka, Steve. 1996. "Political Choice of Bureaucratic Structure." Manuscript. Harvard University.

Key, V. O. 1947. *Politics, Parties, and Pressure Groups*. New York: Thomas Cromwell.

Kiewiet, Roderick, and Mathew McCubbins. 1991. *The Logic of Delegation: Congressional Parties and the Appropriation Process*. Chicago: University of Chicago Press.

King, David C. 1997. *Turf Wars: How Congressional Committees Claim Jurisdiction*. Chicago: University of Chicago Press.

King, Gary, and Lyn Ragsdale. 1988. *The Elusive Executive*. Washington, DC: Congressional Quarterly Press.

Klein, Benjamin, Robert Crawford, and Armen Alchian. 1978. "Vertical Integration, Appropriable Rents, and the Competitive Contracting Process." *Journal of Law and Economics* 21:297–326.

Krehbiel, Keith. 1987. "Why Are Congressional Committees Powerful." *American Political Science Review* 81:929–35.

1990. "Are Congressional Committees Composed of Preference Outliers?" *American Political Science Review* 84:149–63.

1991. *Information and Legislative Organization*. Ann Arbor: University of Michigan Press.

1996. "Institutional and Partisan Sources of Gridlock: A Theory of Divided and Unified Government." *Journal of Theoretical Politics* 8:7–40.

1998. *Pivotal Politics*. Chicago: University of Chicago Press.

Krzanowski, W. J. 1988. *Principles of Multivariate Analysis*. Oxford: Clarendon Press.

Landis, James McCauley. 1938. *The Administrative Process*. New Haven, CT: Yale University Press.

Laver, Michael, and Kenneth Shepsle, eds. 1994. *Cabinet Ministers and Parliamentary Government*. New York: Cambridge University Press.

Lazear, Edward, and Sherwin Rosen. 1981. "Rank Order Tournaments as Optimum Labor Contracts." *Journal of Political Economy* 85:841–64.

Lemieux, Peter, and Charles Stewart. 1990. "A Theory of Supreme Court Nominations." Paper presented at Conference on Political Economy, Cambridge, MA.

Lijphart, Arend. 1984. *Democracies*. New Haven, CT: Yale University Press.

Lohmann, Susanne, and Sharyn O'Halloran. 1994. "Divided Government and U.S. Trade Policy: Theory and Evidence." *International Organization* 48: 595–632.

Londregan, John, and James Snyder. 1994. "Comparing Committee and Floor Preferences." *Legislative Studies Quarterly* 19:233–66.

Lowi, Theodore. 1964. "American Business, Public Policy, Case Studies, and Political Theory." *World Politics* 16:677–715.

———. 1969. *The End of Liberalism: The Second Republic of the United States*. New York: W. W. Norton.

———. 1979. *The End of Liberalism: The Second Republic of the United States*. 2d ed. New York: W. W. Norton.

———. 1988. "Liberal and Conservative Theories of Regulation." In *The Constitution and the Regulation of Society*, ed. G. Bryner and D. Thompson. Albany: State University of New York Press.

Lupia, Arthur, and Mathew McCubbins. 1994. "Learning from Oversight: Fire Alarms and Police Patrols Reconstructed." *Journal of Law, Economics, and Organization* 10:96–125.

Macey, Jonathan. 1988. "Transaction Costs and the Normative Elements of the Public Choice Model: An Application to Constitutional Theory." *Virginia Law Review* 74:471–513.

Maltzman, Forrest, and Steven Smith. 1995. "Principals, Goals, Dimensionality, and Congressional Committees." In *Positive Theories of Congressional Institutions*, eds. Kenneth Shepsle and Barry Weingast. Ann Arbor: University of Michigan Press.

Manne, Henry, and Roger Miller. 1976. *Auto Safety Regulation: The Cure or the Problem?* Glen Ridge, NJ: T. Horton.

Mashaw, Jerry L. 1990. "Explaining Administrative Process: Normative, Positive, and Critical Stories of Legal Development." *Journal of Law, Economics, and Organization* 6:267–98.

Mayhew, David. 1974. *The Electoral Connection*. New Haven, CT: Yale University Press.

———. 1991. *Divided We Govern: Party Control, Lawmaking, and Investigations, 1946–1990*. New Haven, CT: Yale University Press.

McConnell, Grant. 1966. *Private Power and American Democracy*. New York: Vintage Books.

McCubbins, Mathew. 1985. "The Legislative Design of Regulatory Structure." *American Journal of Political Science* 29:721–48.

McCubbins, Mathew, Roger Noll, and Barry Weingast. 1987. "Administrative Procedures as Instruments of Political Control." *Journal of Law, Economics, and Organization* 3:243–77.

———. 1989. "Structure and Process, Politics and Policy: Administrative Arrangements and the Political Control of Agencies." *Virginia Law Review* 75: 431–82.

McCubbins, Mathew, and Thomas Schwartz. 1984. "Congressional Oversight

References

Overlooked: Police Patrols versus Fire Alarms." *American Journal of Political Science* 2:165–79.

McKelvey, Richard. 1976. "Intransitivities in Multidimensional Voting Models and Some Implications for Agenda Control." *Journal of Economic Theory* 12:472–82.

Milgrom, Paul, and John Roberts. 1992. *Economics, Organization and Management.* Englewood Cliffs, NJ: Prentice-Hall.

Miller, Gary. 1992. *Managerial Dilemmas: The Political Economy of Hierarchy.* Cambridge: Cambridge University Press.

Miller, Gary, and Terry Moe. 1983. "Bureaucrats, Legislators, and the Size of Government." *American Political Science Review* 77:297–322.

Mitnick, Barry. 1980. *The Political Economy of Regulation.* New York: Columbia University Press.

Moe, Terry. 1985. "Control and Feedback in Economic Regulation: The Case of the NLRB." *American Political Science Review* 79:1094–1116.

1989. "The Politics of Bureaucratic Structure." In *Can the Government Govern?* eds. John Chubb and Paul Peterson. Washington, DC: Brookings Institution.

1990. "Political Institutions: The Neglected Side of the Story." *Journal of Law, Economics, and Organization* 6:213–53.

Nelson, Garrison. 1993. *Committees in the U.S. Congress: 1947–1992.* Washington, DC: Congressional Quarterly Press.

Nicholson, Shield. 1893. "Scotch Banking." *Journal of Political Economy* 1: 487–502.

Niskanen, William A. 1971. *Bureaucracy and Representative Government.* Chicago: Aldine–Atherton.

North, Douglass C. 1990. *Institutions, Institutional Change and Economic Performance.* Cambridge: Cambridge University Press.

O'Halloran, Sharyn. 1994. *Politics, Process, and American Trade Policy.* Ann Arbor: University of Michigan Press.

Oleszek, Walter. 1984. *Congressional Procedures and the Policy Process.* Washington, DC: Congressional Quarterly Press.

1989. *Congressional Procedures and the Policy Process.* 3d ed. Washington DC: Congressional Quarterly Press.

Ordeshook, Peter, and Thomas Schwartz. 1987. "Agendas and the Control of Political Outcomes." *American Political Science Review* 81:180–99.

Ornstein, Norman, Thomas Mann, and Michael Malbin, eds. 1994. *Vital Statistics on Congress.* Washington, DC: Congressional Quarterly Press.

Pearson, James. 1975. "Oversight: A Vital Yet Neglected Congressional Function." *Kansas Law Review* 23:277–88.

Peltzman, Sam. 1985. "An Economic Interpretation of the History of Congressional Voting in the Twentieth Century." *American Economic Review* 75: 656–75.

Peters, B. Guy. 1997. "The Separation of Powers in Parliamentary Systems." In *Presidential Institutions and Democratic Politics*, ed. Kurt von Mettenheim. Baltimore: Johns Hopkins University Press.

References

Plott, Charles R. 1967. "A Notion of Equilibrium and Its Possibility under Majority Rule." *American Economic Review* 57:787–806.

Polsby, Nelson, ed. 1976. *Congress and the Presidency.* 3d ed. Englewood Cliffs, NJ: Prentice-Hall.

Poole, Keith T., and Howard Rosenthal. 1997. *Congress: A Political-Economic History of Roll-Call Voting.* Oxford: Oxford University Press.

Ramsey, James. 1969. "Tests for Specification Errors in Classic Linear Least Squares Regression Analysis." *Journal of the Royal Statistical Society, Series B* 31:350–71.

Ramseyer, Mark, and Frances McCall Rosenbluth, eds. 1993. *Japan's Political Marketplace.* Cambridge, MA: Harvard University Press.

Ray, Bruce. 1980. "Federal Spending and the Selection of Committee Assignments in the U.S. House of Representatives." *American Journal of Political Science* 24:494–510.

Ripley, Randall, and Grace Franklin. 1984. *Congress, the Bureaucracy, and Public Policy.* 3d ed. Homewood, Ill.: Dorsey Press.

Robinson, James Arthur. 1963. *The House Rules Committee.* Indianapolis: Bobbs-Merrill.

Rohde, David. 1991. *Parties and Leaders in the Postreform House.* Chicago: University of Chicago Press.

Rohde, David, and Dennis Simon. 1985. "Presidential Vetoes and Congressional Response: A Study in Institutional Conflict." *American Journal of Political Science* 29:397–427.

Romer, Thomas, and Howard Rosenthal. 1978. "Political Resource Allocation, Controlled Agencies, and the Status Quo." *Public Choice* 33:27–43.

Rothenberg, Lawrence. 1992. *Linking Citizens to Government: Interest Group Politics at Common Cause.* Cambridge: Cambridge University Press.

Salisbury, Robert. 1969. "An Exchange Theory of Interest Groups." *Midwest Journal of Political Science* 13:1–32.

———. 1990. "The Paradox of Interest Groups in Washington—More Groups, Less Clout." In *The New American Political System,* ed. Anthony King. Washington, DC: AEI Press.

Sartori, Giovanni. 1997. *Comparative Constitutional Engineering: An Inquiry into Structures, Incentives and Outcomes.* 2d ed. New York: New York University Press.

Schattschneider, Elmer Eric. 1942. *Party Government.* New York: Farrar and Rinehart.

Schick, Allen. 1980. *Congress and Money: Budgeting, Spending and Taxing.* Washington, DC: Urban Institute.

Schneier, Edward, and Bertram Gross. 1993. *Legislative Strategy.* New York: St. Martin's Press.

Schoenbrod, David. 1983. "Goals Statutes or Rules Statutes: The Case of the Clean Air Act." *UCLA Law Review* 30:740–70.

———. 1993. *Power without Responsibility.* New Haven, CT: Yale University Press.

Schofield, Norman. 1978. "Instability of Simple Dynamic Games." *Review of Economic Studies* 45:575–94.

Seidman, Harold. 1975. *Politics, Position and Power.* New York: Oxford University Press.

Seidman, Harold, and Robert Gilmour. 1986. *Politics, Position, and Power. From the Positive to the Regulatory State.* 4th ed. New York: Oxford University Press.

Shahn, Ben. 1957. *The Shape of Content.* Cambridge, MA: Harvard University Press.

Shapiro, Martin. 1988. *Who Guards the Guardians?* Athens: University of Georgia Press.

Shefter, Martin. 1978. "Party, Bureaucracy, and Political Change in the United States." In *Political Parties: Development and Decay,* eds. Louis Maisel and Joseph Cooper. Beverly Hills, CA: Sage Publications.

Shepard, Andrea. 1987. "Licensing in the Semi-conductor Industry." Ph.D. diss., Yale University.

Shepsle, Kenneth. 1978. *The Giant Jigsaw Puzzle.* Chicago: University of Chicago Press.

——— 1979. "Institutional Arrangements and Equilibrium in Multidimensional Voting Models." *American Journal of Political Science* 23:27–59.

Shepsle, Kenneth, and Barry Weingast. 1987a. "The Institutional Foundations of Committee Power." *American Political Science Review* 81:85–104.

——— 1987b. "Reflections on Committee Power." *American Political Science Review* 81:935–45.

Shepsle, Kenneth, and Barry Weingast, eds. 1995. *Positive Theories of Congressional Institutions.* Ann Arbor: University of Michigan Press.

Shugart, Matthew, and John Carey. 1992. *Presidents and Assemblies.* New York: Cambridge University Press.

Sinclair, Barbara. 1983. *Majority Leadership in the U.S. House.* Baltimore: Johns Hopkins University Press.

——— 1995. "House Special Rules and the Institutional Design Controversy." In *Positive Theories of Congressional Institutions,* eds. Kenneth Shepsle and Barry Weingast. Ann Arbor: University of Michigan Press.

Skrowronek, Stephen. 1982. *Building a New American State: The Expansion of National Administrative Capacities, 1877–1920.* Cambridge: Cambridge University Press.

Smith, Steven. 1989. *Call to Order: Floor Politics in the House and Senate.* Washington, DC: Brookings Institution.

Smith, Steven, and Christopher Deering. 1990. *Committees in Congress.* Washington, DC: Congressional Quarterly Press.

Spulber, Daniel, and David Besanko. 1992. "Delegation, Commitment, and the Regulatory Mandate." *Journal of Law, Economics, and Organization* 8: 126–54.

Stewart, Richard B. 1975. "The Reformation of American Administrative Law." *Harvard Law Review* 88:1669–813.

Stigler, Joseph. 1971. "The Theory of Economic Regulation." *Bell Journal of Economic and Management Science* 2:3–21.

Strauss, Peter. 1989. *An Introduction to Administrative Justice in the United States.* Durham, NC: Carolina Academic Press.

Strom, Kaare. 1990. *Minority Government and Majority Rule*. New York: Cambridge University Press.

Sundquist, James. 1981. *The Decline and Resurgence of Congress*. Washington, DC: Brookings Institution.

——— 1988. "Needed: A Political Theory for the New Era of Coalition Government in the United States." *Political Science Quarterly* 103:613–35.

Truman, David. 1951. *The Governmental Process*. New York: Knopf.

Weingast, Barry, and William Marshall. 1988. "The Industrial Organization of Congress." *Journal of Political Economy* 96:132–63.

Weingast, Barry, and Mark Moran. 1983. "Bureaucratic Discretion or Congressional Control? Regulatory Policymaking by the Federal Trade Commission." *Journal of Political Economy* 91:775–800.

Weingast, Barry, Kenneth Shepsle, and Christopher Johnsen. 1981. "The Political Economy of Benefits and Costs: A Neoclassical Approach to Distributive Politics." *Journal of Political Economy* 89:642–64.

Wildavsky, Aaron. 1975. *Perspectives on the Presidency*. Boston: Little, Brown.

——— 1992. *The New Politics of the Budgetary Process*. New York: HarperCollins.

Williamson, Oliver. 1975. *Markets and Hierarchies: Analysis and Antitrust Implications*. New York: Free Press.

——— 1979. "Transaction-Cost Economics: The Governance of Contractual Relations." *Journal of Law and Economics* 22:233–61.

——— 1985. *The Economic Institutions of Capitalism*. New York: Free Press.

——— 1989. "Internal Economic Organization." In *Perspectives on the Economics of Organization*, eds. Oliver Williamson, Sven-Erik Sjostrand, and Jan Johanson. Lund, Sweden: Lund University Press.

Wilson, James. 1973. *Political Organizations*. New York: Basic Books.

——— 1974. "The Politics of Regulation." In *Social Responsibility and the Business Predicament*, ed. J. McKie. Washington, DC: Brookings Institution.

——— 1989. *Bureaucracy. What Government Agencies Do and Why They Do It*. New York: Basic Books.

Woll, Peter. 1977. *American Bureaucracy*. New York: W. W. Norton.

Index

313

Continuation of books in series: